family handyman

BEFORE YOU CALL A PRO

![Family Handyman logo](fh family handyman)

Chief Content Officer, Home & Garden Jeanne Sidner
Content Director Mark Hagen
Creative Director Raeann Thompson
Editors Christine Campbell, Sara Strauss
Senior Art Director Kristen Stecklein
Senior Designer Anna Jo Beck
Designer Samantha Primuth
Deputy Editor, Copy Desk Dulcie Shoener
Senior Copy Editor Ann Walter
Associate Assigning Editor Mary Flanagan
Electrical Consultant John Williamson
Plumbing Consultant Bret Hepola, master plumber,
All City Plumbing, Minnetrista, MN

A FAMILY HANDYMAN BOOK

ISBN 978-1-62145-974-3 (hardcover)
ISBN 978-1-62145-975-0 (paperback)
ISBN 978-1-62145-984-2 (e-pub)

Component number 118300122H

We are committed to both the quality of our products
and the service we provide to our customers. We value
your comments, so please feel free to contact us at
TMBBookTeam@TrustedMediaBrands.com.

For more *Family Handyman* products and information,
visit our website: *www.familyhandyman.com*

Printed in China (hardcover)
10 9 8 7 6 5 4 3 2 1

Printed in China (paperback)
10 9 8 7 6 5 4 3 2 1

Text, photography and illustrations for *Before You Call a
Pro* are based on articles previously published in *Family
Handyman* magazine (*familyhandyman.com*).

WARNING

All do-it-yourself activities involve a degree of risk.
Skills, materials, tools, and site conditions vary
widely. Although the editors have made every effort
to ensure accuracy, the reader remains responsible
for the selection and use of tools, materials and
methods. Always obey local codes and laws, follow
manufacturer's operating instructions, and observe
safety precautions.

Photo and Illustration Credits
64 Ray Massey/Getty Images; **68** (br) Sensi; **68** (t)
Paul Tessler/Shutterstock; **84** Xinzheng/Getty Images;
89 JJ Gouin/Getty Images; **101** (tr) Frank Rohrbach III;
111 (b), **112, 114** (b) (5), **115** (t, cr), **116** (br) Courtesy
of Proven Winners—provenwinners.com; **114** (tr)
PATARA/Shutterstock; **114** (tl) Vern Johnson; **116** (cr)
ABO PHOTOGRAPHY/Shutterstock; **116** (t) Viacheslav
Lopatin/Shutterstock; **128** (tl) Snapper; **129** (br) Toro;
129 (tl) WORX; **158** (br) Benjamin Moore; **160** (tl)
ZINSSER; **163** (dark blue paint can) Courtesy of Behr;
194, 202 (t) CreativaStudio/Getty Images; **196** Belinda
Fontes/offset.com; **197** (tl) Judy Lighting; **203** David
Papazian/Shutterstock; **204** Courtesy of Clopay, Inc.;
205 (t) Courtesy of The Home Depot; **206** gpointstudio/
Shutterstock; **207** fstop123/Getty Images; **210** (br)
Lifestyle discover/Shutterstock; **217** Rob Crandall/
Shutterstock; **226** Daniel Jedzura/Shutterstock; **230** (t)
SciePro/Getty Images; **251** driftlessstudio/Getty Images;
256 PM Images/Getty Images; **257** Don Farrall/Getty
Images; **259** Warren Faidley/Getty Images; **266** (t)
AlexMaster/Shutterstock; **266** (bl) Mr. Heater; **267** (tl)
turk_stock_photographer/Getty Images; **268** (bl, br)
Water Bob

All other photographs by Trusted Media Brands, Inc.

SAFETY FIRST—ALWAYS!

Tackling home improvement projects and repairs can be endlessly rewarding. But as most of us know, with the rewards come risks. DIYers use chain saws, climb ladders, and tear into walls that can contain big and hazardous surprises.

The good news is, armed with the right knowledge, tools and procedures, homeowners can minimize risk. As you go about your projects and repairs, stay alert for these hazards:

ALUMINUM WIRING

Aluminum wiring, installed in about 7 million homes between 1965 and 1973, requires special techniques and materials to make safe connections. This wiring is dull gray, not the dull orange characteristic of copper. Hire a licensed electrician certified to work with it. For more information, go to *cpsc.gov* and search for "aluminum wiring."

SPONTANEOUS COMBUSTION

Rags saturated with oil-based paints and stains, and with oil finishes, like Danish oil and linseed oil, can spontaneously combust if left bunched up. Always dry them outdoors, spread out loosely. When the oil has thoroughly dried, you can safely throw them in the trash.

VISION AND HEARING PROTECTION

Safety glasses or goggles should be worn whenever you're working on DIY projects that involve chemicals, dust and anything that could shatter or chip off and hit your eye. Sounds louder than 80 decibels (dB) are considered potentially dangerous. Sound levels from a lawn mower can be 90 dB, and shop tools and chain saws can be 90 to 100 dB.

LEAD PAINT

If your home was built before 1979, it may contain lead paint, which is a serious health hazard, especially for children 6 and under. Take precautions when you scrape or remove it. Contact your public health department for detailed safety information or call 800-424-LEAD (5323) to receive an information pamphlet. Or visit *epa.gov/lead*.

BURIED UTILITIES

A few days before you dig in your yard, have your underground water, gas and electrical lines marked. Just call 811 or go to *call811.com*.

SMOKE AND CARBON MONOXIDE (CO) ALARMS

The risk of dying in reported home structure fires is cut in half in homes with working smoke alarms. Test your smoke alarms every month, replace batteries as necessary and replace units that are more than 10 years old. As you make your home more energy efficient and airtight, existing ducts and chimneys can't always successfully vent combustion gases, including potentially deadly carbon monoxide (CO). Install a UL-listed CO detector, and test your CO and smoke alarms at the same time.

FIVE-GALLON BUCKETS AND WINDOW COVERING CORDS

Anywhere from 10 to 40 children a year drown in 5-gallon buckets, according to the U.S. Consumer Products Safety Commission. Always store them upside down and store ones containing liquid with the covers securely snapped.

According to Parents for Window Blind Safety, hundreds of children in the United States are injured every year after becoming entangled in looped window treatment cords. For more information, visit *pfwbs.org*.

WORKING UP HIGH

If you have to get up on your roof to do a repair or installation, always install roof brackets and wear a roof harness.

ASBESTOS

Texture sprayed on ceilings before 1978, adhesives and tiles for vinyl and asphalt floors before 1980, and vermiculite insulation (with gray granules) all may contain asbestos. Other building materials made between 1940 and 1980 could also contain asbestos. If you suspect that materials you're removing or working around contain asbestos, contact your health department or visit *epa.gov/asbestos* for information.

CONTENTS

AN ELECTRICIAN OR HVAC SPECIALIST

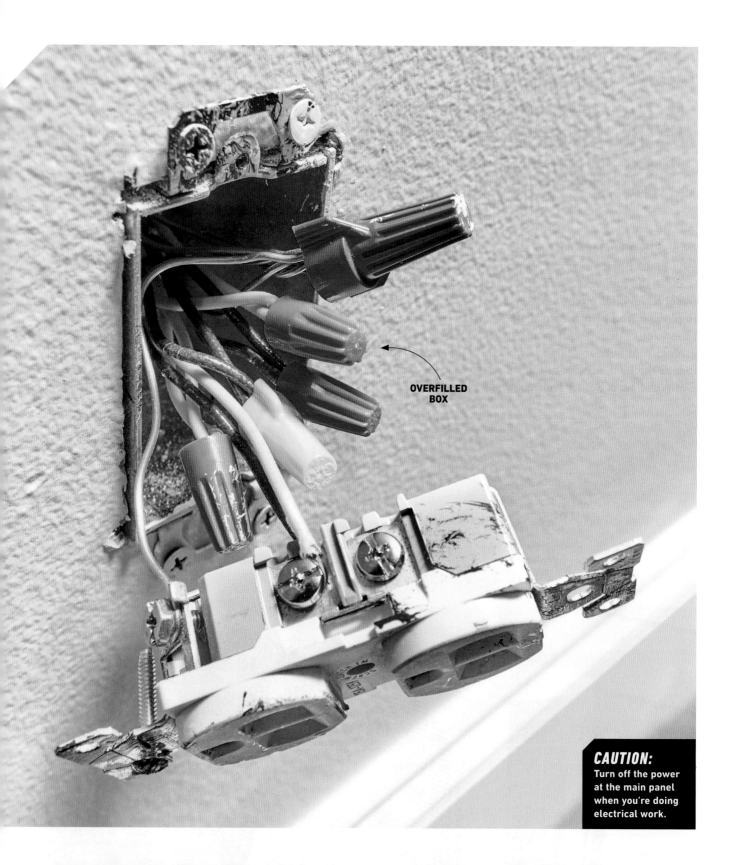

OVERFILLED BOX

AVOID ELECTRICAL MISTAKES

RECOGNIZE AND CORRECT WIRING BLUNDERS THAT CAN ENDANGER YOUR HOME

MISTAKE:
OVERFILLING ELECTRICAL BOXES

Too many wires stuffed into a box can cause dangerous overheating, short-circuiting and fire. The National Electrical Code (NEC) specifies minimum box sizes to reduce this risk.

THE RIGHT WAY:
INSTALL A LARGER BOX

To figure the minimum box size required, assign numerical values to the items in the box:

1 - for each hot wire and neutral wire entering the box
1 - for all the ground wires combined
1 - for all the cable clamps combined
2 - for each device (including a switch or outlet, but not light fixtures)

Multiply the total by 2 for 14-gauge wire and by 2.25 for 12-gauge wire to get the minimum box size required in cubic inches. Then choose a box with at least this much volume. Plastic boxes have the volume stamped inside, usually on the back. Steel box capacities are listed in the electrical code. Steel boxes won't be labeled, so you'll have to measure the height, width and depth of the interior, then multiply to find the volume.

MISTAKE:
REVERSING HOT AND NEUTRAL WIRES

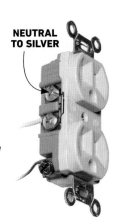

HOT TO BRASS

Connecting the black (hot) wire to the neutral terminal of an outlet creates the potential for a lethal shock. Unfortunately, you may not realize the mistake until someone gets shocked, because lights and most other plug-in devices will still work; they just won't work safely.

THE RIGHT WAY:
IDENTIFY THE NEUTRAL TERMINAL

NEUTRAL TO SILVER

Connect the white wire to the neutral terminal of an outlet and light fixture. The neutral terminal is always marked and usually has silver- or light-colored screws. Connect the hot wire to the other terminal. If there's a green or bare copper wire, that's the ground. Connect the ground to the green grounding screw or to a ground wire or grounded box.

RECESSED LOOSE OUTLET

MISTAKE:
POORLY SUPPORTING OUTLETS AND SWITCHES

Loose switches or outlets look bad and, worse, they're dangerous. Loosely connected outlets move around, causing the wires to loosen from the terminals. Loose wires can arc and overheat, creating a fire hazard.

THE RIGHT WAY:
ADD PLASTIC SPACERS

Fix loose outlets by shimming spacers under the screws to create a tight connection to the box. You can buy spacers at home centers; small washers or coils of wire wrapped around the screws work as well.

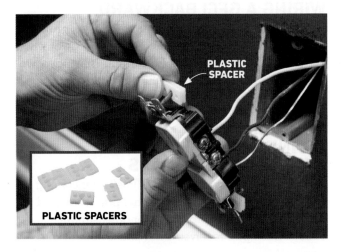

PLASTIC SPACER

PLASTIC SPACERS

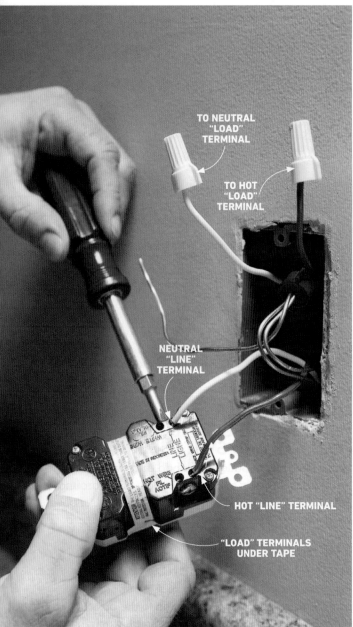

TO NEUTRAL "LOAD" TERMINAL

TO HOT "LOAD" TERMINAL

NEUTRAL "LINE" TERMINAL

HOT "LINE" TERMINAL

"LOAD" TERMINALS UNDER TAPE

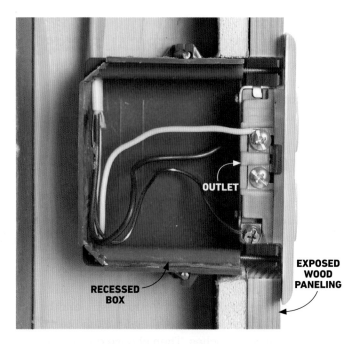

OUTLET

EXPOSED WOOD PANELING

RECESSED BOX

PLASTIC BOX EXTENSION

MISTAKE:
WIRING A GFCI BACKWARD

GFCI (ground-fault circuit interrupter) outlets protect you from a lethal shock by shutting off the power when they sense slight differences in current. They have two pairs of terminals. You'll lose the shock protection if you mix up the line and load connections.

THE RIGHT WAY:
CONNECT POWER TO THE "LINE" TERMINALS

One pair of terminals is labeled "line" for incoming power for the GFCI outlet. The other pair is labeled "load" and provides protection for downstream outlets. Each pair receives a hot and a neutral wire.

MISTAKE:
RECESSING BOXES BEHIND THE WALL SURFACE

Electrical boxes must be flush to the wall surface if the wall surface is a combustible material. Boxes recessed behind combustible materials such as wood present a fire hazard because the wood is left exposed to potential heat and sparks.

THE RIGHT WAY:
ADD A BOX EXTENSION

The fix is to install a metal or plastic box extension. If you use a metal box extension on a plastic box, connect the metal extension to the ground wire in the box using a grounding clip and a short piece of wire.

NO JUNCTION BOX

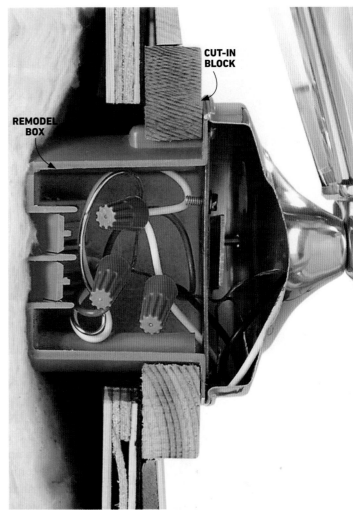

REMODEL BOX

CUT-IN BLOCK

MISTAKE:
MAKING CONNECTIONS OUTSIDE ELECTRICAL BOXES

Never connect wires outside electrical boxes. Junction boxes protect connections from damage and contain any sparks from a loose connection or short circuit.

THE RIGHT WAY:
ADD A BOX

Install a box and reconnect the wires inside it. The photo at right shows one way to do this for an exterior light mounted on wood siding.

MISTAKE:
INSTALLING A FLAT, WEATHER-RESISTANT COVER ON AN OUTDOOR RECEPTACLE

Flat covers provide protection only when a receptacle isn't in use, but it is common for extension cords to be plugged in for extended periods of time—as an example, for holiday lights. Flat covers may still be available at home centers, but they no longer meet code.

THE RIGHT WAY:
INSTALL A BUBBLE COVER

All new exterior outlets must have a "bubble" or "in-use" cover identified as "extra-duty." And don't forget the weather-resistant receptacle. The NEC requires that all 15- and 20-amp receptacles be rated as weather-resistant and tamper-resistant when installed in both wet and damp locations.

BUBBLE COVER

DOES NOT MEET CODE

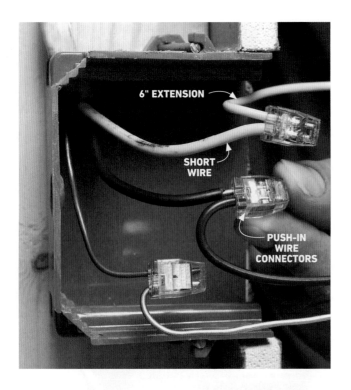

MISTAKE:
CUTTING WIRES TOO SHORT

Wires that are cut too short make wire connections difficult and—since you're more likely to make poor connections—dangerous.

THE RIGHT WAY:
EXTEND WIRES

Leave the wires long enough to protrude at least 3 in. from the box. If you run into short wires, there is an easy fix. Simply add 6-in. extensions to the existing wires. The push-in wire connectors shown below are easy to install in tight spots. You'll find them at hardware stores and home centers.

MISTAKE:
NOT USING A TAMPER-RESISTANT RECEPTACLE

Since conventional receptacles are widely available, many people use them when replacing an outlet.

THE RIGHT WAY:
FOLLOW THE CODE

Per the NEC, when you replace an outlet, the new one must be a tamper-resistant receptacle. The simple swap provides protection against shock and serious injury.

MISTAKE:
INSTALLING CABLE WITHOUT A CLAMP

Cable that's not secured can strain the connections. In metal boxes, the sharp edges can cut the insulation on the wires.

THE RIGHT WAY:
INSTALL A CLAMP

Single-gang plastic boxes do not require internal cable clamps, but the cable must be stapled within 8 in. of the box. Larger plastic boxes are required to have built-in cable clamps, and the cable must be stapled within 12 in. of the box. Cables must be connected to metal boxes with an approved cable clamp. Make sure the sheathing on the cable is trapped under the clamp and that about ¼ in. of sheathing is visible inside the box. Some metal boxes have built-in cable clamps. If the box you're using doesn't include clamps, buy clamps separately and install them when you add the cable to the box (photo right).

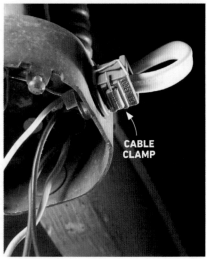

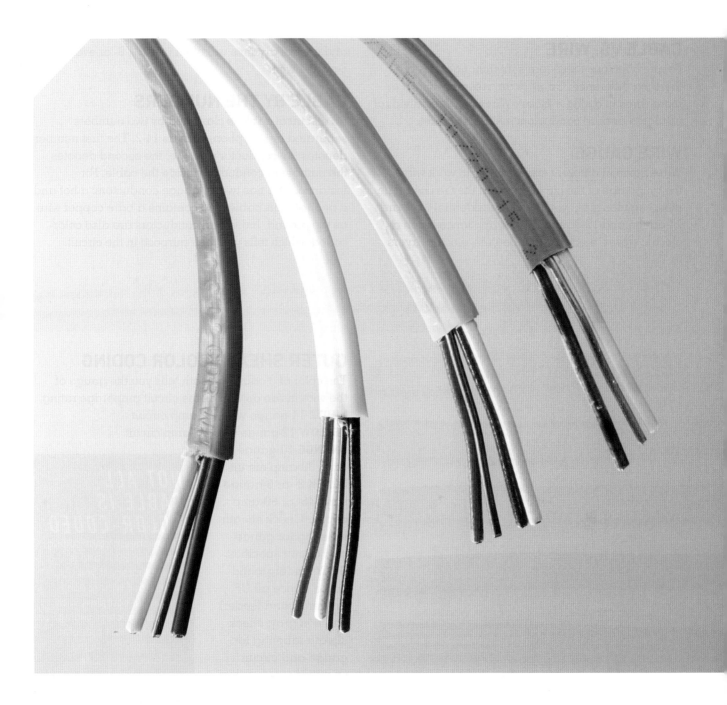

MASTER THE BASICS OF HOME WIRING

//

ARM YOURSELF WITH INFORMATION BEFORE TACKLING ELECTRICAL CABLES

Before you take on your next home wiring project, arm yourself with basic information about the electrical cable or wiring you're likely to see. The wire and cable aisle at your home center can be a pretty confusing place. In this article, you'll learn how to identify different cable types and their uses, as well as how to determine the sizes of individual wires and their purposes. You'll be able to cut through the confusion, get exactly what you need and ensure that your wiring is safe.

CABLE VS. WIRE

People often use these terms interchangeably, but there's a difference: Cable is an assembly of two or more wires in a single jacket. Wires are the individual insulated or bare conductors inside the jacket.

WIRE GAUGE

Wires come in different sizes/gauges to work with the amperage of the circuit in which they're used. The most common sizes you'll find in residential work are 14-gauge and 12-gauge. Larger appliances such as electric stoves, electric water heaters, electric dryers and central air units will often use 10-, 8- or even 6-gauge wire.

CABLE BY THE NUMBERS

An electrical cable is classified by two numbers separated by a hyphen, such as 14-2. The first number denotes the conductor's gauge; the second denotes the number of conductors inside the cable. For instance, 14-2 has two 14-gauge conductors: a hot and a neutral. This cable also contains a bare copper wire as the ground. Individual conductors are also color-coded, which tells you their purpose in the circuit.

TYPE NM-B 14-2 WITH GROUND 600 VOLTS CIRTEX-I

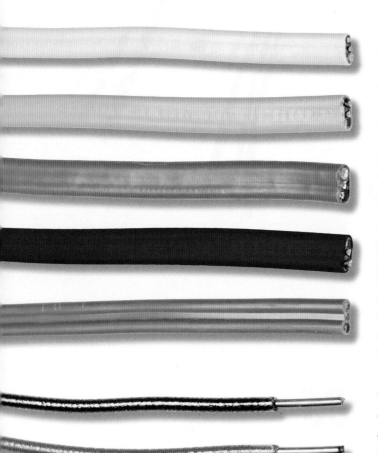

OUTER SHEATH COLOR CODING

The color of a cable's sheath tells you the gauge of the wire inside as well as the circuit amperage rating.
WHITE 14-gauge wire, 15-amp circuit
YELLOW 12-gauge wire, 20-amp circuit
ORANGE 10-gauge wire, 30-amp circuit
BLACK 8- or 6-gauge wire, 45- or 60-amp circuit. Check sheath labeling for gauge and circuit specifics.
GRAY Underground cable. Since all UF (underground feeder) cable is gray, check sheath labeling for gauge and circuit specifics.

NOT ALL CABLE IS COLOR-CODED

Cable-sheath color coding started in 2001 and is still voluntary. If you have older wiring, don't assume it complies with the current color coding. However, most manufacturers now follow the standard color code.

WIRE COLOR CODING

This code is standard for all conductors. Here are the colors you're most likely to find in your home:
BLACK (OR RED) Hot. Hot wires carry current from the panel to the device, which could be a switch, receptacle, light fixture or appliance. There are other colors for hot wires, but they're much less common.
WHITE Neutral. Neutral wires carry the current back to the panel, completing the circuit.
BARE (OR GREEN) Ground. In the event of a ground fault, this wire provides a path for the fault current to return to the panel, opening the breaker or blowing the fuse and cutting off the flow of electricity.

NM-B—NONMETALLIC CABLE

This is the most common type of electrical cable in homes built since the mid-1960s. "Nonmetallic" simply means that the outer jacket is not metal. It's often referred to as Romex, which is a brand name. Typically, NM-B cable has either two conductors and a ground, or three conductors and a ground. The conductors are individually insulated, wrapped in paper and sheathed in plastic. Ground wires are either bare copper or insulated in green.

14-2 Used for general lighting and receptacle circuits, 15-amp circuit maximum

14-3 Used for three-way switches and split receptacle circuits, 15-amp circuit maximum

12-2 Used for 20-amp kitchen, bathroom, laundry and garage receptacles; 230-volt heating circuits up to 3,700 watts; and 115-volt circuits up to 1,800 watts. Can be used anywhere in place of 14-2.

12-3 Same uses as 12-2, with the addition of three-way switches and split receptacle circuits

UF—UNDERGROUND FEEDER CABLE

UF cable is used primarily to bring power to detached garages and outbuildings or to provide outdoor lighting. The insulated conductors are molded into the sheathing. Depending on the situation, UF is either direct-buried or it is run in conduit. Wherever it exits the ground and is exposed, UF must be protected from physical damage by conduit.

MC—METAL-CLAD CABLE

MC cable is common in unfinished areas where the cable would otherwise be exposed and subject to physical damage. It's also sometimes used inside walls. A bare aluminum wire is in continuous contact within the metal sheathing. For MC, the combination of aluminum wire, sheathing and metal boxes grounds the circuit.

STRANDED WIRE VS. SOLID

Stranded wire is more flexible than solid. If you're pulling wire through conduit, stranded wire makes it easier to get around corners and bends in the conduit. However, if the situation requires pushing wires through conduit, you'll want to use solid wire.

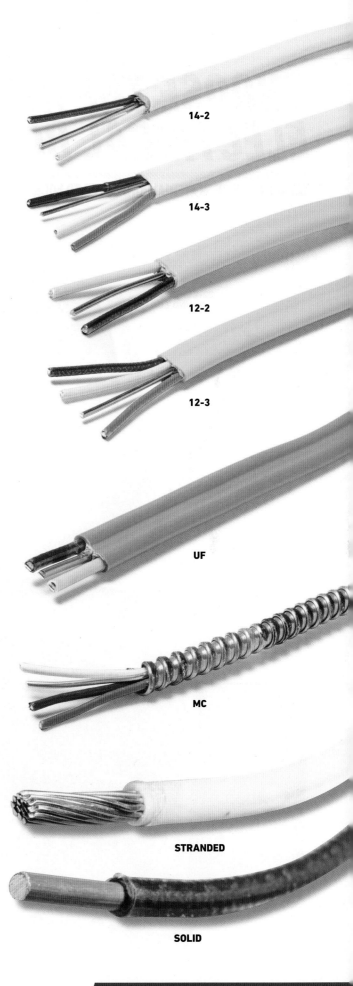

14-2

14-3

12-2

12-3

UF

MC

STRANDED

SOLID

CHOOSE THE RIGHT ELECTRICAL BOX

TAILOR THE SIZE, MATERIAL AND STYLE TO YOUR TASK

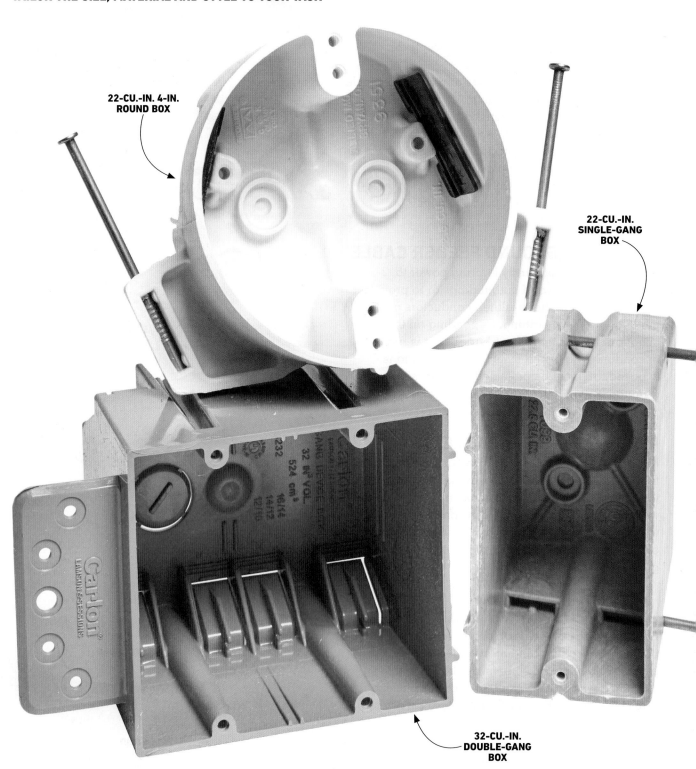

22-CU.-IN. 4-IN. ROUND BOX

22-CU.-IN. SINGLE-GANG BOX

32-CU.-IN. DOUBLE-GANG BOX

WHY USE AN ELECTRICAL BOX?

Wiring connections—where wires join an outlet, switch or other wires—must be inside an electrical box. And here's why: Connections are the weak link in an electrical system. If they get damaged, loosened or pulled apart, you're left without power or, worse, with a fire. Electrical boxes are meant to protect vulnerable connections.

With the variety of different electrical boxes available at home centers, how do you know what to buy? Don't worry; it's not that complicated. We'll whittle it down to about a dozen boxes to cover almost every situation.

NEW WORK: THREE TYPES DO IT ALL

If you have the walls opened up for remodeling or to put on an addition, these three boxes cover about 99% of your needs.

- **22-CU.-IN. 4-IN. ROUND BOX** For ceiling light fixtures, smoke alarms, carbon monoxide detectors and wall sconce light fixtures
- **22-CU.-IN. SINGLE-GANG BOX** For a typical outlet or switch
- **32-CU.-IN. DOUBLE-GANG BOX** For two light switches together in the same box, or two duplex receptacle outlets

BOX SIZE

Wires, receptacles and switches need adequate space. Crowded boxes can damage wires, resulting in a fire or shock hazard. You can use the chart below to calculate a required box size. Add up the numbers for the corresponding components in the box to find how many cubic inches you'll need. Or, in most cases, you can skip the math and just buy the largest volume box available in the style you need. Having a box that is too large is rarely a cause of frustration!

BOX MATERIAL

Indoor nonmetallic boxes are typically plastic or fiberglass. Cheap PVC boxes such as the blue one shown below work fine, but they can move or distort in wood framing as the studs dry. Instead, spend the extra 20¢ per box on heavy-duty thermoset plastic or fiberglass boxes. Unlike PVC boxes, they're super strong and maintain their shape.

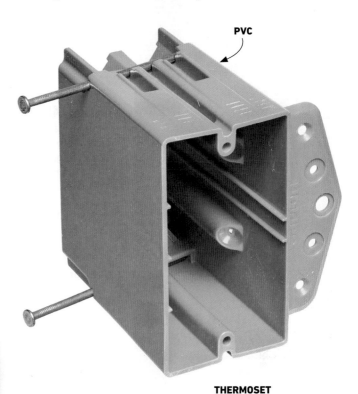

PVC

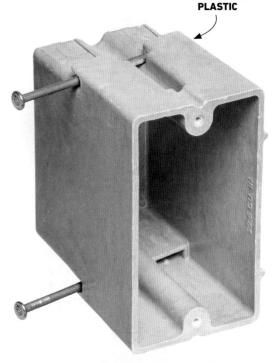

THERMOSET PLASTIC

BOX VOLUME CALCULATOR

Conductor Size	14 AWG*	12 AWG	10 AWG
Each Insulated Wire	2	2.25	2.5
All Grounding Wires Combined	2	2.25	2.5
Each Switch or Receptacle	4	4.5	5
All Internal Cable Clamps	2	2.25	2.5

*American Wire Gauge

EXAMPLE: A Box with Four 14-2 NM Cables with Ground

8 Insulated Wires	16 cu. in.
All 4 Grounding Wires	+ 2 cu. in.
1 Switch	+ 4 cu. in.
1 Receptacle	+ 4 cu. in.
All Cable Clamps	+ 2 cu. in.
Minimum Box Volume	**= 28 cu. in.**

SPECIALTY BOXES

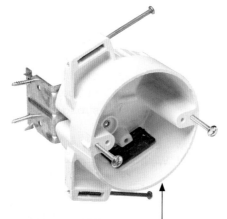

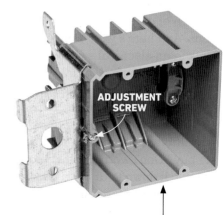

CEILING FAN BOXES

If you're hanging a ceiling fan, you'll need a box designed to support the extra weight. Boxes for ceiling paddle fans are sold as kits, with a wide variety of mounting options for new work and old work (remodeling). Boxes that are the sole support of the fan have to be rated for up to 70 lbs. If the fan is supported independently of the box, you can use a general-purpose box.

ADJUSTABLE BOXES

If you know you'll be installing ceramic tile, wood paneling or wainscoting, buy adjustable boxes. They're mounted to the framing members like any other box but you can just turn a screw to adjust the depth flush with the wall treatment. The adjustment screw is accessible even after the wall treatment is applied.

ADJUSTMENT SCREW

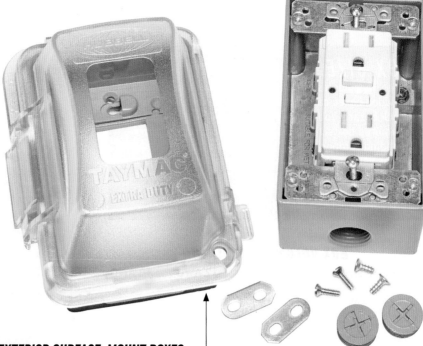

EXTERIOR SURFACE-MOUNT BOXES

Exterior surface-mount boxes—often molded PVC—have either threaded or glued hubs and are used with PVC electrical conduit. Cast-aluminum boxes work well for outdoor projects since they're extra durable and weatherproof. They often come in a kit with a GFCI receptacle and a weatherproof cover, or in a lighting kit with gaskets and lamp holders for floodlights.

SURFACE-MOUNT BOXES

On concrete or block walls, surface-mount boxes and conduit are the way to go. These boxes can be plastic or metal. Because they're exposed, they need to be mounted perfectly plumb and level. They also require conduit to protect the wires.

PAN BOXES

If a ceiling joist is right where you need to install your dining room light fixture, 4-in. round pan (short for "pancake") boxes come in handy. Cutting a notch in the ceiling joist would weaken it. Pan boxes are only ½ in. deep and have a volume of only 6 cu. in., but they will safely accommodate the three wires you need for your light fixture.

GASKET BOXES

FOAM

FOAM GASKET

Energy code boxes are for insulated walls and ceilings. They typically have a molded flange with a foam gasket and foam-lined cable entries that form an airtight seal to keep drafts out. Caulk the flange right to the vapor barrier.

METAL BOXES

You can wire a whole home using only non-metallic boxes, but metal boxes still come in handy for certain situations. They are extremely sturdy and work well where you need lots of volume—for example, for a welder receptacle in your work-shop or for a hub where multiple cables meet. As with nonmetallic boxes, get the large ones, which are 4 in. square by 2⅛ in. deep. You'll find cover options for most configurations of switches and receptacles, as well as mud rings.

OLD WORK BOXES

FLANGE

TAB

Old work boxes come in several types for walls covered with drywall or other material. The boxes don't need to be fastened to a stud, so you can install them anywhere. The one shown has flip-out tabs that squeeze the box flanges against the drywall. Use the box face as a marking template to get a nice, close fit.

LOW-VOLTAGE BRACKETS

Unlike in the old days when homes had one or two phone jacks, today we have much more low-voltage wiring for computers, cable TV, home entertain-ment systems, and whole-house audio, security and tempera-ture control systems. Save time and money by installing low-voltage brackets instead of electrical boxes. Low-voltage wiring doesn't necessarily need an enclosed box. In fact, you often don't want an enclosed box because it may require the wires to make a sharp bend, which impedes the performance of some cables.

RESET A CIRCUIT BREAKER

///

A FEW SIMPLE STEPS WILL HAVE YOUR LIGHTS AND APPLIANCES UP AND RUNNING AGAIN

You may already know how to reset a circuit breaker, but you're not always around. Show everyone in your household where the main panel is, and post these steps near it.

1 DON'T WORRY!
All the dangerous parts are behind the breaker switches. You can't get a shock by flipping breaker switches.

2 FIND THE TRIPPED BREAKER
Open the panel's door and look for the breaker switch that's out of line with the others. It will be about midway between the "off" and "on" positions. You may have to look closely to spot it.

3 RESET THE BREAKER
To reset a breaker, move the switch all the way to its "off" position, then back to "on." You might hear a few beeps from smoke detectors and appliances when you turn the power back on, but that's normal.

4 BE PREPARED IF IT TRIPS AGAIN
If it happens again, the circuit is probably overloaded. To reduce the load, unplug or switch off items that are using the circuit. If that doesn't work, your electrical system may have a problem. If you lack the know-how to troubleshoot your wiring, it's time call an electrician.

FIND THE SWITCH THAT'S OUT OF LINE

SWITCH TO "OFF"

THEN "ON"

REPLACE A NOISY BATH FAN

//
THE JOB IS MUCH EASIER THAN YOU THINK

If the bath fan in your home is more than 20 years old, chances are it's pretty loud. A loud fan may be good for masking bathroom noise, but the jet engine roar is downright annoying the rest of the time. Worse yet, your old bath fan may not be moving enough air to keep your bathroom free of mold and mildew.

Newer-style bath fans, on the other hand, are so quiet you can hardly hear them running, and they cost very little to operate. It's easier than you think to replace that noisy, inefficient bath fan, especially if you choose a new one that's designed to be installed without ripping apart the bathroom ceiling.

Of the many replacement models to choose from, one good choice is the Broan No. RB110 Ultra Pro Series (about $170 at *supplyhouse.com*) because the fan can be installed from inside the bathroom. It's not the quietest model available, but at 0.6 sones (about 25 decibels), it's a huge improvement over the old 4-sone (about 60-decibel) fan we're replacing. If you can locate a joist, cut drywall and handle basic electrical work, you can do the whole job in about two hours and save about $200 on the installation. You'll need a stud finder, a drywall saw, a drill and screws, and aluminum duct tape.

BUY THE RIGHT SIZE FOR YOUR BATHROOM

A one-size-fits-all bath fan doesn't exist. For bathrooms up to 100 sq. ft., calculate the required cubic feet per minute (cfm) by multiplying the room's length x width x height. Multiply that result by 0.13 and round up to the nearest 10. Example: 9 ft. long x 10 ft. wide x 9 ft. high x 0.13 = 105. Round up to 110 and buy a 110-cfm bath fan. For bathrooms larger than 100 sq. ft., simply add up the cfm requirements for each of these plumbing fixtures: toilet, 50 cfm; shower, 50 cfm; bathtub, 50 cfm; jetted tub, 100 cfm.

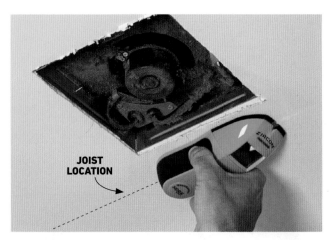

1 FIND THE JOISTS

Slide a stud finder along the ceiling until you find the joist nearest the old fan. Mark the location. Then find the joist on the opposite side of the fan.

JOIST LOCATION

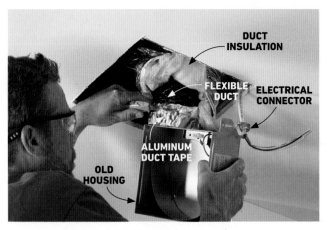

DUCT INSULATION

FLEXIBLE DUCT

ELECTRICAL CONNECTOR

ALUMINUM DUCT TAPE

OLD HOUSING

3 DISCONNECT AND REMOVE THE OLD PARTS

Unscrew the old fan housing from the joist. Then disconnect the electrical connector from the housing. Slice through the aluminum duct tape with a utility knife and disconnect the duct.

2 MARK AND CUT THE CEILING OPENING

Using the template provided, trace the new opening onto the ceiling. Then cut along the lines using a drywall saw. Cut shallower strokes around the flexible duct so you don't puncture it.

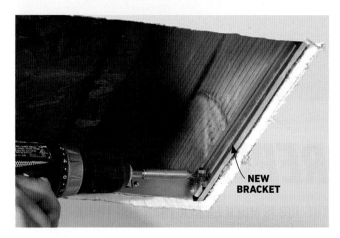

NEW BRACKET

4 MOUNT THE BRACKET

Slide the bracket through the opening and extend it so it contacts the joists on each side of the opening. Secure both sides to the joists with drywall screws.

TURN OFF THE POWER BEFORE PROCEEDING

You'll have to remove the power cable from the old unit and connect it to the new fan. This must be done with the power off. Don't rely on turning off the fan switch; flip the breaker as well. Then double-check that the power is off with a voltage sniffer. If you're not comfortable working with electricity, hire an electrician to remove and connect the wires.

FIND THE JOISTS AND DUCT, THEN ENLARGE THE OPENING

Most bath fans are mounted to a ceiling joist with the duct running parallel to the joist. Start by locating the direction of your ceiling joists (Photo 1). Then locate the damper (you may have to remove the fan motor and blade from the housing). That'll tell you where the duct lies in the ceiling. Mark the duct location. Then enlarge the opening (Photo 2).

REMOVE AND REPLACE THE HOUSING, DUCT AND FAN

With the opening now enlarged, you'll have room to disconnect the old housing, electrical cable and old duct (Photo 3). Install and secure the new mounting frame (Photo 4). Connect the electrical cable to the

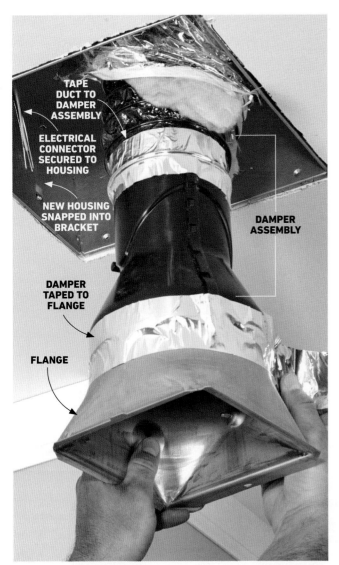

TAPE DUCT TO DAMPER ASSEMBLY

ELECTRICAL CONNECTOR SECURED TO HOUSING

NEW HOUSING SNAPPED INTO BRACKET

DAMPER ASSEMBLY

DAMPER TAPED TO FLANGE

FLANGE

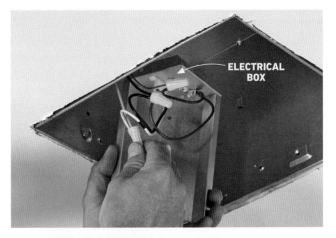

ELECTRICAL BOX

6 CONNECT THE WIRES
Secure the hot, neutral and ground wires with wire nuts. Then slide the metal electrical box into place in the housing and attach it with the screw provided.

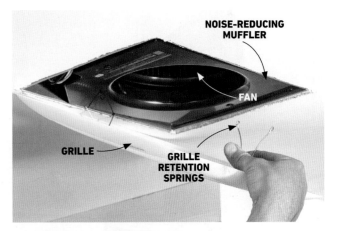

NOISE-REDUCING MUFFLER

FAN

GRILLE

GRILLE RETENTION SPRINGS

5 CONNECT THE DUCT
Pull the old duct through the housing and into the room. Then tape the duct to the damper assembly. Slide the damper onto the flange and secure with aluminum duct tape. Push the duct, damper and flange back into the ceiling and secure the flange to the housing using the screw provided.

7 INSTALL THE FAN AND GRILLE
Slide the fan assembly into the housing until it snaps in place. Secure with screws. Plug the electrical connector into the electrical box mounted earlier. Then screw in the noise-reducing muffler. Squeeze the grille springs and snap the grille into place.

new housing and snap the housing into the frame so the duct opening is facing the existing duct. Then connect the duct, damper and flange using aluminum duct tape (Photo 5). Finish the rough-in by connecting the power wires and ground to the electrical box provided (Photo 6). Then slide the fan into the housing and add the muffler and grille (Photo 7). Turn on the power and test. Apply a bead of fire-resistant (intumescent) caulk around the fan housing and drywall to prevent moisture intrusion into the attic.

IS YOUR ATTIC ACCESSIBLE?
The installation we show here is all done from inside a bathroom with a floor above it. If you're replacing a bath fan in a bathroom with an accessible attic above it, you have the option to do some of the work from up there. You may save some mess by going into the attic and moving the insulation aside before you remove the old fan. Then rearrange the insulation after the installation is done. Or, eliminate the second trip by making the electrical and vent connections at the same time.

FLOOD YOUR KITCHEN WITH LIGHT

//

TRANSFORM THE ROOM INTO A PLACE YOU'LL LOVE TO BE

We have tackled several kitchen projects over the years, but we've never made such a major improvement with so little time and money. We spent less than $350 and just four hours brightening this kitchen. Our original intent was strictly practical: better light to make food prep and cleanup easier. But replacing a single fixture with bright LEDs transformed the room.

USE LOW-PROFILE LEDS

Initially, we thought we'd install recessed can lights for a sleek look and lots of light. Then we ran across these ultra-slim Halo LEDs (about $20 each). Several similar products are available, but these were in stock at the local home center. These LED lights are super bright (940 lumens) and have such a low profile (less than ½ in.) that you can even locate them directly under a joist if needed. They're rated for insulation contact and wet locations, so you can use them in a shower or even outdoors. A switch on the side of the box lets you adjust the color temperature. They're also dimmable.

All you need is a power supply, a means to cut round holes, 14-2 NM-B cable, basic electrical tools and a drill. The transformer box converts 120V to low voltage, and it's UL-listed as a junction box with room for power in and power out. That lets you take power from the first box and string together as many lights as you want. You might need to fish wire, but aside from that, installation is easy.

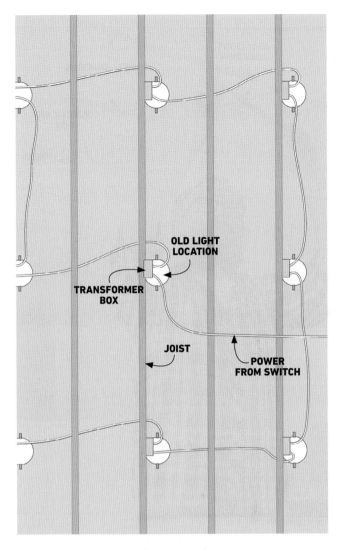

OLD LIGHT LOCATION

TRANSFORMER BOX

JOIST

POWER FROM SWITCH

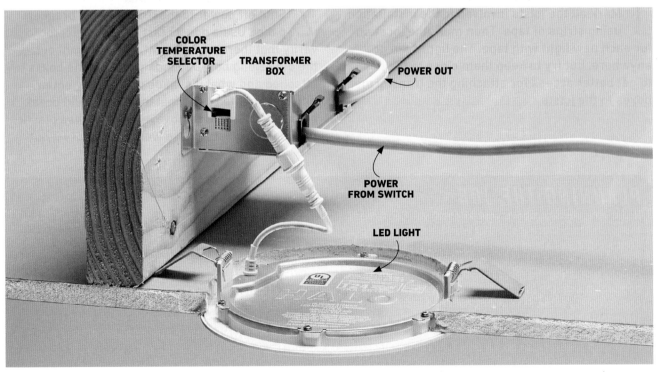

COLOR TEMPERATURE SELECTOR

TRANSFORMER BOX

POWER OUT

POWER FROM SWITCH

LED LIGHT

NEW LIGHT
LOCATION

JOIST LOCATIONS

OLD CEILING
BOX

OLD CEILING
BOX

1 LAY OUT THE NEW LIGHT LOCATIONS

Mark all the joists involved in the installation using strips of tape. Then mark the location for each new light with tape. The lights can go anywhere, but try to keep them close to the joists to get better access for attaching the transformer boxes to the joists.

2 REMOVE THE OLD CEILING BOX

Shut off power to the fixture at the breaker panel. Use a noncontact voltage detector to verify that there's no current, and then pull out the old ceiling box. Depending on how the box is attached and what it's made of, this may entail different methods. For instance, you could break a fiberglass box to remove it. This box was plastic, nailed to the joists, so we were able to pry it out.

PLANNING THE JOB

If you have an attic above your kitchen, you can access the joists from there instead of working from below. That simplifies fishing wires, but you'll still have to dig through insulation.

Before starting the job, remove the ceiling fixture and look inside the junction box. Our box had just one incoming cable. If your box contains more cables, wiring will be a bit more complicated. You may need to install a second junction box because the box for these LED fixtures can house only two 14-2 cables.

We replaced the existing fixture with an LED like all the others.

If you want a standard fixture in the center of your ceiling, you'll still have to remove the existing junction box (Photo 2) to access the joists. Then, after installing the new lights, install a remodeling box in the same hole. We found everything we needed at a home center. Two special tools made the project much easier: an adjustable drywall circle cutter (about $30) and a 54-in. flexible drill bit (about $60).

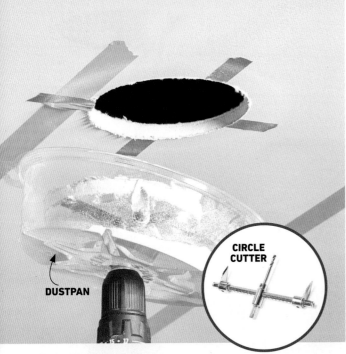

CIRCLE CUTTER

DUSTPAN

3 CUT NEW HOLES

Cut all the holes for the new lights. An adjustable drywall circle cutter **(above)** slices out perfect holes, saving lots of time. It includes a pan to catch the dust. But it can't be used to enlarge the existing hole that held the old box. For that, trace the provided template and cut it out using a manual drywall saw. Now it's time to fish wires.

JOIST

SKIL

4 DRILL THROUGH THE FIRST JOIST

Drill through the joist at least 2 in. from its bottom edge. Drill a 1-in.-dia. hole to make it easier to maneuver the long, flexible bit in the next step. But if you're just going through one joist, you won't need the flexible bit.

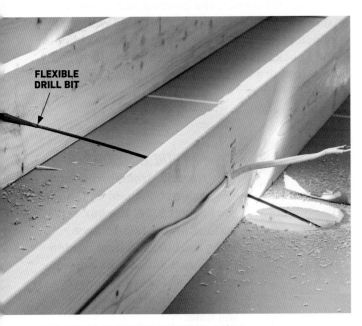

FLEXIBLE DRILL BIT

5 DRILL THROUGH THE NEXT JOIST

Pass a flexible bit through the hole you just drilled until it hits the next joist. Flex the bit downward to get close to the center of the joist. Unless you have access from above, this is guesswork. Drill through the joist, and then loosen the drill's chuck and set the drill aside, leaving the bit in the hole.

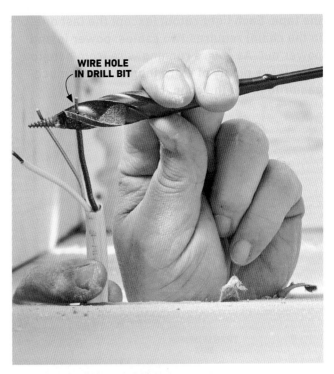

WIRE HOLE IN DRILL BIT

6 FASTEN CABLE TO THE DRILL BIT

Run one of the wires from a new cable through the hole in the bit's tip and bend it over. Twist the other wires together and wrap everything with electrical tape.

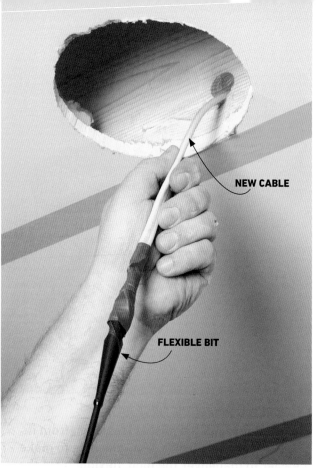

NEW CABLE

FLEXIBLE BIT

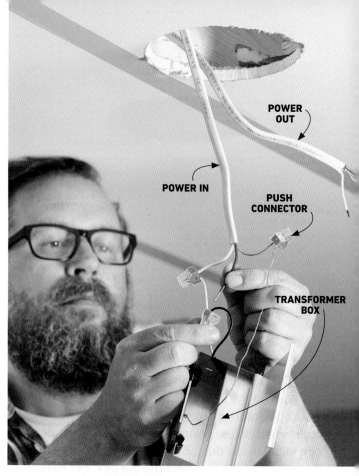

POWER OUT

POWER IN

PUSH CONNECTOR

TRANSFORMER BOX

7 PULL IN THE NEW CABLE

Pull the flexible bit back through the hole along with your new cable, and then unwrap the tape. Each light cutout (except the last one in the chain) requires two cables: power in and power out. As you're running wire from hole to hole, leave plenty of extra length. It'll be much easier to make the connections.

8 CONNECT POWER TO THE TRANSFORMER

Connect the power source to first transformer box, and connect the downstream cable to the next box in line. The lights are outfitted with push connectors. Secure the cables using cable clamps in the knockouts or built-in cable traps. Here, code doesn't require the cables to be secured to joists.

TRANSFORMER BOX

9 HANG THE TRANSFORMER

Hold the transformer box against the joist and mark the keyholes. Set the box aside and install the two screws. Hang the box, and then tighten the screws with a screwdriver. Working space is limited, so hang the box directly above the hole.

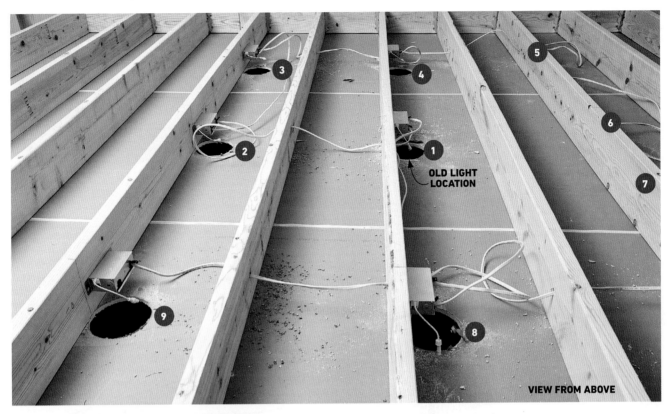

VIEW FROM ABOVE

OLD LIGHT LOCATION

10 CONNECT ALL THE TRANSFORMERS
Connect power to each box and hang all the transformers. Each box except for the last one has power in and power out.

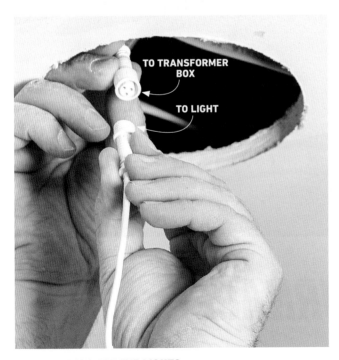

TO TRANSFORMER BOX

TO LIGHT

RETAINING SPRINGS

11 CONNECT THE LIGHTS
Plug the low-voltage cables from the lights into the cables from each transformer box. Set the desired color temperature using the switch on the side of each transformer box.

12 SNAP IN THE LIGHTS
Press the retaining springs upward and pop each light into place, and then switch the power back on at the breaker panel. If you want to change the color temperature after the lights are installed, carefully pull down on each light's flange to remove it, keeping your fingers clear of the mousetrap-like retaining springs!

PROTECT YOUR FURNACE

//
FILTER FAILURE CAN COST YOU THOUSANDS

If you're negligent about replacing your furnace filter regularly or you're not using the correct one, listen up. You're not just compromising your indoor air quality. You're also spending more money than necessary on utility bills and repairs, and you may even have to replace your furnace.

BE WARY OF WASHABLE FILTERS

Washable, reusable filters require far more effort than simply swapping a dirty disposable filter for a new one. Plus, it's difficult to get washable filters completely clean. Most washable filters offer MERV ratings only in the 1 to 4 range, so they don't provide good filtration either. Since they cost a bit more than disposable, you'll have to decide if the benefit is worth the price, trouble and substandard filtration. If you choose this route, shop around to find a washable filter with a MERV rating of about 9.

CONTINUE TO GET YOUR FURNACE SERVICED

You might think frequent filter switch-outs would keep your furnace in tiptop condition, but you'd be wrong. It's still a good idea to have your furnace professionally serviced. The technician will clean internal components and the condensate line, as well as perform a combustion analysis for O_2, CO and CO_2 to make sure your furnace is performing safely and up to par.

Most importantly, the technician will ensure your heat exchanger is intact, and that's a big safety issue. If you live in an exceptionally clean house, you may be able to go two or more years between services. Ask the technician for advice.

DON'T USE FIBERGLASS FILTERS

Light passes through fiberglass filters so well for a reason: they're very porous. That's why they last so much longer than pleated filters—since they don't capture the finer debris, they don't clog as fast as higher-quality filters. That fine dust stays in your indoor air and also circulates within the furnace, where it will damage mechanical and electronic parts. Use pleated paper filters instead.

CHOOSE A FILTER WITH THE BEST RATING FOR YOUR HOUSEHOLD

Furnace filters are "MERV" rated according to the size and quantity of particles they filter. MERV stands for Minimum Efficiency Reporting Value, and the range is from 1 to 16, with 1 being the most porous and 16 the finest. One might think that the higher the MERV rating, the better. But for most homes, a filter in the 7 to 11 range is plenty good and will trap the vast majority of airborne particles (enough for those with seasonal allergies) and protect furnace components.

MERV filters rated higher than 11 plug faster and need more frequent replacement. Only households with members with respiratory issues, serious allergies or low-immunity issues should bother with those, and you really have to stay on top of filter changes.

MERV RATINGS

Filter Quality	Pollen	Dust & Lint	Smoke	Pet Dander	Bacteria	Virus Carriers	Mold	Microscopic Allergens	Odor	Dust Mites
MERV 13	x	x	x	x	x	x	x	x	x	x
MERV 11	x	x	x	x	x	x	x	x		x
MERV 8	x	x		x	x		x			x
MERV 6	x	x		x						x

PRO TIP: HOME DEPOT RATES FILTERS DIFFERENTLY

If you shop at Home Depot, you'll find the filter aisle dominated by filters made by 3M and Honeywell. And you'll be confused because the MERV ratings are replaced by an "FPR" (Filter Performance Rating). That is Home Depot's own rating system—you won't find it at other stores. FPRs are not equivalent to MERV ratings. Roughly, a MERV rating of 8 matches an FPR of 5, and a MERV 11 is close to an FPR of 7. Our advice? Next time you have your furnace serviced, ask the technician to recommend a filter to suit your home air-quality needs and protect your furnace.

MERV	FPR
13	10
11	7
8	5
6	N/A

KNOW WHEN TO REPLACE YOUR FILTER

You should change your filters when you need to—not on some arbitrary schedule. Depending on your filter and home environment, filters may need replacing anywhere from every 20 days to once a year.

How do you tell? First of all, always have at least one new replacement filter on hand. Every 20 to 30 days, take a few seconds to pull the filter from your furnace and compare it with the new one. You'll be able to tell whether the filter is covered with dust and needs to be replaced. Never go more than 60 days between changes for any 1-in. filter.

BUY IN BULK

Here's why it pays to have extra filters on hand: When you buy in bulk, you'll save money. And when you're checking a filter to see if it needs replacement, you'll have a new one for comparison and you'll be able to install a new filter right away.

REPLACE FILTERS IN SUMMER TOO

Whenever your HVAC system is running, the filter is getting dirty. That's not only during the heating season but also through the warmer months. During the cooling season, air flows through the furnace exactly the same way it does when you're heating the house. So it's important to check your filter all year long. However, if you live in a mild climate where the furnace is off for long stretches, you can skip the regular filter checks during those periods.

INSTALL DUCTLESS AIR CONDITIONING

///

DIY COOLING IS SURPRISINGLY EASY WITH A MINI-SPLIT SYSTEM

Adding an A/C system sounds like a job for pros only. And usually it is. But two non-pros installed this ductless mini-split system in a garage in one day.

The installation was fast and easy because of the special line set **(see right)**. It comes prefilled, or "precharged," with refrigerant and includes connectors that don't require special skills or tools. Just mount the two main units and connect the line set to the condenser. Some mini-splits include an easy-install line set, but most don't.

A mini-split system can be installed in a home, a garage, a cabin or a shed. Some offer heating as well as cooling, and some include multiple evaporators to serve multiple rooms. Depending on features and size, most DIY mini-splits cost from about $700 to $3,000.

CHOOSE THE SYSTEM

Very few brick-and-mortar stores carry DIY systems, so online shopping may be your only option. Luckily there are many online suppliers. The size of the system is listed in BTUs (British thermal units). The higher the number, the greater the cooling capacity. To select the right size mini-split, calculate the heat loss of the room. Several websites simplify these calculations. Don't just guess; an undersized system won't keep up, and an oversized system will cycle on and off too frequently, shortening the condenser's service life. We installed a 12,000-BTU heating and cooling system that costs about $1,100 at *climateright.com*. The other necessary materials totaled about $275.

PROVIDE POWER

Usually the biggest challenge is running power to the system. A typical small mini-split system will probably need a dedicated 20-amp, 240-volt circuit. Larger systems may require a 30- or even 40-amp dedicated 240-volt circuit. Installing a new circuit can

HOW IT WORKS
A mini-split system has two main components: an indoor evaporator, which cools the air, and an outdoor condenser, which dissipates heat. They're connected by a line set, a tube that passes through a baseball-size hole in the wall, carrying hot refrigerant outside and cold refrigerant in. Our line set also included cable to power the evaporator and a drain line to carry condensation outside.

WARM AIR
EVAPORATOR
COOL AIR
LINE SET
CONDENSER

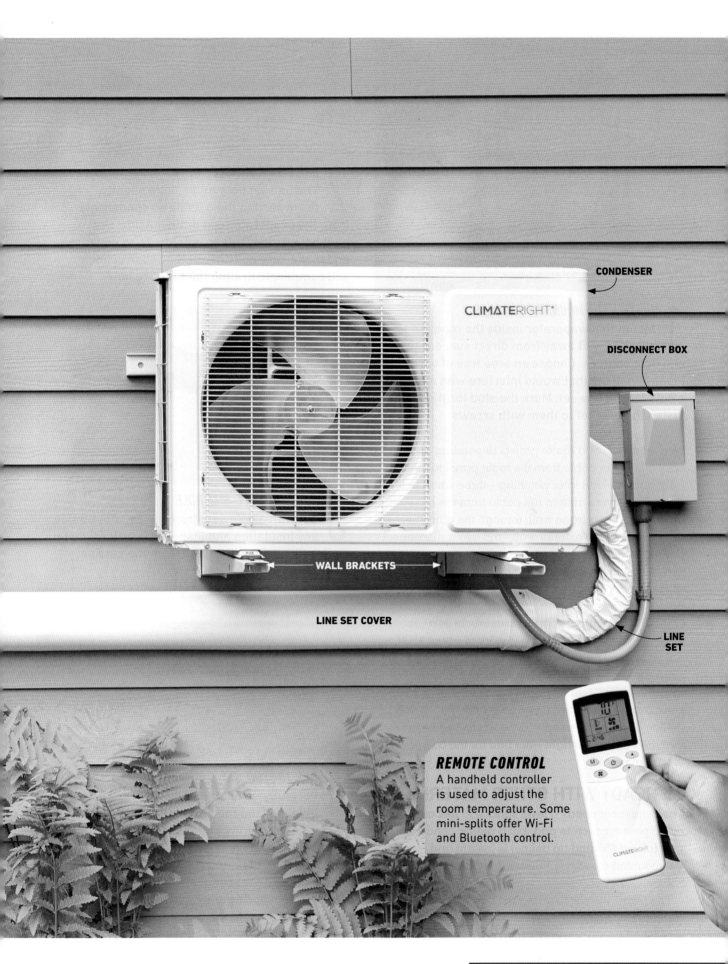

CONDENSER

DISCONNECT BOX

CLIMATERIGHT®

WALL BRACKETS

LINE SET COVER

LINE SET

REMOTE CONTROL
A handheld controller is used to adjust the room temperature. Some mini-splits offer Wi-Fi and Bluetooth control.

CLIMATERIGHT

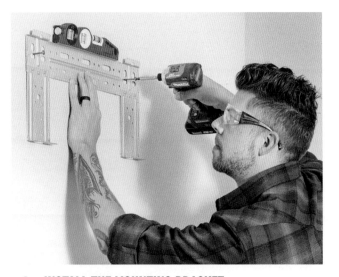

1 INSTALL THE MOUNTING BRACKET

Mount the evaporator inside the room on an exterior wall away from direct sun, doorways and dust sources. Choose an area free of wires, pipes and ducts that would interfere with making a hole for the line set. Mark the stud locations and fasten the bracket to them with screws.

be a small job or a major project depending on how easy it is to run cable from the main panel to the unit.

By cutting—and later patching—three small holes in drywall, we were able to run cable from the basement up through the garage wall, through the attic, then down and out the exterior wall, and into a disconnect box. (The disconnect provides an easy, certain way to turn off power when servicing the unit.) Power then runs from the disconnect to the condenser. Cable running alongside the line set powers the evaporator. Our bill for electrical supplies was about $160. A local electrician estimated that work at about $500.

If you have some electrical know-how but need extra guidance, don't forget your local electrical inspector. It's not an inspector's job to act as a consultant, but most will give you some advice and outline code requirements. Expert help and certainty that the job is done right—not bad for the cost of an electrical permit.

BE READY WITH OTHER MATERIALS

The condenser needs a level surface to rest on. You could pour a concrete pad, but a plastic condenser pad (about $50 and up online) is instant and easy. We mounted ours on condenser wall brackets (about $50 online).

The fabric sleeve covering the line set isn't attractive or easy to keep clean. The solution is a plastic line set cover kit (about $40 online).

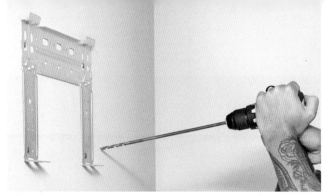

2 DRILL A PILOT HOLE

The line set hole must slope slightly downward to the outside so condensate from the evaporator can drain outside. Drill a pilot hole from inside to outside. Then go outside and make sure no trim or other obstructions will complicate drilling the full-size hole.

3 BORE THE FULL-SIZE HOLE

Cut with a hole saw from inside, move aside any insulation and inspect the wall cavity for obstructions. Finish drilling from the outside.

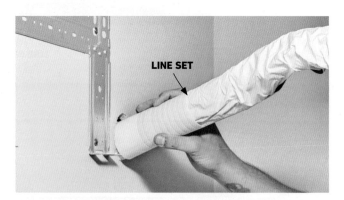

LINE SET

4 RUN THE LINE SET

Carefully uncoil the line set. With a helper outside, feed the line set through the hole. The helper should gently bend the line set downward and to the side as needed to reach the condenser. Keep the rigid plastic collar surrounding the line set on the end that connects to the condenser. The drain line is shorter and goes through last, below the other lines. Add the drain extension and wrap the joint with electrical tape to keep it secure.

5 INSTALL THE EVAPORATOR

Wrap the foam sleeve around the section of line set within the hole and replace any insulation in the wall cavity that was disturbed. Then hang the evaporator on the mounting bracket. Your helper may need to feed a few more inches of the line set outside as you do this. On the outside, insert the two-piece plastic trim into the hole to prevent any rough edges from damaging the line set.

6 INSTALL THE CONDENSER

Set the condenser on a pad on the ground or mount it on a wall bracket so the refrigerant lines can reach it easily. Route the line set so it stays tight to the building exterior and doesn't leapfrog any obstructions. This makes it easier to install a cover. Ensure the condenser has the recommended clearance from walls and bushes.

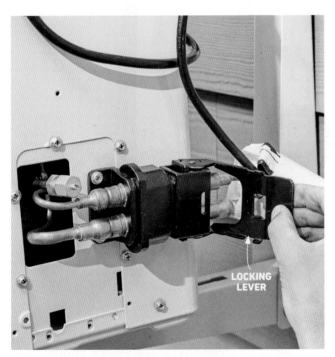

LOCKING LEVER

LINE SET COVER

DRAIN LINE

7 CONNECT THE REFRIGERANT LINES

This step varies by manufacturer. With this system, a locking lever presses the line connections together. Before powering up, inspect the refrigerant lines for kinks and verify the electrical connections. Then go inside and set the temperature using the handheld controller.

8 COVER THE LINE SET

Insulate and seal the hole in the outside wall, then cover the line set using sections of plastic or metal channel cut to length. Place the back half of the channel behind the line set, plumb it and anchor it to the wall with self-tapping screws. Our line set travels horizontally to the condenser, so when we added the channel corner, we drilled a hole in it to allow the drain line to exit straight down.

GET WIRED FOR A SMART THERMOSTAT

A SIMPLE FIX CAN HELP LAUNCH YOUR SYSTEM INTO THE MODERN ERA

If you're replacing an old dial thermostat with a smart thermostat, you may find that you're missing a wire. Don't worry. Usually all you need is an adapter kit to add a C-wire. These are often included with a smart thermostat, and they're easy to install.

1 CHECK FOR A C-WIRE

Cut power to your furnace. Remove the old thermostat and label the wires according to the terminals they're attached to. If there is a wire in the "C" terminal, you're good. If not, you'll connect the adapter to your furnace's control board.

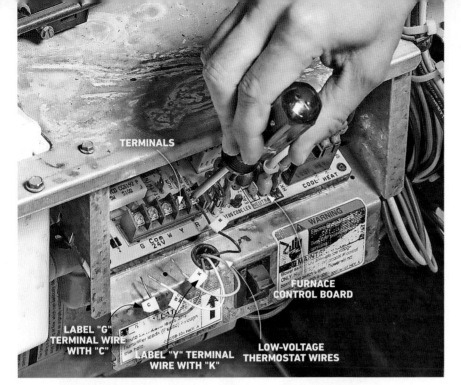

TERMINALS

FURNACE
CONTROL BOARD

LABEL "G"
TERMINAL WIRE
WITH "C"

LABEL "Y" TERMINAL
WIRE WITH "K"

LOW-VOLTAGE
THERMOSTAT WIRES

2 LABEL AND REMOVE THE WIRES AT THE FURNACE

Find the furnace control board and take a photo of the wire arrangement. Label the wires according to which terminals they're in, except for the "G" and "Y" terminal wires. Label the "G" terminal wire with a "C" and the "Y" terminal wire with a "K." Unscrew the terminals and remove the wires. If there are wires that aren't connected to anything, leave them alone.

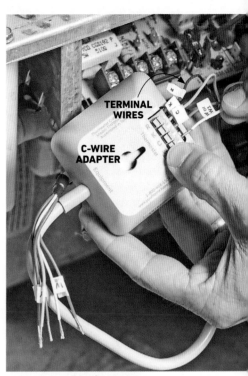

TERMINAL
WIRES

C-WIRE
ADAPTER

3 WIRE THE ADAPTER

Connect the wires to their corresponding terminals on the C-wire adapter.

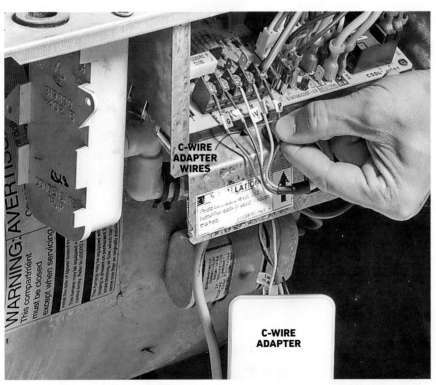

C-WIRE
ADAPTER
WIRES

C-WIRE
ADAPTER

4 CONNECT THE ADAPTER TO THE FURNACE

Connect the wires from the adapter to their corresponding terminals on the furnace control board. Mount the adapter inside the furnace and close the furnace cover.

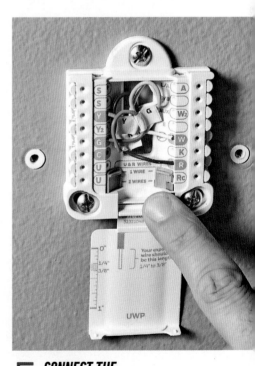

5 CONNECT THE NEW THERMOSTAT

With the new wall plate fastened to the wall, connect the wires to the corresponding terminals.

A PLUMBER

FIX A LEAKY TOILET

EVEN A SMALL TOILET LEAK CAN LEAD TO BIG PROBLEMS—HERE'S HOW TO FIX IT YOURSELF AND SAVE

If your toilet is leaking around the base, there's likely a problem with the toilet-to-flange connection. The solution may be as simple as replacing a wax ring, but whatever the case, it's important to stop leaks as soon as possible—even minor ones can cause substantial damage over time. These tips and reminders can help you detect and address the most common problems under the toilet.

1 BUY A VARIETY OF FLANGE FIXES

You never know what you're going to find when you pull the toilet, so you have to be prepared in order to get your toilet working again fast. You can always return the items you don't use. (Don't buy the cast-iron repair parts unless you have cast-iron drain lines.) In addition to the flange fixes (see p. 45), get two wax rings, a new set of brass toilet flange bolts, plastic toilet shims and a tube of tub/tile caulk.

TOILET SHIM

2 DON'T IGNORE A ROCKING TOILET

If your toilet is rocking or wobbling, don't ignore it, even if it's not leaking. Eventually the wax ring/toilet base seal will fail, and you'll have a leak. To prevent a leak and fix the rocking, shim under the toilet with plastic toilet shims until it's steady. Then trim the shims and snug up the flange nuts. Finally, caulk around the base of the toilet with tub/tile caulk.

STAINLESS STEEL RIM

3 CHOOSE FLANGES WITH STAINLESS STEEL RIMS

If you have access under the toilet, replacing a bad or corroded flange is sometimes the best and easiest solution. Because all plastic flanges are prone to breakage, and plastic flanges with ordinary steel rims are prone to rotting away, the best choice is a plastic flange surrounded with stainless steel. Go downstairs and investigate. Depending on access, you may need elbows, more pipe and a coupling to tie in the new one.

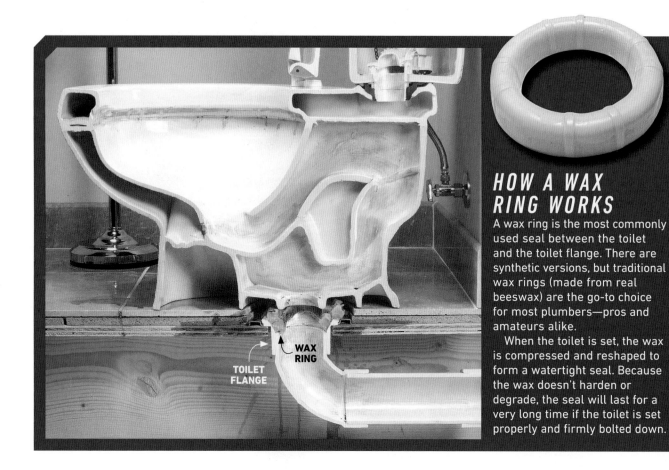

HOW A WAX RING WORKS

A wax ring is the most commonly used seal between the toilet and the toilet flange. There are synthetic versions, but traditional wax rings (made from real beeswax) are the go-to choice for most plumbers—pros and amateurs alike.

When the toilet is set, the wax is compressed and reshaped to form a watertight seal. Because the wax doesn't harden or degrade, the seal will last for a very long time if the toilet is set properly and firmly bolted down.

WAX RING

TOILET FLANGE

4 ASSESS THE LEVEL OF FLOOR ROT

If your toilet has been leaking for some time, you're likely to have rot. Finished flooring traps water, which accelerates and spreads the problem. The rot can range from a little bit around the flange to a full-blown case that requires tearing up the flooring and replacing subflooring and possibly framing.

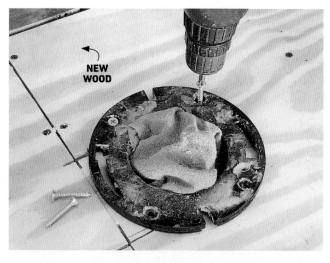

NEW WOOD

FLANGE SUPPORT BRACKET

MODERATE ROT If the rot extends beyond the range of an eared flange but is still contained within the footprint of the toilet, step up to a flange support bracket. These transfer the load past the rotted areas of the subfloor.

EXTENSIVE ROT Don't freak out if you have bad floor rot. It's easier than you think to cut out the bad flooring and replace it with new wood and additional framing if needed. Just make sure you go far enough to cover the entire area of rotted wood. Bad framing can usually be left in place and reinforced with new 2-by material, if you can screw it into solid wood. Don't worry about removing the rotted framing. With the leak fixed, the rot won't continue. The worst part is that you'll also need to replace the finished floor.

FLANGE FIX-IT OPTIONS

TWO-PART REPAIR RING

Steel flanges that surround plastic flanges can rust away. The easiest solution is to install a two-part (or hinged) ring that locks under the plastic rim. Badly corroded steel rings can be pried and peeled away. If you have to get aggressive, cut it away with an angle grinder or oscillating tool fitted with a metal-cutting blade.

EARED REINFORCEMENT RING

If you have just a bit of rot around the flange, or screws won't be able to grip the wood under a repair flange, try an eared reinforcement ring. The ears may extend beyond the rot enough to get a good grip in the subfloor for the screws. Anchor the ring to wood with six 1½-in. No. 8 oval-head stainless steel screws, and to concrete with 1¼-in. flat-head concrete screws.

EAR

BROKEN FLANGE

REPAIR RING

Plastic flanges often bend or break. To fix one, screw a stainless steel repair ring over the plastic flange with at least four 1½-in. stainless steel screws. Consider doing this even if the flange is in good shape and you only need to replace the wax ring. It's cheap insurance against trouble. The repair ring raises the flange about ¼ in., so before you install the ring, rest it over the flange and then see if the toilet rocks when you set it on top. If it does, shim under the toilet to allow for the extra height.

STAINLESS STEEL RING

BROKEN FLANGE

REPAIR BRACKETS

BROKEN FLANGE

REPAIR BRACKET

Cast-iron flanges often break on one or both sides. If only the bolt slot is damaged, slip a repair bracket under the cast-iron lip. It will be held in place by the unbroken cast-iron lip and provide a new slot for the flange bolt.

REPAIR FLANGE

REPAIR FLANGE

If the flange is in bad shape, you can install a plastic flange that slips inside (shown above). Home centers carry one or two versions of these. Or you can add a brass ring similar to the stainless steel ring shown at left. If necessary, break away the cast-iron flange with a cold chisel.

CHOOSE THE RIGHT TOILET PAPER

//
SHOP WISELY TO STOP CLOGS BEFORE THEY START

Toilets clog for a number of reasons, but one reason few consider is the type of toilet paper that's used. While all toilet paper dissolves eventually, how fast it breaks down is what matters.

Slow-dissolving toilet paper can get caught in your pipes and build up, creating a clog. If you have an old toilet, bad pipes, a septic tank or a kid who loves to watch streamers of toilet paper disappear down the toilet, it's even more important you buy the right stuff. So, to get to the bottom of that problem, we went to a local store, loaded a cart with popular toilet paper brands and put them to the test. As you might imagine, we received a lot of strange looks, but we didn't let that deter us; we were on a mission.

THE PROCESS

Because we were testing how fast toilet paper disintegrated in water, we didn't consider other factors such as the environment, cost or comfort. We just needed to find the toilet paper with the fastest breakdown. The process was straightforward: We gathered nine rolls from popular toilet paper brands, dropped two squares of each in water, and let them sit for 15 minutes. Afterward, we stirred to simulate a single flush. Then we tried to scoop the scraps out of the water. The samples that barely remained intact were the winners. The results were stunning and clear—keep them in mind on your next trip to the store.

TOILET PAPER BREAKDOWN

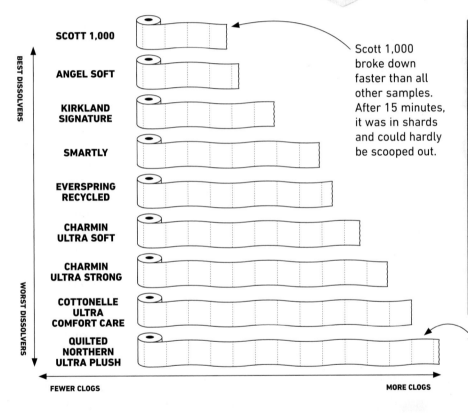

BEST DISSOLVERS
- SCOTT 1,000
- ANGEL SOFT
- KIRKLAND SIGNATURE
- SMARTLY
- EVERSPRING RECYCLED
- CHARMIN ULTRA SOFT
- CHARMIN ULTRA STRONG
- COTTONELLE ULTRA COMFORT CARE
- QUILTED NORTHERN ULTRA PLUSH
WORST DISSOLVERS

FEWER CLOGS → MORE CLOGS

Scott 1,000 broke down faster than all other samples. After 15 minutes, it was in shards and could hardly be scooped out.

1-PLY VS. 3-PLY

Toilet paper comes in 1-, 2- and 3-ply versions. With 1-ply paper, you might expect that people would simply use more and end up with the same clogging problems caused by thicker paper. But we found that 1-ply paper breaks down better, even if more is used. For example, we tested three times as much of the Scott 1,000 1-ply as the Quilted Northern Ultra Plush 3-ply to see if it made any difference in breakdown. It didn't. More sheets of Scott 1,000 still broke down faster than the equivalent of Quilted Northern Ultra Plush.

The Quilted Northern sheets came out of the water thick and almost fully intact. There's little doubt they would clog a toilet.

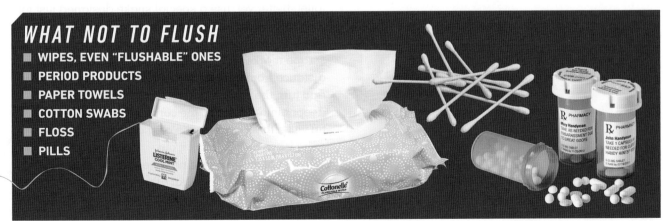

WHAT NOT TO FLUSH

- WIPES, EVEN "FLUSHABLE" ONES
- PERIOD PRODUCTS
- PAPER TOWELS
- COTTON SWABS
- FLOSS
- PILLS

UNPLUG A TOILET

SIMPLE TOOLS AND EASY TECHNIQUES YIELD FAST RESULTS

A plugged toilet can require professional intervention. But in the vast majority of cases, you can do exactly what a plumber would do. That means starting with a plunger and then, maybe, using a "snake." Until you've tried those methods, don't schedule an expensive house call.

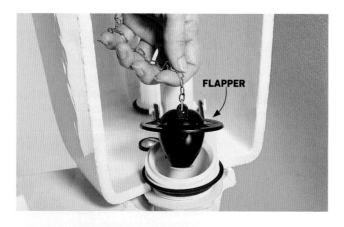

FLAPPER

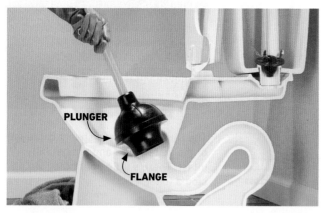

PLUNGER

FLANGE

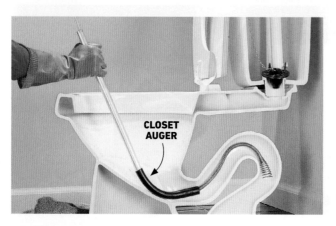

CLOSET AUGER

DON'T FLUSH!

When a flush seems weak, you'll wonder whether the toilet is plugged. Don't find out by flushing again—you could end up with an overflow. Instead, lift the lid off the tank and raise the flapper by hand for a few seconds. That will release some water into the bowl so you can see whether it flows down the drain. Adding dish soap to the bowl before lifting the flapper—and then letting the soapy water sit in the drainpipe for a couple hours—can sometimes help get a clog moving. For a faster fix, locate your plunger.

PLUNGER POINTERS

- If the bowl is nearly overflowing, wait. In most cases, the water level will slowly fall. That may take 15 minutes or more, but better to delay than to slop sewage all over the floor.
- Use a plunger with a fold-out flange. It will seal better around the toilet drain for a more powerful—and more effective—plunge.
- Start gently. Before your first push, the plunger is full of air, so a hard push will blast out a messy sewage explosion. Slowly increase the force of your thrusts until you know how hard you can push.
- You need water in the bowl. Driving air down the drain won't work. So if the water level drops too low, add some by lifting up the flapper.
- Don't give up. Clearing a stubborn clog can take 20 pushes or more.

SEND IN THE SNAKE

You can use a standard drain snake to unplug a toilet. Better yet, use a special snake designed just for toilets: A "closet auger," available at home centers, has a rubber sleeve to protect the toilet bowl from scrape marks and a long handle that gives you more distance from the splashy action. Just insert the snake and turn the handle that spins the snake. As it twists deeper into the drain, the corkscrew tip will either break up the clog or snag it so you can yank it out. When snaking fails, the next step is to remove the toilet. That allows easier access to the clog, whether it's in the toilet or in the drain lines.

DRAIN SNAKE

GET OUT OF PLUMBING JAMS

OVERCOME COMMON SETBACKS WITH EXPERT-APPROVED SOLUTIONS

Sometimes even the best-laid plumbing plans go awry. Your project can come to a screeching halt when a vital piece breaks off, gets stuck or is too rotten or corroded to work with. Then what? Sure, cursing might make you feel better, but you need a real solution that gets your project back on track. We consulted a plumbing expert and found the best ways to tackle problems encountered by pros and amateurs alike.

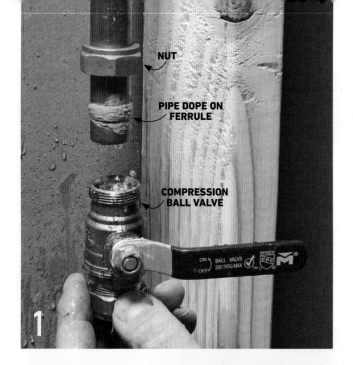

NUT

PIPE DOPE ON FERRULE

COMPRESSION BALL VALVE

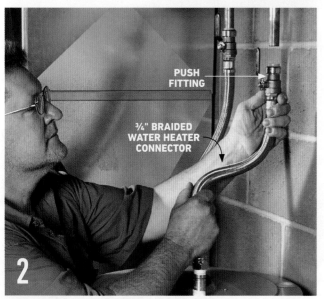

PUSH FITTING

¾" BRAIDED WATER HEATER CONNECTOR

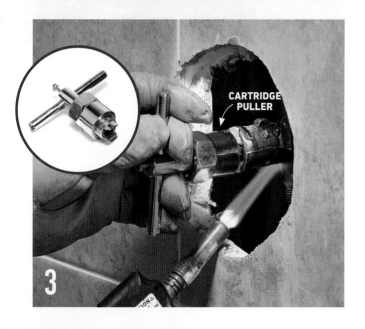

CARTRIDGE PULLER

1 INSTALL A COMPRESSION FITTING FOR EASIER SOLDERING

You know that it's nearly impossible to sweat (solder) joints when there's the least bit of water inside the lines. So don't sweat it (plumbers' humor). Install a compression fitting or a push fitting instead. Neither requires any heat, solder or flux. Compression fittings just tighten with a wrench; push fittings simply slide on and seal themselves. Neither is affected by a little water. When you're installing compression fittings, lubricate the ferrule with a bit of pipe dope so it slides in and seats straight into the nut. Mechanical (shutoff) fittings like this need to be accessible, so don't bury them behind drywall.

2 MAKE A SUPER-FAST WATER HEATER CONNECTION

Most folks "can't live" without hot water, and when a water heater conks out, getting the new one installed is a high priority. There's no faster or easier way to install water heater supply lines than by using specially designed braided stainless steel water lines with a push-fitting shutoff valve on one end. All you need to do is apply a little pipe dope or plumbing tape to the water heater nipples, fasten the female ends to the water heater, and then just push the push fitting onto the water supply lines. But this convenience comes with a price. The ¾-in. x 18-in. connectors shown here cost about $36 each at a home center.

3 USE A CARTRIDGE PULLER FOR STUCK CARTRIDGES

Some shower cartridges pull right out, but some need a little convincing with a cartridge puller. Others are even more stubborn and need a puller and some heat to persuade them to break free. Heat expands the valve body, decreasing the pressure on the cartridge. Heat also softens the rubber seals. Hook up the cartridge puller and put the flame on the valve body of the cartridge. Add pressure to the puller as you apply the heat. Set a heat shield on the back of the cartridge so you don't start a fire. And have a fire extinguisher at hand just in case.

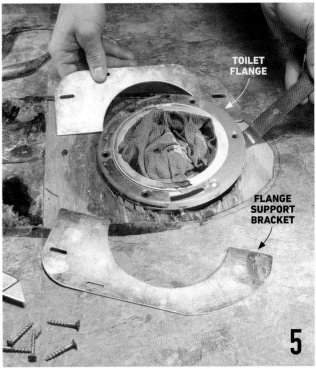

TOILET FLANGE

FLANGE SUPPORT BRACKET

5

CUTTING BLADES

GUIDE

SOCKET SAVER

M18 LITHIUM XC

4

REAM OUT BROKEN HUBS

4 You can reuse an existing hub by reaming out the old pipe that's glued inside it. This PVC fitting saver will do the trick. It has a guide that rides inside the pipe you're removing so the hub won't get wrecked. Since replacing a hub can mean having to open up a finished wall—or worse, busting up concrete—this affordable tool can save you a lot of time and money. The Socket Saver by Jones Stephens is available at home centers and online for about $20.

USE A FLANGE SUPPORT BRACKET FOR ROTTED FLOORS

5 If the floor is too spongy to screw down a toilet flange, attach a flange support bracket to the floor and then secure the toilet flange to that. This fix will work only if the majority of the floor under the toilet is solid. Probe the floor by poking it with a screwdriver. If more than an inch or so around the flange is rotten, you'll need to repair the floor itself.

The bracket shown in **Photo 5** is part of the Quick-Fix Floor Flange Support Kit. You can find the kit online at *quickfixplumbingproducts.com*. It will also work over holes in the floor that have been cut a bit too large.

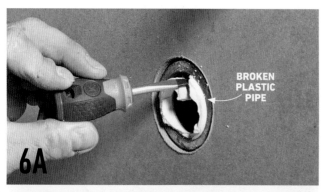

6A

BROKEN
PLASTIC
PIPE

6B

½" INTERNAL PIPE
WRENCH

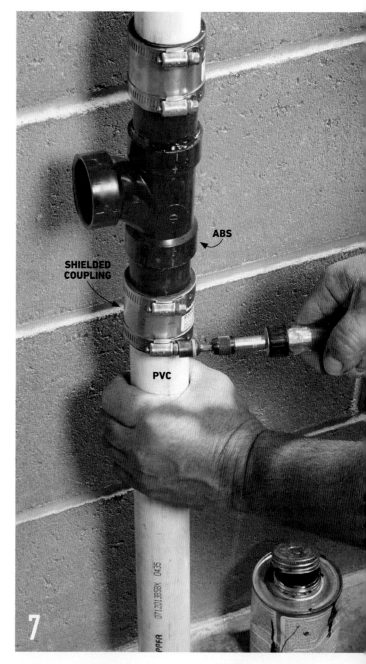

ABS

SHIELDED
COUPLING

PVC

7

6A CUT AND PRY BROKEN THREADS ...

Pipes sometimes break off when you're trying to separate them, leaving the threads stuck inside the other pipe. When removing threads from steel pipes, carefully make two cuts with a hacksaw and then pry the piece loose with a screwdriver **(Photo 6A)**. The top side of the pipe is subjected to much less water and is less likely to leak, so always make cuts on the top side of the pipe in case the steel threads get nicked a little. And make sure to use pipe dope or tape on the new pipe.

6B OR REMOVE THEM WITH AN INTERNAL PIPE WRENCH

You can use an internal pipe wrench to remove small supply-line pipe threads **(Photo 6B)**. A knurled cam slides out when the wrench is twisted, grabbing hold of the old threads from the inside. The one shown costs about $10 at home centers. Another trick that sometimes works is to grab hold of the end of the thread with needle-nose pliers. Twist the pliers clockwise and the thread will wind out like a spring.

½" MALE
PIPE THREAD

CAM

7 JOIN INCOMPATIBLE PIPES WITH A SHIELDED COUPLING

If you need to tie into a white PVC pipe but the closest plumbing supplier carries only black ABS, you don't have to run all over town. Install a shielded rubber coupling between the two pipes. Shielded couplings are often referred to as "mission couplings," and they work great to connect other dissimilar pipes: galvanized steel to plastic, cast iron to plastic, ABS to PVC. Make sure you use a "fully banded" coupling because the couplings with just the two individual hose clamps may not be allowed in some situations.

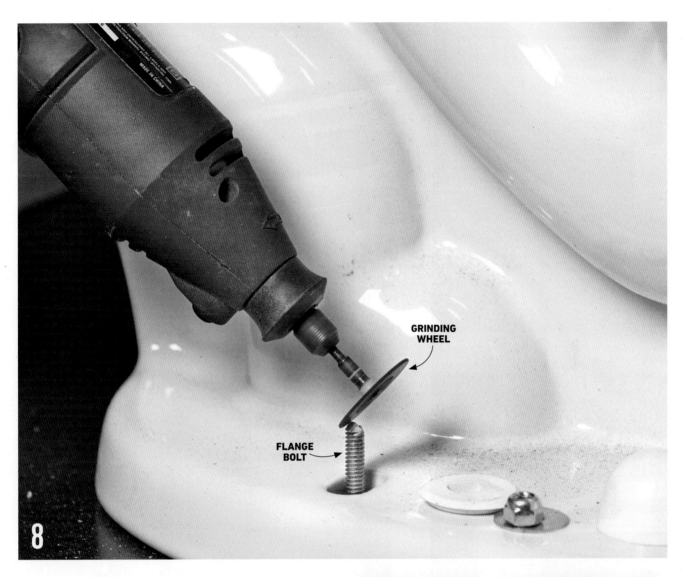

GRINDING WHEEL

FLANGE BOLT

8

8 SMOOTH BOLTS WITH A ROTARY TOOL

Sometimes a toilet can be reset using the existing flange bolts, but often the ends of the soft brass bolts are damaged, making it difficult to get the nut started. Clean up the ends of the bolts with a rotary tool fitted with a grinding wheel. You can use the same tool to cut off new flange bolts to the proper height if they're too long. Clean up the ends of the bolts to ease future repairs.

9 DROP IN A REPLACEMENT CLOSET FLANGE

If the old toilet flange is broken beyond all hope of repair, drop in a replacement flange. The expert we consulted prefers replacement flanges with a rubber compression gasket that expands. There are several styles, but the gasket on this one expands as you twist it into place. It's available for both 3-in. and 4-in. waste pipes at home centers and plumbing supply stores.

9

REPLACEMENT FLANGE

BROKEN CAST IRON CLOSET FLANGE

UPGRADE YOUR SHOWER IN A WEEKEND

//

ADD LUXURY TO YOUR BATHROOM, FASTER AND WITH LESS MESS

Bathrooms are often high up on the renovation wish list, but the thought of demolishing a bathroom and putting it out of commission—or having a contractor trekking in and out for weeks—scares off many a homeowner. Luckily, we've dreamed up a few ways to get big upgrades in less time and with less disruption.

4 FANCY FEATURES

These are the features we were able to add to our bathroom inside the drop ceiling. This would also be a great space for a heater or even speakers.

■ **LIGHTED BATH FAN** A slim-fit fan allowed us to maintain enough ceiling height and use 2x6s for the ceiling frame. The Aero Pure fan we chose includes an LED light.

■ **RAINFALL SHOWER** The epitome of luxury in a bathroom is an overhead shower. The plumbing is easy to run down the wall; all you need is a hole big enough for the pipe.

■ **LED ACCENT LIGHTS** These 12-volt dimmable LED light strips can be cut to any length and are easy to wire together. Most importantly, they're rated for damp areas such as a shower. Made by various manufacturers, a 16-ft. strip costs about $40. The lights are powered by a switch that has a built-in transformer to convert 120-volt power to the 12 volts needed for the LED light strips. Made by Kichler, the switch cost us about $150.

■ **3-WAY SHOWER VALVE** This Grohe Grohtherm SmartControl valve (about $600) lets you use the shower wand, tub spout and rainfall showerhead all at the same time, individually or in any combination of the three.

MATERIALS LIST

ITEM	QTY.
2x6 x 8'	3
2x4 x 8'	6
4' x 8' PVC sheets	2
Drop ear elbow	1
Cortex screws	1 box
½" PEX pipe	25'
14-2 NM cable	25'
Low-voltage cable	25'

Figure A Drop Ceiling
OVERALL DIMENSIONS: 12½" T X 35¾" W X 60" L

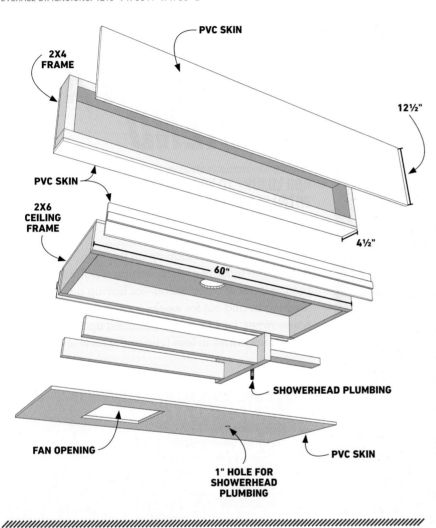

- PVC SKIN
- 2X4 FRAME
- 12½"
- PVC SKIN
- 2X6 CEILING FRAME
- 4½"
- 60"
- SHOWERHEAD PLUMBING
- FAN OPENING
- 1" HOLE FOR SHOWERHEAD PLUMBING
- PVC SKIN

Figure B Plumbing & Electrical Plan

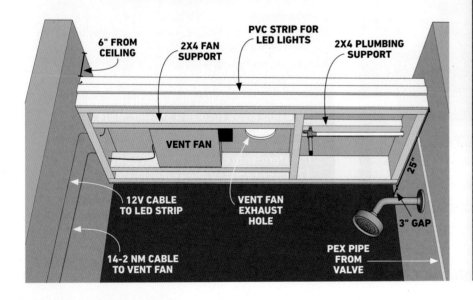

- 6" FROM CEILING
- 2X4 FAN SUPPORT
- PVC STRIP FOR LED LIGHTS
- 2X4 PLUMBING SUPPORT
- VENT FAN
- 25"
- 12V CABLE TO LED STRIP
- VENT FAN EXHAUST HOLE
- 3" GAP
- 14-2 NM CABLE TO VENT FAN
- PEX PIPE FROM VALVE

WHY A DROP CEILING?

Drop ceilings are common in kitchens and basements, where they hide ductwork, plumbing or beams. Building one above the bathtub might seem a little odd, but it's a perfect way to add luxury features without tearing apart your bathroom. We built this ceiling from PVC sheet material, which is waterproof, paintable and easy to work without special tools.

BEFORE

AFTER

2X6 CEILING FRAME

2X4 SUPPORTS ALLOW CABLES TO CROSS

1 BUILD A BOX

Build the ceiling frame by screwing 2x6s together. To determine the length of this simple box, measure between the two walls and subtract ¼ in.

2 ADD SUPPORTS FOR THE FAN AND SHOWERHEAD

Set the bath fan and showerhead in the ceiling frame. We placed the center of the showerhead 20 in. from one side (one-third of the total length) and then centered the fan between the opposite side and the showerhead. Screw the 2x4s and 2x6s into place from the outside of the frame.

COMPOSITE SCREWS FOR PVC

Cortex screws have a reverse thread near the head that pulls the material tightly to the frame and prevents the material from coming loose. The special bit drives the screw to the correct depth, leaving a recess for the plugs.

CORTEX COMPOSITE SCREWS

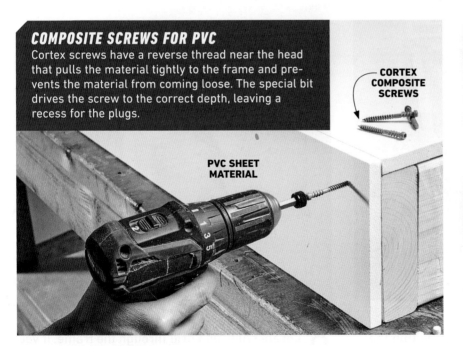

PVC SHEET MATERIAL

3 COVER THE BOX WITH PVC

Cut a sheet of ½-in. PVC to fit the top and sides of the frame. Fasten this PVC skin to the frame with composite screws, then plug the holes to hide the screw heads. Carefully position the PVC before driving screws; removing a composite screw leaves a hole that you can't screw back into.

4 CUT A HOLE IN THE TOP

Using a jigsaw, cut out a 6-in.-diameter hole in line with the fan's exhaust port to run flexible duct through.

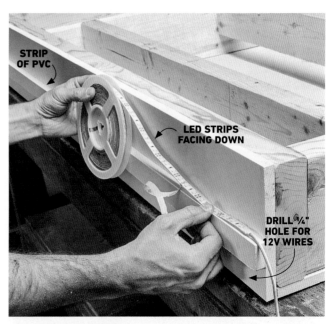

5 INSTALL PLUMBING ELBOW

Install a drop ear elbow centered in the frame 20 in. from the side. This fitting holds the rainfall showerhead in place. PEX pipe will be attached to it later to supply the water.

6 INSTALL LIGHTS

Screw a strip of PVC along the side of the ceiling frame toward the top. Stick on the damp-rated LED strip so it faces down. Drill a ¼-in. hole above the strip and feed the low-voltage cable inside the ceiling frame for connections later.

7 POSITION THE CEILING FRAME

With a helper, position the frame within the shower walls with 6 in. of space below the ceiling, to make room for the fan's duct, and 3 in. from the back wall. Prop the frame into position with a few 2x4s, then wedge it into place with shims.

8 SECURE THE FRAME

Locate studs and drill through the frame. If you can't find studs through the tile, track them down on the back side of the wall and transfer the measurement to the front. Then use a tile bit to drill holes so the frame can be fastened with large screws into the studs. You'll need to drill through the tile for the plumbing and electrical cable too.

GROHE RAPIDO ROUGH-IN BOX

BLOCKING FOR TUB SPOUT

PVC CUTTER

PEX EXPANDER TOOL

TRACE THE VALVE

9 CUT THE TILE TO FIT THE NEW VALVE

To make room for the Grohe rough-in box, we cut a hole 5¾ in. in diameter. The best tool for this is a diamond hole saw, but one that big can be expensive. We opted to use an angle grinder with a diamond blade. This cut can be tricky; take your time.

10 INSTALL THE VALVE

We cut an access hole in the wall behind the shower and installed the three-way shower valve. Then we used PEX pipe to supply the new rainfall showerhead and to connect to the old copper pipe. Secure the valve with 2x4 blocking.

11 COVER THE ACCESS HOLE

We fastened a frame to the drywall that we'd cut out earlier and attached the frame to the wall with trim screws. To make the frame easy to remove, we didn't plug the screw holes.

ROUTE CABLES DOWN THE WALL

PEX PIPE INSTALLED AND ROUTED DOWN THE WALL

OPENING FOR VENT FAN

1" HOLE FOR SHOWERHEAD PLUMBING

12 CAP THE FRAME

Cut a hole in the final PVC sheet for the fan and drill a 1-in. hole for the showerhead plumbing. Route electrical cables into the wall, then cap the frame with the PVC.

ATTACH DUCT AND INSTALL WIRING

13 INSTALL THE BATH FAN

Make the electrical connections to the fan and attach the flexible exhaust duct to the fan. Slide the fan into the opening, screw it to the blocking and install the grille.

KEEP BOTTOMS FLUSH

FASTEN TO STUDS

3" GAP

14 COVER IT ALL WITH A PANEL

Build a panel to be fastened 3 in. from the front of the drop ceiling. Use PVC to wrap the back and bottom, then screw the panel to the walls between the shower. After covering the front with the final sheet of PVC, caulk the corners and paint it to match the rest of your wall. No one will ever know your trick to an easy bathroom upgrade!

INSTALL FAUCETS

///
THE PROCESS CAN BE QUICK, EASY AND LEAK-FREE

Today's faucets are easier than ever for DIYers to install. In fact, you can even buy faucets that install entirely from the top of the sink so you don't have to crawl underneath. But there are still some things you should keep in mind. Here are our best tips for helping you with your next faucet installation.

1 CUT OUT THE OLD FAUCET

Even with a basin wrench, it can be nearly impossible to break loose corroded nuts holding older faucets to the sink. If you don't care about wrecking the faucet, cut off the nuts instead. You can use either a rotary tool (Dremel is one brand) with a metal-cutting disc or an oscillating tool with a metal-cutting blade. Cut through one side of the nut. Then use a screwdriver to pry the nut away from the faucet body. You can also cut off other stubborn parts, such as the pop-up drain assembly on a bathroom sink.

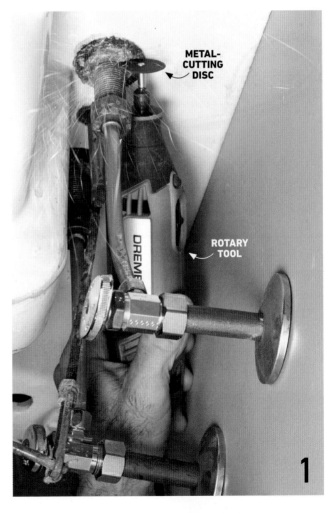

METAL-CUTTING DISC

ROTARY TOOL

1

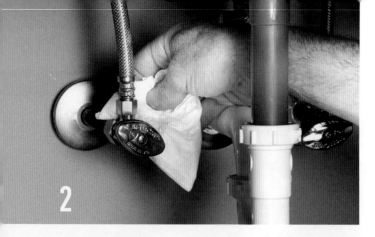

2

CLEAR
SILICONE
CAULK

3

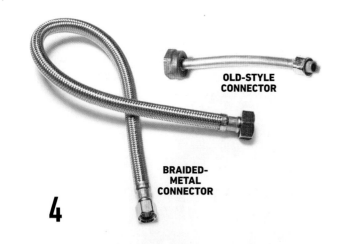

OLD-STYLE
CONNECTOR

BRAIDED-
METAL
CONNECTOR

4

SHUTOFF
VALVE

5

2 CHECK FOR LEAKS

When you're done with the faucet installation, check for leaks. Fill up the sink to the overflow two to three times and then drain the sink. The extra head pressure will show a leak more readily than just running a stream of water from the faucet. Then crawl underneath the sink with some tissue and wipe around the joints with it. Even a tiny leak will show up as a wet spot on the tissue. Tighten the connection near any leak you find.

3 MOUNT THE FAUCET WITH SILICONE

If water gets under your faucet, it can corrode the faucet, or worse, damage your countertop or cabinet. Most new faucets include a gasket of some type to create a seal between the faucet and the sink, but it's still a good idea to apply a bead of clear silicone caulk to the bottom of the faucet and the bottom of the gasket to ensure a good seal. Also, the silicone acts as an adhesive to prevent the faucet from moving around if the connection nuts loosen. Clean up any silicone that oozes out, first using just a paper towel, then mineral spirits.

4 UPGRADE YOUR SUPPLY LINES

One of the most difficult parts of installing a new faucet used to be connecting the supply lines so they didn't leak. But the new-style connectors with braided jackets have gaskets built into each end that make connections virtually foolproof. They cost more but are worth every penny. You don't need to crank the nut very tight for an effective seal. Just thread it finger-tight and then add about a half-turn with a wrench. So save yourself headaches and replace those old supply lines with braided stainless steel connectors.

5 MEASURE FOR THE SUPPLY LINES

Many new faucets include supply lines, but they may not be long enough, or they may not have the right threads to connect to your shutoff valves. To determine the length of the supply lines you'll need, measure from the underside of the sink near where the faucet connects to the shutoff valve and add a few inches. If the supply lines included with your new faucet aren't long enough, buy extensions. To make sure the threads on your new supply lines match those on your shutoff valves, take one of your old supply lines with you to the store and match it with the new supply lines.

6 LOOSEN STUCK SHUTOFF VALVES

If your shutoff valve is stuck open, you can often free it by loosening the packing nut slightly. This relieves pressure on the valve stem and allows you to turn the valve more easily. Retighten the nut just enough to prevent leaks around the valve stem.

7 REMOVE THE AERATOR BEFORE YOU TURN ON THE WATER

Messing around with plumbing often dislodges minerals or other debris that has built up inside the pipes and valves. To prevent that stuff from clogging the aerator in your new faucet, remove the aerator before turning the water back on. Most aerators simply unscrew counterclockwise. Some new faucets include a special tool for removing the aerator.

If you're installing a pullout faucet, the aerator can be tricky to remove. If this is the case, simply unscrew the entire spray head from the supply tube and point the tube into the sink while you turn on the water. Let the water run a few seconds. Then replace the aerator or spray head.

8 SAVE THE INSTRUCTIONS AND PARTS IN A FREEZER BAG

Many new faucets include wrenches, aerator removal tools, and other parts or tools that you should keep. Put it all in a big freezer bag and hang it inside the sink cabinet, where you'll always be able to find it.

9 PREMOUNT THE FAUCET ON NEW SINK INSTALLATIONS

If you're installing a new sink along with your faucet, mount the faucet to the sink before you install the sink. It's much simpler than lying on your back inside the sink cabinet. Even if you're not installing a new sink, you may find it easier to remove the old sink to get better access for removing the old faucet and installing the new one.

10 KEEP A BASIN WRENCH HANDY

A basin wrench is a standard plumbing tool that is indispensable for removing and installing most faucets. The wrench allows you to reach into the cramped area behind the sink to loosen or tighten the nuts that hold the faucet to the sink, and the nuts that connect the supply lines. You may not need a basin wrench if you can get the old faucet out by cutting the nuts (see Tip 1) and if the new faucet includes a wrench or some other means of installing the faucet. Check inside the package when you buy the faucet to see what's required.

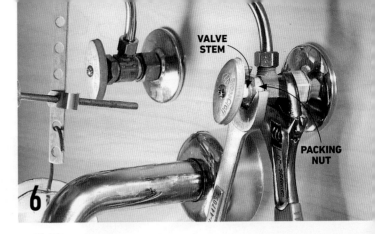

VALVE STEM

PACKING NUT

6

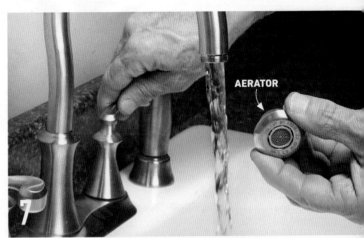

AERATOR

7

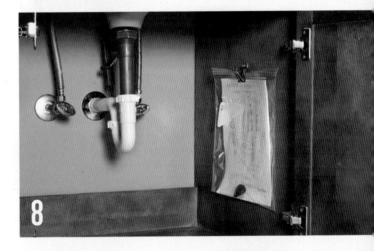

8

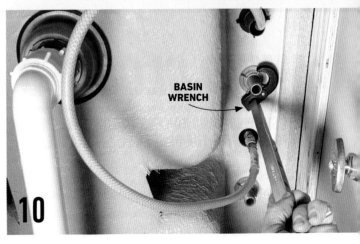

BASIN WRENCH

10

AVOID CLOGGED DRAINS

FROM SHOWERS AND TOILETS TO THE KITCHEN SINK, ALL HOUSEHOLD DRAINS CAN RUN FREELY WITH THE PROPER MAINTENANCE

Drains always seem to clog at the worst possible time, like when you have a houseful of overnight guests or a big party. And while you may not be able to stop every drain clog, there are steps you can take to prevent most clogs and nasty backups. These 10 tips will save you big headaches down the line.

WASHING MACHINE DISCHARGE HOSE

MESH LINT TRAP

LINT TRAPPER

1 INSTALL A LINT CATCHER ON YOUR WASHING MACHINE HOSE

If the drain for your washing machine hasn't ever backed up, you're lucky. Lint, bits of fabric, facial tissue and even the occasional sock can sneak through your washer's drain hose and cause trouble in your drain.

To keep this stuff from plugging your drain, put a lint trap on the end of the drain hose. You can buy mesh lint traps for your washer's discharge hose at home centers and hardware stores, or you can simply use an old nylon stocking. Use a zip tie to hold the lint trap in place. Keep an eye on the trap and replace it when it's full. For extra insurance, buy a Lint Trapper (shown above). This reusable cone-shaped trap snaps into your laundry tub drain hole. It's available for about $13 online and at some home centers and hardware stores.

2 PUT BACTERIA TO WORK

Whether it's hair, grease or food, some sort of organic matter causes most drain clogs. Fortunately, there's a type of bacteria that breaks down organic matter in your drains. Adding the bacteria to your drains will start to consume organic matter and prevent clogs. You can buy drain-cleaning bacteria in granular or liquid form.

Bacterial drain cleaner is noncorrosive, so it won't harm pipes, and the bacteria won't interfere with the bacteria in your septic system. Follow the instructions on the package. Add the bacteria when drains won't be used, like right before everybody goes to bed, to allow it time to work. One-pound packages of drain and trap cleaner are available at home centers and hardware stores. They should last several months, depending on how many drains you treat.

3 COLLECT GREASE—DON'T DUMP IT

One of the worst things you can pour down your drain is grease. Warm grease runs down your drain until it cools in the pipe, where it congeals to start forming a clog. Then other stuff gets stuck in it, and before you know it you've got a major issue.

The best solution is to avoid pouring any grease or oil down your drain. Just keep a jar handy to collect the grease, and throw it into the trash when it gets full. Or, if you're one who likes to cook with leftover bacon grease, you can buy a container that's designed to save the grease for reuse.

4 DON'T WAIT FOR A MAIN LINE BLOCKAGE

If you have a clogged sewer line every year or two, don't just keep getting it cleaned. Most sewer service companies will "scope" the line to see what's causing the problem. That entails sending a remote camera down the line for a visual inspection.

The recurring issue could be tree roots entering through clay tile joints, a partially collapsed pipe or even rotted-out cast iron that allows soil to fall into the line and create a blockage. It's worth paying to find out the cause and get it fixed rather than hassling with frequent sewer backups and sewer-cleaning bills.

5 DON'T RINSE CEMENT, GROUT OR JOINT COMPOUND DOWN THE DRAIN

Setting-type joint compound hardens by a chemical reaction and will set up even underwater, so obviously if it settles in your drain you're in for a rock-hard clog. Sand is another building product that is notoriously bad for drains. Sand is heavy and settles quickly in traps and pipes to form clogs that are difficult to remove.

To avoid these problems, never rinse setting compound, grout, mortar mix or concrete down the drain. Instead, save rinse water in a container until the solid materials settle out. Then decant the water in an out-of-the-way area in your yard, and dump the remaining sludge into your garbage can.

6 FLUSH YOUR DRAINS

Low-flow toilets and faucets are great for saving water but not so good for keeping drains clear. The lower volume of water often doesn't carry away debris, and instead leaves it to collect in your pipes. You can counteract this problem by occasionally flushing the pipes with a large flow of water. Fill a 5-gallon bucket with water and pour it into your toilet while simultaneously flushing to help keep the large main drain line clear. Also, fill your bathtub and sinks with hot water and release it down the drain.

7 CATCH HAIR BEFORE IT REACHES THE DRAIN

Hair and soap combine in your tub or shower drain to create clogs that could end up requiring a drain snake to remove. But you can avoid that task by catching the hair before it reaches the drain.

Various sizes of mesh screens well-suited for this purpose are available at home centers and online. We recommend using a stainless steel strainer **(Photo 7A)** in both bath and laundry tub drains.

Another option is to replace the stopper assembly with one that includes a built-in screen. One choice is the DrainEASY Bathtub Stopper **(Photo 7B)**. It's designed to replace stopper assemblies that screw into the drain.

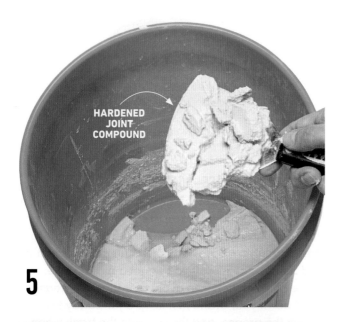

HARDENED JOINT COMPOUND

5

6

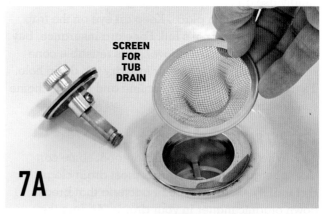

SCREEN FOR TUB DRAIN

7A

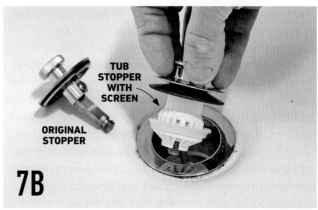

TUB STOPPER WITH SCREEN

ORIGINAL STOPPER

7B

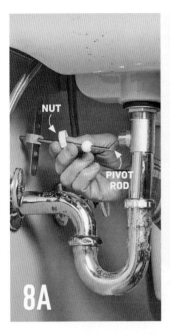
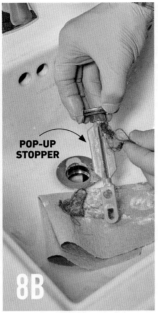

8A

NUT

PIVOT ROD

8B

POP-UP STOPPER

9

8 KEEP YOUR POP-UP STOPPER CLEAN

The pop-up stopper on your bathroom sink is a magnet for hair, dental floss and other yucky stuff. And it's probably a good thing, because it keeps all of that out of your drains. But allowing this waste to build up for too long can cause the sink to drain slower and slower and eventually not empty at all. And because the water flow down the drain is also slowed, clogs in the drain lines can form more easily.

When you notice that your bathroom sink is draining slowly, remove the stopper and clean it. Most pop-ups can be installed two ways. They can either be hooked into the pivot rod that lifts them, or simply rest on it. If your pop-up stopper is hooked in, you'll have to unscrew the nut on the back of the tailpiece (under the sink) and pull out the pivot rod to release the pop-up **(Photo 8A)**. When you reassemble it, try reinstalling the rod without running it through the hole in the pop-up stopper. Then drop the stopper into the drain hole. In most cases, it will work fine this way, and you'll be able to remove the pop-up stopper for cleaning without removing the rod.

9 COLLECT YOUR FOOD WASTE

Grinding up food in a disposer and sending it down the drain is convenient, but it can clog drains. A better idea is to collect your organic waste in a container and add it to a compost pile. Many cities collect organic waste for composting, but if yours doesn't, consider building your own compost bin. Avoid putting meat or other greasy food in the compost collection—it takes too long to break down.

10

10 DON'T USE THE TOILET AS A WASTEBASKET

It's tempting to throw all kinds of personal care products into the toilet. After all, there's a big drain hole and the stuff usually goes down OK. But just because dental floss goes down the toilet drain doesn't mean it'll make it to the main sewer. It's possible it will get snagged on something in your pipes and start a clog.

In addition to the fact that many of these products don't decompose readily, adding an unnecessary burden to the water treatment facility, they can clog drains. So avoid using the toilet as a wastebasket. It's better for the environment and better for your drains.

PREVENT FROZEN PIPES

DON'T LET WINTER'S ARRIVAL SPELL DISASTER—PREPARE YOUR PLUMBING INSTEAD

We all know that water expands when it freezes. That's not a problem when it comes to the ice cubes in your freezer, but if that ice forms in your plumbing, it's a potential disaster. A frozen pipe can crack, spewing hundreds of gallons of water into your home. Fortunately, you can take steps to help prevent a catastrophe and put your mind at ease.

1 GET AN EARLY WARNING
A Wi-Fi thermostat lets you conveniently control and monitor your home's temperature using a smartphone. If the temperature in your house drops, you'll get an email or text alert. Other types of alert systems are also available. Some send alerts to your cellphone via a phone jack in your house. Others send an alert to a landline or cellphone. To learn more, visit *familyhandyman.com* and search for "smart thermostat." Wi-Fi thermostats are available online and at home centers for $100 to $500.

1

2 SHUT OFF OUTDOOR FAUCETS

Turn off outdoor faucets at their shutoff valves. Open the faucet and then open the bleeder cap on the shutoff valve to drain any water out of the pipe. If you don't drain the pipe, it can still freeze and crack. Leave the bleeder cap open with a bucket underneath to catch any drips. If the dripping continues, your shutoff valve needs to be replaced.

3 INSTALL FROST-FREE SILL COCKS

Unlike a typical faucet, the working parts of a frost-free sill cock—valve, seat and washer—are located up to 18 in. inside the wall instead of right at the faucet. When the sill cock is properly installed, with a slight downward pitch, water drains from the pipe every time you turn off the knob at the faucet. Frost-free sill cocks can be purchased at home centers.

4 DISCONNECT HOSES

A water-filled hose left out in cold weather will freeze solid. If the hose is still connected to the faucet, ice can back up into the pipe inside your house, causing the pipe to crack. Disconnect all hoses from their faucets, drain them and store them for the winter.

5 COVER HOSE BIBS

Insulated covers slow the heat loss from a pipe as it travels through the wall out into the cold. They provide some protection for very little cost (about $3 at home centers).

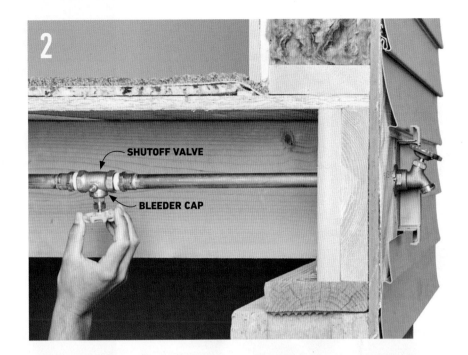

2

SHUTOFF VALVE

BLEEDER CAP

3

FROST-FREE SILL COCK

VALVE

4

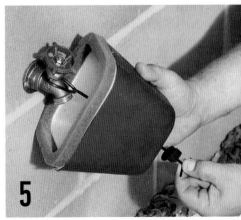

5

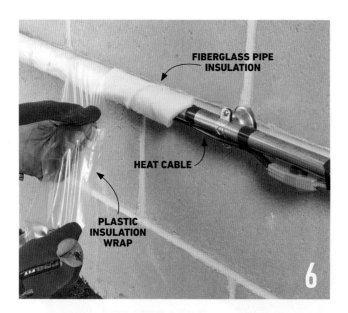

FIBERGLASS PIPE
INSULATION

HEAT CABLE

PLASTIC
INSULATION
WRAP

6

RIM JOIST
INSULATION

7

MAIN
SHUTOFF

8

THERMOSTAT

9

6 INSULATE PIPES

If you have pipes in an unheated area, such as a crawl space, an attic or a garage, use heat cable (see Tip 9) and cover it with pipe insulation. Pipe insulation alone does little, as it's only a matter of time before cold air can reach the pipe. Insulating pipes without also using heat cable can even prevent warm air from getting to them. Many types of pipe insulation are available at home centers for about $2 to $6.

7 SEAL AROUND RIM JOISTS

The rim joist is a likely area for cold air intrusion. Seal cracks or holes using expandable foam and then insulate between the floor joists. Be sure not to insulate a pipe from the heat in the rest of the house. Also, inspect around holes where cables, wires or pipes pass through an exterior wall. Insulate where you can, and seal drafts with caulk or expandable foam. After insulating, be sure you have combustion air for the furnace coming in through a makeup air pipe.

8 SHUT OFF THE WATER IF YOU LEAVE TOWN

If you're leaving town for a few days or more, turn the water off at the main shutoff. That way, if a pipe does freeze and crack, you'll have far less damage when you return. We also recommend shutting off your automatic icemaker so it doesn't continually try to make ice, burning out the motor. Even if the ice bin is full, the ice will evaporate and the icemaker will try to make more.

9 INSTALL HEAT CABLE

Heat cables can help protect vulnerable pipes. They have an integral thermostat that senses pipe temperature, turning the heat on and off as needed to keep the pipe from freezing. Heat cables are available at home centers. You'll need an accessible outlet to plug in the cable. Note: Do not install heat cable on PEX or plastic water piping—the piping can melt.

10 INSULATE YOUR GARAGE DOOR

If you have water lines in the garage, insulate the garage door, if not the whole garage. Consider a combination of heat cable and insulation as well. If it's really cold, put a portable heater in the garage.

INSULATION RETAINER PIN

10

DURING A COLD SNAP

What constitutes a cold snap depends on both your local climate and your home's insulation. A temperature of 32 degrees F isn't cause for alarm in Minnesota, but it might be in Mississippi.

■ **KEEP THE TEMPERATURE STEADY** During extreme cold, bypass your thermostat's program and leave the temperature steady. You may even want to turn it up a couple of degrees.

■ **OPEN KITCHEN CABINET DOORS** Being behind closed doors, kitchen plumbing pipes are vulnerable, as the heat from the rest of the house can't reach them. Open the cabinet doors to allow heat to circulate into the cabinets. A fan or portable heater pointed inside the cabinet also helps circulate warm air.

■ **LEAVE FAUCETS RUNNING** A trickling faucet acts as a relief valve for the pressure that builds up if a pipe does freeze. That pressure relief can prevent a frozen pipe from cracking. A slow trickle is all you need. It'll bump up your next water bill a bit, but compared with major home repairs, that's an easy price to pay. Don't leave a faucet running if the drain is on an exterior wall, though; the drain can freeze, causing the sink to overflow.

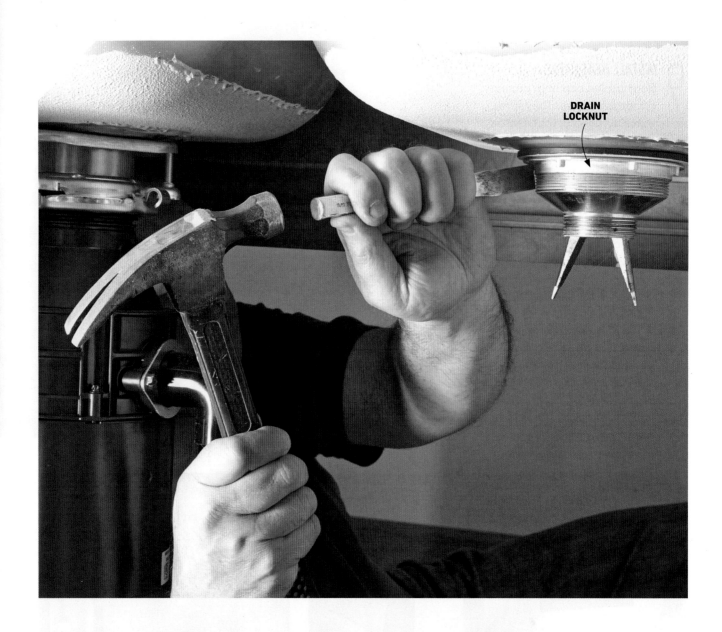

DRAIN
LOCKNUT

REPLACE A SINK STRAINER

THE RIGHT TECHNIQUES WILL SAVE YOU A BUNDLE

Kitchen sink basket strainers/drain assemblies work great when they're new. But with daily use and cleaning, the chrome or painted finish starts to wear off. The basket strainer stopper may also start leaking. Once that happens, you can forget about soaking pots and pans overnight. You might think that the solution is to buy a new basket strainer. Good luck finding one that fits and seals. You can buy a "universal" replacement that'll work as a strainer. But it usually doesn't seal well because it's not an exact fit. So your best option is to replace the entire drain assembly.

You can replace the drain assembly yourself, but it's a much easier job with two people. The hardest part of the job involves removing the old drain locknut. If your locknut comes off easily, you can finish the entire job in less than an hour. However, a drain locknut that's corroded is tougher to deal with. Either way, you'll save enough money on labor costs to make it worth your while. We'll show you two quick ways to conquer stubborn locknuts, and we'll offer some tips on shopping for a new, longer-lasting basket strainer/drain assembly.

REMOVE THE DRAINPIPES

To begin, place a bowl under the P-trap. Then use slip-joint pliers to loosen the compression nuts at the drain tailpiece and both nuts on the trap. Completely unscrew the tailpiece nut and swing the P-trap out slightly. Then unscrew the trap nuts completely and remove and drain the entire trap and tailpiece assembly to give yourself more working space.

LOOSEN AND REMOVE THE DRAIN LOCKNUT

Crawl under the sink and check for corrosion on the large drain locknut. If it's corroded, spray all around the nut with rust penetrating oil and allow it to soak for at least 15 minutes. Then have a friend hold the drain so you can loosen the locknut **(Photo 1)**. Loosen the locknut with a hammer and chisel **(Photo 2)**. If the locknut won't loosen or the entire drain spins and your helper can't hold it, cut it off **(Photo 3)**.

If you don't have either a helper or a rotary cutoff tool and you've tried but can't loosen the locknut yourself, there's still another option to try. Head to the home center or hardware store and purchase a sink drain wrench to loosen the nut and a plug wrench to help hold the drain **(Photo 4)**. Once you get the locknut off, pull the entire drain up and out of the sink.

CLEAN THE SINK FLANGE AND INSTALL THE NEW DRAIN

Scrape off the plumber's putty or silicone from around the drain flange in the basin and under the sink. If the old drain was caulked with silicone, use silicone remover to clean it. Then apply a fresh bead of silicone around the flange in the basin and insert the new drain. Next, install the new O-ring and locknut in the order shown **(Photo 5)**. Tighten the locknut until the rubber O-ring compresses slightly. Then reassemble the trap and tailpiece and attach it to the new sink drain. Clean off any excess silicone in the basin with a paper towel. Then clean off the O-ring and locknut.

Test the new drain assembly for leaks by filling the sink with water and releasing it while you check the pipes under the sink.

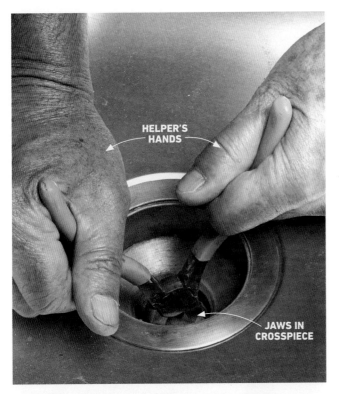

HELPER'S HANDS

JAWS IN CROSSPIECE

1 **_HOLD THE DRAIN TO LOOSEN THE LOCKNUT_**
Jam needle-nose pliers into the crosspiece section at the bottom of the drain. Have a pal spread the pliers and hold it tightly to prevent the drain from turning while you loosen the locknut. A basket strainer wrench also works for this task.

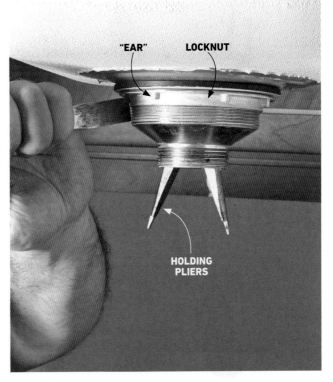

"EAR"   LOCKNUT

HOLDING PLIERS

2 **_LOOSEN THE LOCKNUT_**
Place the chisel tip against a locknut "ear." Then smack the chisel with a hammer. Move the chisel to the next ear and repeat until the nut spins by hand.

CARDBOARD
O-RING

3 DRASTIC MEASURES FOR STUCK NUTS

If all else fails, chuck a metal cutoff wheel into a rotary tool and cut the locknut. Cut until you reach the cardboard ring above the nut. Don't cut into the sink. If the nut still doesn't spin, fit your chisel into the cut area and smack it with a hammer to crack it open. Wear eye protection.

BUYING TIPS

Don't just pick up the cheapest option—spend a bit more for a high-quality strainer/drain assembly with a durable finish and a reliable stopper mechanism. The best strainers have either a spin-lock or a twist-and-drop style stopper. The spin-lock stopper doesn't have any parts that can wear, but screwing it in and out can be annoying. The twist-and-drop style is much easier to use but requires occasional O-ring replacement.

Avoid push-in style strainers that have a nonreplaceable neoprene stopper or a plastic knob. The plastic parts break and can lose their sealing ability if exposed to boiling water.

SPIN-LOCK STOPPER TWIST-AND-DROP STOPPER PUSH-IN STOPPER

SCREW LOCK   STAINLESS SEALING DISC   REPLACEABLE O-RING SEAL   NEOPRENE SEALING DISC

PLUG WRENCH

SINK DRAIN WRENCH

4 NO HELPER? NO PROBLEM!

You can buy these tools at any home center. Loosen the locknut with the sink drain wrench while you hold the drain with pliers and the plug wrench.

CARDBOARD O-RING

NEW LOCKNUT

RUBBER O-RING

5 INSTALL THE NEW STRAINER

Slide the rubber O-ring on first. Then add the cardboard O-ring and the locknut. Tighten the nut until it starts compressing the rubber O-ring.

REPLACE SHUTOFF VALVES

SWAP OLD MULTI-TURN VALVES FOR A MORE RELIABLE OPTION

If you're servicing or replacing a toilet or sink faucet, the first step is to shut off the water supply valve that feeds the fixture. But the simple task of shutting off the valve can be the start of a whole set of unexpected headaches.

Unless your house is fairly new, chances are you have multi-turn shutoff valves at every toilet and faucet. Shutoff valves perform flawlessly for years. But when they aren't opened or closed for a long time, you may find that the valve handle either won't turn or will turn but won't stop the water flow completely. And even if the valve does shut off the water, it may leak when you reopen it—the last thing you need after finishing a plumbing repair!

You can spend time rebuilding the old valve, but the problems will just reappear years from now. The best way to deal with bad valves is to replace them with modern quarter-turn ball valves. They rarely lock up, leak or wear out; they're inexpensive; and they'll take just an hour or so to install. Here's how to put them in.

IDENTIFY THE VALVE CONNECTION STYLE

Shutoff valves connect to copper plumbing pipes in one of two ways: compression fitting or sweat fitting. Identify the connection type used in your home by referring to the photos on p. 76. If you have an older home with galvanized pipes, we suggest hiring a plumber to do the switch-out. Unscrewing the old valve and screwing on a new one may seem easy enough. But if the pipe is rusted internally or the threads are rotted, this "simple" plumbing job can turn into a plumbing nightmare. If your home is plumbed with PEX or plastic pipe, these instructions don't apply.

Once you identify the connection type, buy a quarter-turn shutoff ball valve to match the size of the incoming copper pipe and the size of the supply tube connection. If you're replacing a sweat valve, you'll need a torch, flux, solder, emery cloth, wire brushes and a flame-protection cloth to shield the wall. This is also a good time to replace an old supply tube and a corroded escutcheon (wall trim plate).

PREPARE FOR VALVE REPLACEMENT

Shut off the water at the main shutoff valve. If you have a gas water heater, turn the knob to the "pilot" position. Shut off the circuit breakers to an electric water heater. Then open a faucet on the lowest level of your house and another faucet on an upper level to drain the pipes. Finally, disconnect the supply tube from the shutoff valve. Now you can replace the valve.

AFTER REPLACEMENT

Close the new valve. Then open the water-main shutoff valve and let the water run until all the air is out of the pipes. Then shut off the upper and lower faucets. Check the new valves for leaks. Turn the water heater gas valve back to "on" or flip on the circuit breakers to the electric water heater.

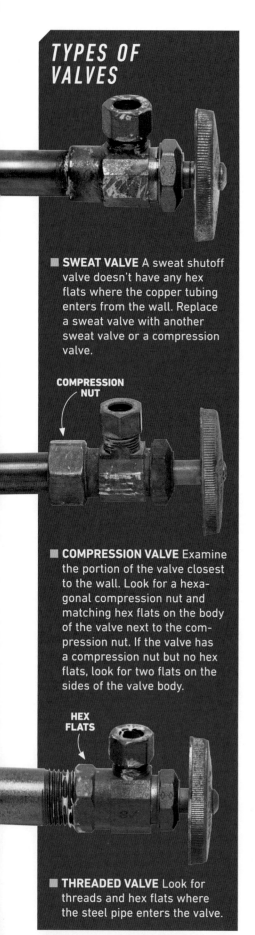

TYPES OF VALVES

■ **SWEAT VALVE** A sweat shutoff valve doesn't have any hex flats where the copper tubing enters from the wall. Replace a sweat valve with another sweat valve or a compression valve.

COMPRESSION NUT

■ **COMPRESSION VALVE** Examine the portion of the valve closest to the wall. Look for a hexagonal compression nut and matching hex flats on the body of the valve next to the compression nut. If the valve has a compression nut but no hex flats, look for two flats on the sides of the valve body.

HEX FLATS

■ **THREADED VALVE** Look for threads and hex flats where the steel pipe enters the valve.

REPLACE A SWEAT VALVE

Hold the valve with a pliers, loosen the packing nut and unscrew the entire valve stem. Peek inside and remove the old washer if it's stuck on the seat. Removing the valve stem allows any remaining water to drain out, making the unsweating process easier. Before you do any torch work, make sure there's a fire extinguisher nearby and safeguard the wall with a flame-protection cloth. Then remove the old valve **(Photo 1)** and the remaining solder **(Photo 2)**.

Clean the tubing with emery cloth. If you're replacing a sweat valve with a compression valve, sand off all traces of solder before adding the new escutcheon, nut and sleeve. Otherwise, remove enough old solder to allow the new sweat valve to slide onto the tubing. Remove the stem and wire-brush the opening in the new quarter-turn valve and apply flux to the valve and the copper tubing. With the flame-protection cloth in place, heat the valve just enough to draw in the solder.

NEW SWEAT VALVE

FLAME PROTECTION CLOTH

1 REMOVE THE OLD SWEAT VALVE
Drape the flame-protection cloth over the copper tubing and tape it to the wall. Adjust the torch to a small flame and aim it toward the body of the valve. As soon as the solder melts, twist and pull the valve off the copper tubing with a pliers.

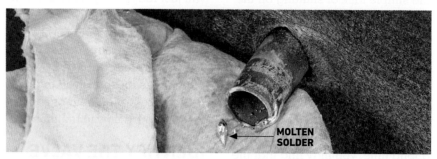

MOLTEN SOLDER

2 CLEAN EXCESS SOLDER
Put on a leather glove and grab a damp cotton rag (microfiber cloth will melt). Heat the remaining solder with the torch until it's molten. As soon as the solder melts, wipe away the excess solder with a damp rag. Be sure to wear leather gloves to prevent steam burns.

REPLACE A COMPRESSION VALVE

To remove a compression-style shutoff valve, hold the valve body with an adjustable or open-end wrench, or a slip-joint pliers. Grab the compression nut with another wrench, and begin turning the nut clockwise to loosen it. Then pull the valve off the copper tubing.

Remove the old compression sleeve and nut. Grab the old sleeve with a pliers, using minimal pressure to avoid distorting the copper tubing. Then rotate and pull it off the tubing. If the sleeve is stuck, saw it **(Photo 1)** and break it **(Photo 2)**.

Slide the new escutcheon and compression nut onto the copper tubing. Then add the new compression sleeve **(Photo 3)**. Insert the new valve and apply a very light coating of pipe dope to the compression sleeve. Next, screw the compression nut onto the valve until snug. Hold the valve with a wrench or a pliers and tighten the nut a one-half to three-quarters turn (follow the manufacturer's tightening instructions). Connect the supply tube and test for leaks.

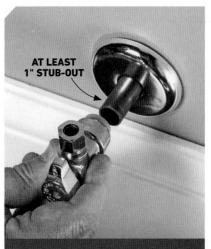

AT LEAST 1" STUB-OUT

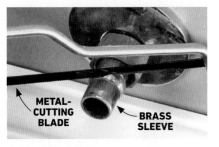

METAL-CUTTING BLADE

BRASS SLEEVE

1 SAW PARTIALLY THROUGH THE SLEEVE

Use a hacksaw to cut partially through the sleeve at an angle. Use short strokes to avoid cutting into the copper tubing. Check your progress and stop cutting before you reach the copper.

2 TWIST AND BREAK THE SLEEVE

Insert a flat-blade screwdriver into the cut and twist the screwdriver to break the sleeve. Slide off the old sleeve, old compression nut and the escutcheon (if you're going to replace it).

PREVIOUS SLEEVE DEPRESSION

3 POSITION THE NEW COMPRESSION SLEEVE

Slide the new compression sleeve onto the copper tubing. If the old sleeve left depression marks, locate the new sleeve slightly forward of the marks.

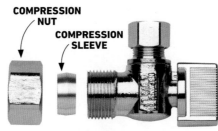

COMPRESSION NUT

COMPRESSION SLEEVE

NEW COMPRESSION VALVE

CAN YOU USE A PUSH-FIT VALVE?

Several companies make quarter-turn push-fit ball-style shutoff valves that install without tools. They're a good alternative to sweat and compression fittings if you have enough tubing projecting out from the wall and if that tubing is in good shape. They make the job even simpler. If your stub-out tubing is perfectly symmetrical, long enough and has a square-cut end, you might be able to use a push-fit valve to replace your old compression or sweat valve.

Most push-fit valves require at least 1 in. of stub-out tubing. So measure the length of the stub-out and refer to the valve manufacturer's length requirements before buying. If your tubing will work, shop for a valve that meets your configuration needs (straight or angled). Push-fit valves are available with and without a permanently mounted supply tube. We don't recommend the permanently installed supply tube version because you have to shut off the water and replace the entire unit if the supply tube ever needs replacement.

Before installing a push-fit valve, remove any burrs from the open end. If you're replacing a sweat valve, remove all traces of solder and ensure the tubing is perfectly round. Then mark the installed length on the tubing and push the valve onto the tubing until it reaches the mark.

A MECHANIC OR AUTO DETAILER

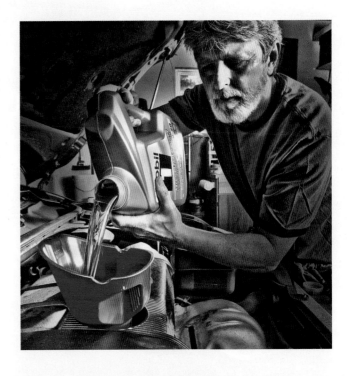

MAXIMIZE SMALL ENGINE PERFORMANCE

THE RIGHT CARE KEEPS SMALL ENGINES RUNNING AT THEIR BEST

Battery-powered yard tools are taking over, but it's not quite the end for gasoline and small engines. You can keep yours running smoothly for years with regular maintenance and some inside knowledge.

We talked with Dave Cheney of DC Carburetor Restoration to get his best advice on small engine maintenance. Plus, he showed us how to rebuild a carburetor, which is not as scary at it sounds.

KEEP YOUR SMALL ENGINES HEALTHY

1 CHECK FOR A SPARK

A spark plug checker can provide critical information. First, it will tell you if electricity is getting to the spark plug. Second, if there is no spark, it gives you the ability to determine the cause of failure.

2 INSPECT THE SPARK PLUG DIODE

If the spark plug looks slightly brown—not too dark—simply clean it with a soft wire brush, check the gap and reinstall. If the spark plug has an oil-fouled and deteriorated electrode, however, it needs to be replaced. A new spark plug typically costs less than $10 and will create the right spark to best ignite the fuel/air mix in the combustion chamber.

3 FEED YOUR MACHINE FRESH AIR

Small engines need clean air. A clean air filter allows maximum airflow and the optimum fuel/air mixture. You can and should clean the air filter. If the air filter is too far gone or if it's made of paper and it's clogged, it needs to be replaced.

4 DON'T ADD FUEL STABILIZER TO OLD GAS

Stabilizer won't bring gas back to life. Add stabilizer only to fresh gas to extend its use.

5 ALWAYS USE NEW GAS

Small engines love fresh fuel. If you have a can of gas that has been sitting around for more than four months,

LOOK FOR A SPARK HERE

PET-4000

ECHO.

1

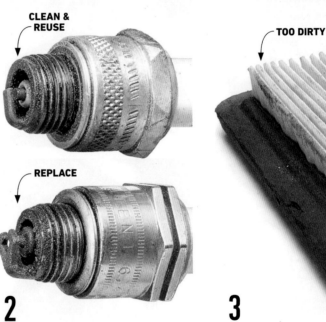

CLEAN & REUSE

TOO DIRTY

REPLACE

2

3

recycle that old gas. Ethanol blends have an even shorter life. Through oxidation and evaporation, gasoline becomes less combustible, leading to poor performance, rough idling and varnish deposits.

6 AVOID ETHANOL BLENDS

Small engines prefer ethanol-free gas. Ethanol attracts moisture from the air, separates from the gas and sinks to the bottom of the tank. This can cause ignition problems. But that's not the worst of it—ethanol is also corrosive and burns very hot, which can cause overheating and severe engine damage.

7 REPLACE A CARBURETOR THAT'S TOO FAR GONE

If your carburetor has reached the point of no return, finding a new replacement online is easy. According to Dave, Amazon and eBay are great places to start looking.

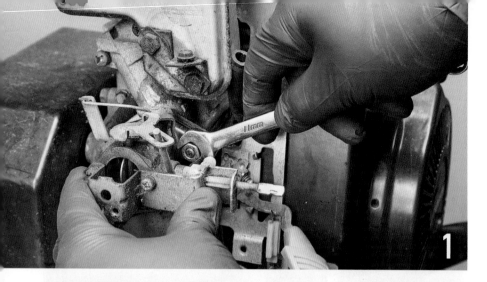

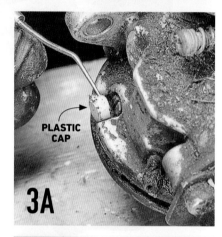

CLEAN/REBUILD THE CARBURETOR

We've all done it—delayed fall maintenance until spring. The engine might fire up, but it won't stay running for long. It's time to disassemble and clean the carburetor.

1 REMOVE THE CARBURETOR

Disconnect the fuel line, and if there is still fuel in the tank, crimp the line to avoid leaks. Most of the time, you'll find two bolts holding the carburetor to the engine. Remove these bolts and the carburetor.

2 DISASSEMBLE

After removing the main jet and the float bowl, Dave pokes out the float hinge pin with a nail set. Take the float off with care; the inlet needle and spring clip are under the float and are easy to lose.

3 REMOVE THE IDLE JET

A dirty idle jet causes small engines to pulse and surge instead of idle smoothly. On this carburetor, the idle jet is behind a small plastic cap. Dave uses an old dental pick to pop out the cap **(Photo 3A)** and then removes the idle jet with a small flat-head screwdriver **(Photo 3B)**.

4 SOAK THE PARTS IN CARB CLEANER

A 15-minute soak in Berryman Chem-Dip cleaner takes care of most surface grime. After soaking the parts, use a brush to clean off any remaining debris.

PLASTIC CAP

3A

IDLE JET

3B

FLOAT HINGE PIN

2

4

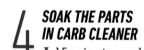

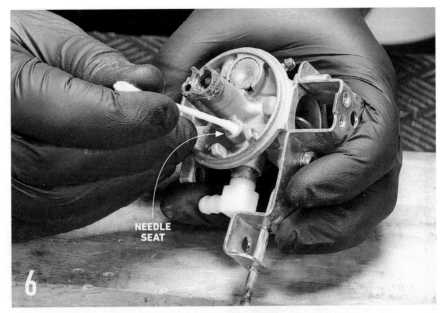

NEEDLE SEAT

5 DEEP CLEAN
A deep clean removes debris not reachable by soaking. Dave uses an ultrasonic cleaner, but you can place parts in a pot of boiling water for 15 minutes.

6 CLEAN THE NEEDLE SEAT
To make sure the needle seats cleanly, use a cotton swab to clear debris out of the needle seat.

7 REASSEMBLE AND INSTALL
Lay the clean parts out on your bench and do one final inspection. Reassemble the carburetor, bolt it to your machine and don't forget to prime it!

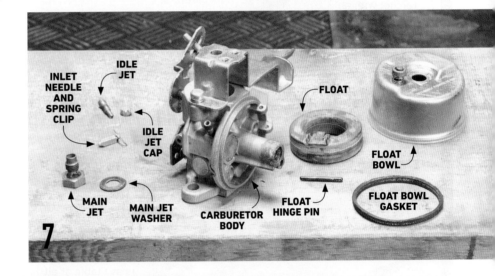

IDLE JET

INLET NEEDLE AND SPRING CLIP

IDLE JET CAP

FLOAT

FLOAT BOWL

MAIN JET

MAIN JET WASHER

CARBURETOR BODY

FLOAT HINGE PIN

FLOAT BOWL GASKET

RULES FOR SEASONAL STORAGE

■ **DRAIN THE CARBURETOR** You need to take one more important step after running your small engine out of fuel for the season. Some gas will remain in the carburetor's float bowl, and you need to drain it completely. Many carburetors have a small drain plug on the bottom of the float bowl for this purpose. If left to sit, the gas will varnish and you'll need to remove the carburetor to clean it.

■ **DON'T WINTERIZE—EXERCISE** Perhaps the easiest way to avoid the downside of seasonal maintenance tasks is to "exercise"

your engine. Instead of draining the engine of all gas, keep the fuel tank full in the off-season and run the engine once a month for about 10 minutes. Dave has used this technique for years; it saves him time and provides peace of mind. He knows his small engines always have good gas and the internal workings are always coated in fresh oil. Seems like a no-brainer.

■ **CHANGE THE OIL** Change the oil in your small engine every season. Fresh, clean oil keeps sludge from building up and helps maintain good compression.

PLASTIC BAG

OIL FILL TUBE

PRO TIP
Some lawn mowers don't have an oil drain plug; the oil is drained out of the fill tube at the top of the engine. Before you tip over your lawn mower to drain the oil, unscrew the gas cap and stretch plastic over the gas tank opening, then screw the cap back on. The plastic will prevent gas from leaking out the cap vent.

DAVE'S BENCH KIT

Dave depends on these tools the most in his shop.

SPARK TESTER
This adjustable-gap inline spark plug checker from Echo costs about $70 online.

FLEXIBLE PRY BAR
A strong, non-marring poly/nylon pry bar won't damage brass or aluminum.

SCREWDRIVERS
Basic? Yes. Indispensable? Also yes.

NEEDLE-NOSE PLIERS
You will always need a pair when working on carburetors.

RATCHET DRIVER
This ¼-in.-drive ratchet with an extension gets the socket into tight places.

DENTAL PICK
An old dental pick can poke, pull and clean where other tools simply can't.

WRENCH
Dave has a set of combination wrenches in both imperial and metric.

JET-CLEANING BRUSHES
These micro-wire brushes remove debris from jets.

CARB CLEANER
Gumout carb cleaner is available at all auto parts stores.

SLIP JOINT PLIERS
These adjustable pliers can play many roles.

HOSE PINCH
These locking pliers will clamp on a hose without causing damage.

HOSE CLAMP PLIERS
Removal of flat-type or ring-type hose clamps is much easier with these.

WIRE CUTTERS
Dave uses these for snipping linkages.

NITRILE GLOVES
Dave prefers these tough, black nitrile gloves.

WIRE BRUSH
It's a must-have for cleaning small parts.

KNOW YOUR MOTOR OIL

BAD OIL ADVICE ABOUNDS, BUT EXPERT WISDOM CAN SET THE RECORD STRAIGHT

Motor oil has gotten much better over the years. And, with oil-life indicators on newer cars, drivers don't have to guess when to change their oil. Yet even with better oil and oil change reminder lights, repair shops are reporting a shocking increase in the number of engines damaged by wear and sludge buildup.

It turns out that many DIYers and even some oil change shops are using the wrong oil, and drivers are simply going too long between oil changes. Just

as troubling, many drivers have almost completely abandoned the job of checking their oil level when gassing up, and many more are causing engine damage by driving with low oil levels. Too many drivers seem to follow their own ideas about which oil they can use and how long they can run it in their engine. But that leads to trouble. Whether you change your own oil or take your vehicle to a shop, you need factual information right from the experts. Buckle up. It's time to get smart about oil.

OIL-CHANGING TIPS

- If the engine is cold, start it and let it run for five minutes to warm the oil. If it's hot, wait at least 30 minutes to avoid getting burned.
- Never use an adjustable wrench or socket on the drain plug. Use the proper size box-end wrench, usually metric, for the plug.
- Always use jack stands. Never work under a car that's supported by a jack only.
- Use new oil to coat the oil filter gasket before spinning it on.
- Always hand-tighten the filter. Never use a filter wrench.
- Find an oil/oil filter recycling center near you (see p. 88).
- Line up all the oil bottles you'll need for the fill so you don't lose count as you pour.

UNDER-HOOD LABEL

Engine Oil   Huile moteur
Use only oil that expressly complies with VW 502 00.
Utilisez uniquement de l'huile qui satisfait expressément à VW50200
For a list of approved oils: Pour une liste d'huiles approuvées: > 1-800-822-8987 > www.vw.com > www.vw.ca

OIL BOTTLE LABEL

And All Preceding API Gasoline Categories.
ADDITIONAL SPECIFICATIONS: VW 502.00, 505.00, 505.01
MB 229.51, BMW LL-04, PORSCHE A40

CAUTION: Avoid prolonged or repeated skin contact with used engine oil. Used

1 FIND THE ENGINE-SPECIFIC OIL

The label under the hood of this VW says to use only oil that complies with VW specification 502.00. To find oil that meets that standard, look for the specification on the oil bottle label.

IT'S MORE THAN JUST VISCOSITY

Every owner's manual lists the recommended oil viscosity for the engine. But knowing the correct viscosity is just the starting point. Your car may also require synthetic oil or oil that meets a specific industry service rating (API and ILSAC are two examples). The most recent ratings are API-SN PLUS and ILSAC GF-5. Both are backward-compatible, so if your manual shows a lower rating, you can safely substitute the newer oil.

But not all carmakers use those two industry rating services. European carmakers may require a regular ACEA-rated oil in some engines and a different oil that meets more rigid specifications in another engine. Manufacturer-specific and engine-specific oil is a growing trend, and when a carmaker specifies a particular oil for an engine, that's the only oil you can use **(Photo 1)**.

Ultimately, engine designers know more than you or your buddies. If you use the wrong oil, you can destroy your engine. The damage won't be covered by the factory powertrain warranty or your extended warranty, even if the oil changes were done by a pro.

If you do use a shop for oil changes, make sure it has the correct oil on hand. The shop may charge more for the special oil, but it'll keep your engine running longer. When changing your own oil, you may have trouble finding the proper oil at big box stores, but you can always get it (or order it) at any auto parts store.

SHOULD YOU USE SYNTHETIC OIL?

Even if your car doesn't require synthetic oil, you should switch to it anyway. Synthetic oil is made

2 OLDER ENGINES NEED STRONGER MEDICINE

Fill older engines with high-mileage synthetic oil to keep them running cleaner and provide maximum protection against wear.

from natural gas or crude-oil feed stocks that go through a chemical reaction that results in uniformly sized molecules. The uniform size reduces friction, heat and wear in your engine. Name-brand synthetic oil has higher-quality and longer-lasting additives that keep your engine cleaner. And, since it doesn't contain paraffin (wax) like conventional oil, it flows faster and builds pressure faster on cold starts. Sure, it costs a couple bucks more per quart, but it's a far better lubricant. It's worth the extra cost, especially if you love your car and/or plan to keep it for years to come.

WHAT ABOUT OIL FOR OLDER CARS?

You can argue that your old car racked up 100,000 miles just fine with conventional oil. Great. But now it has some wear on the piston rings, and it's generating more "blow-by" (combustion gas slipping by the piston rings). That increase in blow-by means more acid, soot, corrosion, varnish and sludge formation throughout the engine. That's precisely why switching to synthetic oil makes so much sense for older cars. The more robust additive package is especially well suited to keeping an older engine cleaner and running longer. If you change your own oil, switching to synthetic costs only about $10 per change. We think it's well worth the cost.

Internet lore advises performing an engine flush before switching to synthetic, but that's a bad idea. Just drain the old oil and remove the old filter. Then pop on a premium filter and pour in the synthetic oil. It's also time to discontinue the age-old practice of adding a higher-viscosity oil to combat low oil pressure. Higher-viscosity oil actually increases friction and reduces flow rate, causing the oil (and engine) to run hotter. So you wind up with lower gas mileage, more wear and sludge buildup.

High-mileage synthetic oil contains film-strengthening additives to improve ring sealing and oil pressure. Many brands also include seal conditioners to soften stiff seals, as well as extra antioxidant, anticorrosion, antiwear and detergent additives to handle all the crud in the crankcase. If you have more than 100,000 miles on your engine, switch to a high-mileage oil **(Photo 2)**. It costs only about $1 per quart more than regular synthetic.

WHEN SHOULD YOU CHANGE THE OIL?

Everybody's full of advice about how long you can go between oil changes. But unless they know your driving habits, that advice is just hot air. Frequent cold starts, short trips (less than 4 miles), stop-and-go driving, hauling heavy loads and lead-foot starts are incredibly hard on oil and deplete the additives quickly. Your owner's manual lists a different oil change schedule for this kind of severe driving, a category that includes most drivers. Unfortunately, those same drivers tend to change their oil according to the optimistic "normal" schedule. So follow the oil change schedule that applies to your driving style. Or, if you have a newer vehicle with an oil-life monitor, rely on that.

TRUST THE OIL-LIFE MONITORING SYSTEM IF YOU HAVE ONE

Some vehicles have an oil change reminder light that turns on when you've reached a set mileage. Those systems don't take your driving habits into account. So you have to adjust your oil change intervals according to how you drive. However, oil-life monitoring systems do track your driving habits. The computer records the number of cold starts, ambient and engine temperatures during startup, driving time between starts, engine load and whether the miles are highway or stop-and-go. It runs that data through an algorithm to estimate the remaining oil life. If you do a lot of short-trip city driving, the light will come on sooner than if you make long commutes.

You can trust the carmakers' oil-life monitoring systems only if you use the recommended oil and don't use any aftermarket additives. Pour in some miracle oil stabilizer, and all bets are off.

WHAT ABOUT THOSE LONG-DISTANCE OILS?

What about those claims that certain oils can go 15,000 or 25,000 miles between changes? Is there really an oil with a 300,000-mile engine guarantee? Because severe driving degrades oil

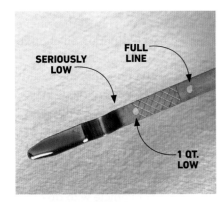

SERIOUSLY LOW — FULL LINE — 1 QT. LOW

3 CHECK THE OIL LEVEL EVERY 500 MILES

Add more oil to bring the level up to the FULL line, even if the dipstick shows the oil is down only a half quart. This will prevent rapid oil degradation.

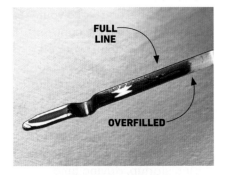

FULL LINE — OVERFILLED

4 OVERFILLING DAMAGES THE OIL AND ENGINE

Overfilling creates foam, which rapidly degrades the oil and causes additional engine wear. Foam doesn't remove heat as efficiently as liquid oil, so the engine and the oil get much hotter. The extra heat and air rapidly degrade the oil.

additives faster, oil manufacturers often qualify their oil change recommendations in the fine print. In some cases, your driving habits may require you to reduce the advertised mileage interval by as much as half. So don't assume you qualify for the best-case scenario: Read the instructions and the warranty terms. And no matter what the companies' promises

GET THE MOST OUT OF YOUR OIL CHANGE
Put your time and money to good use with these pointers

■ **PROTECT YOUR WARRANTY**
If you do your own oil changes and want to maintain your factory or aftermarket warranty, you'll have to prove you changed your oil on time. That's easy to document.

If you have a shop do your oil changes, make sure the receipt shows the oil viscosity and the service rating.

■ **BUY THE RIGHT FILTER** Select an oil filter that's designed to last as long as your oil change interval. Economy oil filters last about 3,000 miles. So if your change interval is 7,000 miles, it won't do its job for the last

4,000 miles. Look for terms such as "extended performance" or "extended life" on the box.

■ **SAVE MONEY ON OIL** Buying oil by the jug saves about $17 per oil change. Pour the used oil into an empty jug and drop it at a recycling center. To find the nearest recycling center for used motor oil, go to *search.earth911.com*, enter "motor oil" and your ZIP code into the search fields, and then click "search." Auto parts stores, oil change shops and municipal recycling centers are common locations that accept used motor oil.

OIL FILTER BOX TOP   UPC LABEL FROM OIL BOTTLE

OIL + FILTER CHANGED
MAY 28TH 2021
41,642 MILES

are, if you skip the carmakers' recommended change intervals, your factory or extended warranty will be void. So you would have to depend on the oil manufacturer to pay for repairs.

CHECK YOUR OIL LEVEL

Unless you own a luxury vehicle equipped with an oil level sensor, your vehicle won't tell you when it's low on oil because its warning light only indicates oil pressure. By the time the warning light comes on, you're already dangerously

low on (or completely out of) oil.

Here's the bottom line: All engines burn oil. And with longer intervals between oil changes, you can count on losing up to a full quart before it's time for your next oil change. Driving a quart low puts tremendous stress on the remaining oil, dramatically reducing its useful life. So get into the habit of checking the dipstick every other fill-up. Add oil to raise the level to the full mark, even if it's down just a half quart **(Photo 3)**. But don't overfill **(Photo 4)**.

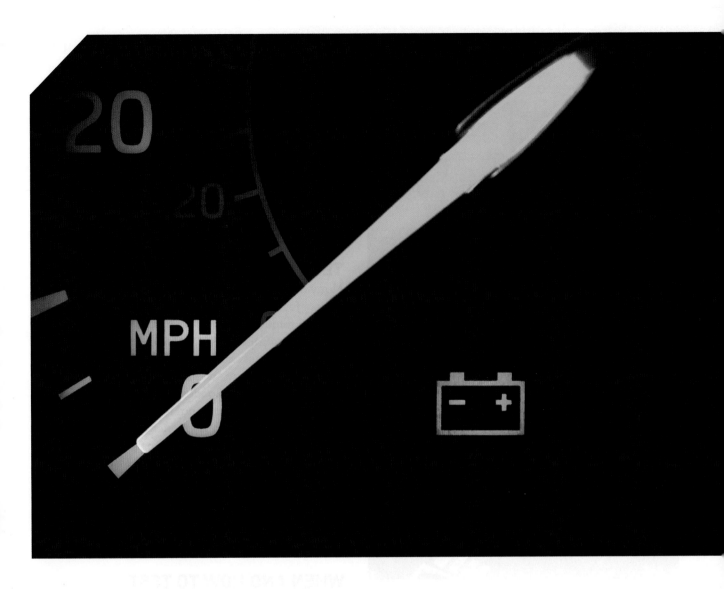

DON'T GET STRANDED BY A DEAD BATTERY

//
TEST NOW TO AVOID SURPRISES LATER

If you're like most other car owners, you just start your car every morning until the day you turn the key and find out your battery has died. But you shouldn't be shocked when it drops dead out of the clear blue. All car batteries wear out eventually, and about half of them die without any advance warning. So how are you supposed to know when to replace a battery?

Our battery expert, Dale Gospodarek, says there's an easy way to avoid the surprise of a dead battery.

He recommends getting a battery checkup at every oil change to monitor its health. That way you'll know when it would be wise to replace it. Combine that with regular battery maintenance, and you'll never get stranded. We'll walk you through the battery testing procedure and relay Dale's best battery-buying advice and tips for getting the longest life out of your battery. So don't get all charged up—leave the jumper cables in the trunk and enjoy the ride.

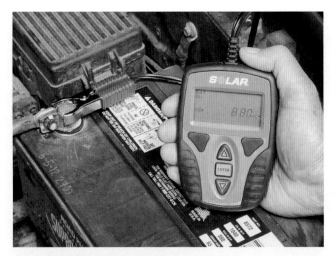

1 PROGRAM THE TESTER
Program the battery type first, then set the CCA rating.

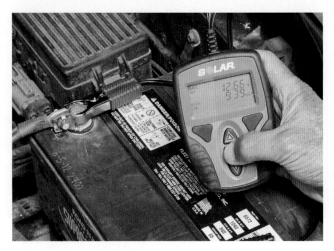

2 READ THE RESULTS
Scroll through the different tests and read the results for state of health, state of charge and internal resistance.

> **CAUTION:**
> Never disconnect the battery terminals on a late-model vehicle (2000 and later) without first providing backup power to the vehicle's diagnostic port. Loss of battery power for even a few seconds can cause an electronic throttle body to forget its "home" position, resulting in a no-start, rough-idle or limited-acceleration condition when you connect the new battery.
>
> Depending on the vehicle, you may have to tow it to a shop to have the throttle body reprogrammed. Disconnecting the battery without proper backup power will also wipe out the memory for all your electrical accessories (seats, mirrors, radio station presets, etc.).
>
> If your vehicle is equipped with start-stop technology (engine turns off when stopped and restarts when you press the gas pedal), battery replacement is more complicated because the computer MUST be reprogrammed. That's a job best left to a qualified repair shop.

TESTING YOUR BATTERY

NEW TESTERS CAN PREDICT PROBLEMS
Newer digital battery testers are light-years beyond the obsolete testers that just measured the battery's state-of-charge and load potential. Newer testers still check for charge and load, but they also perform resistance and conductance tests that can determine the condition of internal cell plates and all electrical connections, so they're much better at determining a battery's overall health.

TEST FOR FREE OR BUY A TESTER
Many auto parts stores and repair shops offer free battery testing while it's in your car, or if it's dead, you can remove it from your car and bring it in. But if you own several vehicles, consider buying your own digital tester. Just choose one that can test all the types of batteries you may encounter over the next 10 years, including traditional flooded lead acid, absorbed glass mat (AGM—traditional rectangular shape and spiral wound), start/stop batteries and gel cell.

In addition, look for a unit that performs a starting and charging system test. That way you'll be able diagnose starting problems if the battery is still good. Digital battery testers are available at auto parts stores and online. We're using the SOLAR BA9 because it's reasonably priced, tests all battery types and tests the starting and charging systems.

WHEN AND HOW TO TEST
Most batteries are damaged by excessive engine compartment heat, but they don't quit until the first cold snap. So it's always smart to test your battery before winter. Before you start, you'll need to know the battery type and its cold cranking amp (CCA) rating.

If you have an older vehicle (pre-2015), chances are you have a standard flooded lead-acid battery, but many late-model luxury vehicles have an AGM battery. Vehicles with start/stop technology (shuts off engine at every stop and then restarts) usually have either an enhanced flooded or a special AGM-type battery. Find the specs for yours on the battery label.

Clean the battery posts and terminals to get the most accurate results (see caution at left). Then, turn off all electrical accessories, remove the key from the ignition and close the doors to eliminate all electrical power draw. Connect the tester directly to the battery posts and enter the type and CCA rating **(Photo 1)**. Activate the battery test and read the results **(Photo 2)**. If the battery fails any tests, shop for a replacement.

BATTERY CARE TIPS

EXTEND THE LIFE OF YOUR BATTERY

■ Reuse factory battery insulators when you replace a battery. They protect the battery against high temperatures under the hood.

■ Keep battery posts and terminals clean and protected against corrosion **(Photos 1 and 2)**. A small amount of corrosion can have a huge impact on the charging system's ability to recharge the battery. Prolonged undercharged conditions dramatically reduce battery life.

■ If you take lots of short trips in winter weather and use your lights, seat heater, blower and defogger, you'll drain more power from your battery than the charging system can replace. That will leave your battery in a discharged state, which can shorten its life. After several short trips in cold weather, make a longer trip at higher speeds to top off your battery.

■ If you drain your battery, use a battery charger at its lowest setting to bring it back to full charge. It's bad practice to charge a dead battery just enough to start the engine—driving fast for short periods on a barely charged battery can shorten its life.

■ Connect a battery maintainer if you're not going to drive for more than a month. Car computers draw power (even when the engine isn't running) and can drain a battery in about three weeks. Plus, all lead-acid batteries lose up to 25% of their charge per month even in warm weather even if they're disconnected from the car. A lead acid battery at 70 degrees F self-discharges about 1% a day just sitting on the shelf at the store.

HOW TO BUY A NEW BATTERY

The old folklore was to buy a battery with the most CCAs. That's bad advice, according to Dale. Refer to your owner's manual to find the factory-recommended CCA rating and battery "group" size and buy a battery with those same specs—period. A battery with a higher or lower CCA may not perform as well and may actually have a shorter life span.

DO YOU NEED AN AGM BATTERY?

AGM batteries are designed to withstand deeper and more frequent discharge rates/cycles. If your vehicle is loaded with high-draw electrical accessories like heated seats, high-wattage sound systems, snow plows or winches and you're experiencing short battery life, consider upgrading to a standard AGM or a yellow-top spiral-wound AGM battery (Optima by Johnson Controls is one popular brand).

SAFE JUMP-STARTING

If you find yourself stranded with a dead battery or want to be a good Samaritan and help someone jump-start their car, follow these safety tips.

■ Never smoke when jump-starting a vehicle. Dead batteries can explode and cause severe injuries.

■ Turn off all electrical accessories in both vehicles before connecting the jumper cables.

■ Connect the positive cable clamp to the positive terminal on the dead vehicle and the clamp on the other end to the positive battery terminal on the good vehicle. Then connect the negative cable clamp to a metal engine part far away from the dead battery before connecting the other clamp to the negative battery post on the good vehicle. Remove the cables in reverse order.

■ Let the dead vehicle charge for at least five minutes before you try starting. If the dead vehicle won't start after 15 minutes, it's never going to start with a jump. Call a tow truck.

1 CLEAN IT UP
If you have corrosion on your battery, remove the terminals and clean with a battery brush. Then clean the posts. Spray battery neutralizer/cleaner on the battery and hold-down hardware.

2 PROTECT AGAINST CORROSION
Spray the battery posts and terminals with battery protectant spray. Allow it to dry before driving (some sprays are flammable).

SURVIVE A FLAT TIRE

GET BACK ON THE ROAD SAFELY BY EXPECTING THE UNEXPECTED

Your car owner's manual shows you how to change a flat tire, assuming a best-case scenario. But the real world can bring stuck lug nuts, a wheel that's rusted to the hub, or another nasty surprise. So although you may think you can change a flat, you'll probably run into things you're not prepared for. Even drivers with roadside assistance can get stuck in an area with no cell coverage or face lengthy wait times.

To help you survive a flat-tire ordeal, we've collected these tips. Some we've taken from our own ugly encounters, and others we've learned from our readers.

CAUTION: SPACE-SAVER SPARES WON'T LAST LONG

Get your flat tire repaired or replaced right away, because space-saver spares are designed to run for only 50 to 70 miles. And the spare-tire manufacturers are serious about their 50-mph maximum speed limit. So slow down!

1

KEYED
LUG NUT

KEYED
SOCKET

1 DO YOU KNOW WHERE YOUR KEYED SOCKET IS?

To avoid theft, many cars have one special lug nut on each wheel that requires a special "keyed socket" to loosen it. If you can't locate the key when you have a flat tire (or another driver in the family isn't aware of it), it won't be possible to remove the wheel. You'll have to use Fix-A-Flat (see p. 94), call for roadside service or have the vehicle towed to a shop. That can cost upward of $200. So make a point of keeping the key in a safe place, like the glove box, that is known to everyone who drives the car.

2 PACK A TIRE INFLATOR

If you don't routinely top off the air pressure in your spare tire, don't be surprised if it's severely underinflated when you need it. Driving on a severely underinflated full-size spare is unsafe, and driving on an underinflated space-saver spare is downright dangerous. Solve that problem by keeping a plug-in tire inflator in your vehicle at all times (one choice is the Slime 12-Volt Digital Tire Inflator, No. 40022; about $40 at auto parts stores). Start the engine, plug the unit into your power port and bring the spare tire up to the recommended pressure (found on the decal inside the driver's door area) before installing it on the hub.

3 DON'T BREAK YOUR PLASTIC WHEEL COVERS

Carmakers use two methods to secure plastic wheel covers: spring clips and screw-on plastic lug nuts. If you don't know which type is on your vehicle, try turning one of the plastic nuts with the socket end of your tire iron. If it rotates, you have the screw-on type. Unscrew all the plastic nuts and lift off the cover.

If the nut doesn't turn, you have the snap-on style. Those have to be pried off, and that's where some people get into trouble. If you jam the tapered end of your tire iron into a weak area on the cover, you'll break it to pieces. So be sure to pry behind one of the larger spokes and twist until the cover pops off.

4 REMOVE A STUCK WHEEL WITH THE SPARE

If you don't rotate your tires every 5,000 miles, your wheels may be bonded to the hub by rust. Here's a way to knock the wheels loose, submitted by a reader.

With the lug nuts loosened about three-quarters of the way, grab the spare by the center hole and use it as a battering ram. Swing it horizontally with all your might so it strikes the stuck wheel at the 12 o'clock position. Repeat the blows at the 3 o'clock and 9 o'clock positions until the wheel breaks free from the hub.

PLUG INTO POWER PORT ON DASH

LARGEST SPOKE

ASSEMBLE A MISSION-CRITICAL KIT

Whether you change your tire yourself or rely on a tire sealant, keep these "mission-critical" items in your vehicle at all times.

- **WHEEL CHOCKS** Chocks keep your car from falling off the jack, especially on slopes.
- **GLOVES** These are helpful all year round and critical for handling cold metal in icy temps.
- **PLUG-IN FLASHLIGHT** Dark nights can make it impossible to see what you're doing.
- **TIRE INFLATOR** You'll need this to fill low spares and top off tires repaired with Fix-A-Flat.

5 GET OUT OF A JAM WITH FIX-A-FLAT

If you're not confident that you or the driver can change a flat tire, buy two cans of aerosol tire sealer from any auto parts store (Fix-A-Flat is one well-known brand) and keep them in the vehicle. The cans are sold in several sizes for compact, standard and truck-size tires. Tire sealants work on tread punctures 3/16 in. or less in diameter. They won't work on sidewall punctures, blowouts or any other catastrophic failures. You've got little to lose by trying sealant.

You can greatly increase your chances of a successful seal if you can find the puncture site and move the vehicle until the leak is facing down. If you see the culprit, don't remove it; it'll help seal the hole. If the can is frozen, thaw it with the defroster or floor heater vents until the contents move freely when shaken. Then fill the tire following the directions on the can. If the rim doesn't lift off the ground after using a second can, the puncture is too large to be sealed and you'll have to call for help.

Top off the air pressure as soon as possible. If you have a tire inflator on hand, do it now. This is a very temporary fix, so get the tire repaired professionally ASAP. Tire sealant must be removed within three days or 100 miles, whichever comes first. Inform the tire shop that you've used tire sealant so no one breathes in the propellants (not flammable, but not healthy either). The shop may charge extra for cleaning the sealant from the tire.

6 SPARE YOUR LIMBS WHEN INSTALLING THE SPARE

Truck and SUV tires are really heavy. Some DIYers sit on the ground with their knees under the wheel so their legs can help with the lifting. That's a great way to lose a limb or two if the vehicle falls off the jack (which happens more often than you think). Instead, raise the vehicle just enough to get a 1-in. clearance between the tire and the ground.

Rotate the hub until one of the studs is in the 12 o'clock position. Roll the spare tire next to the vehicle and position it so the holes line up with the studs. Then grab the wheel by the rim, lift it up and hang the tire on the top stud. Then align the rest of the holes with the studs and push it on.

7 SAVE YOUR BACK WHEN LOOSENING LUG NUTS

There's no way you can loosen the lug nuts once you raise the vehicle—the tire will just spin. Instead, break loose—but don't remove—the lug nuts while the tire is still on the ground. To save your back, place the tire iron on each lug nut so the handle is in the 9 o'clock position. Place both hands on the tire iron and push down with all your might. If that doesn't work, use a downward bouncing motion with your weight to break the nut loose.

WHAT'S THE DEAL WITH TIRE PLUGS?

Many DIYers think they can permanently repair tire punctures with just a plug. They're wrong. A tire plug is just half of the repair. The tire's interior liner must also be repaired with a patch, and that means a trip to the tire store. Skip the patch and you risk a catastrophic blowout.

PERFORM YOUR OWN FRONT BRAKE JOB

BANISH BRAKE NOISE AND PEDAL PULSATION WITH A STEP-BY-STEP APPROACH

If you've done some basic wrenching like replacing starter motors, alternators or even mufflers, you're completely capable of doing your own brake job. In this story, we'll show you how to do the front brakes on a late-model vehicle. The job takes about four hours and will save you hundreds in shop labor.

Rear disc brakes are far more complex, so that's a job you should leave to the pros. (To learn how to

tell whether your front or rear brakes need replacing, go to *familyhandyman.com* and search for "how to check your brakes.")

A car that's used mostly for driving in the city will need new front brakes and rotors about every 40,000 miles. But cars that are driven mostly on highways can go almost 80,000 miles before the front brakes wear out.

CALIPER BOLT

BLEEDER SCREW

ANTI-RATTLE CLIP

CALIPER BOLT

1 REMOVE THE CALIPER

Loosen the caliper bolt heads with a ratchet. Then remove and store the rubber cap on the bleeder screw (if equipped) and loosen the bleeder screw with a box-end wrench. Reseat the bleeder screw and remove the caliper bolts.

GET THE PARTS AND GATHER THE TOOLS

A shop can determine whether a rotor can be reused as is or resurfaced with an on-car brake lathe. Since you don't have access to an on-car lathe and probably don't own a brake micrometer, just plan on buying new rotors and brake pads. Choose the premium offerings from a name brand manufacturer to get the longest life and best service out of your new brakes. (Bendix, Raybestos, EBC, Wagner, Brembo and Akebono are examples of well respected brands.) Buy the same type of brake pad that was installed at the factory—the auto parts store has that information.

You'll also need a small packet of synthetic high-temperature brake grease, aerosol brake cleaner, polishing pads, a tube of nickel anti-seize and a packet of blue and red thread locker (Loctite is one brand).

Next, gather your socket set, torque wrench and screwdrivers, along with a drill and wire wheel, an 8-in. C-clamp, a small spool of mechanic's wire, 2 ft. of ¼-in.

vinyl tubing and a jar to hold the brake fluid that bleeds out as you compress the caliper piston.

WORK ON ONE SIDE AT A TIME

Brakes on late-model vehicles include clips and springs that must go back in exactly the same position. If you remove both brakes at the same time and forget how to reinstall the small parts, you won't have the other side to use as a reference (a common DIY mistake). So replace the brakes one side at a time.

Start by loosening (not removing!) the lug nuts while the tire is on the ground. Raise one side of the vehicle with a floor jack or spare-tire jack. Then place a jack stand under the engine cradle for added safety. Then remove the tire and proceed with the brake job.

UNBOLT THE CALIPER

Once you'ved removed the tire, loosen the caliper retaining bolts with a socket and ratchet (Photo 1). Next, loosen the caliper bleeder screw and lightly reseat

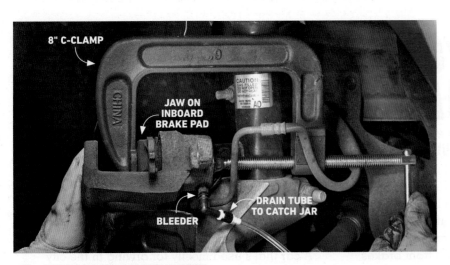

8" C-CLAMP

JAW ON INBOARD BRAKE PAD

DRAIN TUBE TO CATCH JAR

BLEEDER

2 RETRACT THE CALIPER PISTON

Place the inboard pad against the piston and center the C-clamp jaw on the pad. Locate the clamp screw on the back side of the caliper. Open the bleeder and retract the piston.

YOU MIGHT NEED HEX- OR STAR-SHAPED SOCKETS

The brake caliper bolts on older vehicles usually have an internal hex or internal star-shaped head. You won't have enough leverage to remove an internal hex-head caliper bolt with an ordinary L-shaped Allen wrench. So before you begin the job, turn the front wheels all the way to one side and crawl under the vehicle with a light. Check the caliper bolts to see if they're internal hex or internal star. Then buy a complete set of the correct sockets to have on hand when you start the job.

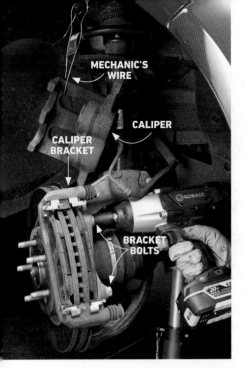

MECHANIC'S WIRE

CALIPER

CALIPER BRACKET

BRACKET BOLTS

HOLD-DOWN SCREW

3 UNBOLT THE CALIPER BRACKET

Break the caliper bracket bolts loose with an impact wrench or a breaker bar. Store the bolts and lift the bracket off the steering knuckle.

4 REMOVE THE ROTOR HOLD-DOWN SCREW

Smack the rotor hold-down screw with a hammer to shock it. Then insert a Phillips or star socket. If the screw doesn't loosen, try tightening. Rock the socket back and forth until it comes out. Then wiggle the rotor to remove it from the hub.

5 CLEAN OFF THE RUST

Toss the old anti-rattle clips (see **Photo 1**). Remove all traces of surface rust in the pad slide areas using a wire brush or a drill with a wire wheel. Coat the areas with a light film of brake grease.

it. You'll loosen it again when you retract the caliper piston. Then lift the caliper off the rotor and set it on top of the caliper bracket.

REMOVE THE CALIPER, RETRACT THE PISTON

Connect one end of the drain tube to the bleeder screw and place the other end in a catch jar. Then open the bleeder and force the caliper piston back into the bore with the C-clamp (**Photo 2**). When you're done, tighten the bleeder and disconnect the drain tube. Secure the caliper to the coil spring or strut with mechanic's wire while you complete the brake job. Never let the caliper dangle by its hose.

Next, remove the caliper bracket so you can replace the rotor. The caliper bracket bolts are quite large and are usually coated with thread locker, so you'll need a large ratchet or breaker bar or an impact wrench to remove them (**Photo 3**).

As you remove the bolts, note whether they've been coated with red or blue thread locker. Recoat the threads with the same type when you reinstall them.

REMOVE THE ROTOR

Many carmakers secure the rotor to the hub with a screw, and it rarely comes out without a fight. So assume it's rusted in place and soak it with spray rust penetrant before you try to remove it. If you don't, you can strip the head, and you'll be forced to drill it out. Let the penetrant work for 15 minutes. Then remove the screw (**Photo 4**) and pull the rotor off the hub.

IT'S ALL ABOUT CLEAN

Brake noise, vibration, harsh braking and brake pedal pulsation are the most common brake complaints, and they're all caused by improper cleaning and installation procedures. So trust us on this point and follow

all of our cleaning and greasing instructions.

Remove the old anti-rattle clips and toss them. Then clean all the rust off the caliper bracket (**Photo 5**). Next, clean the caliper bolts with aerosol brake cleaner and check for corrosion. Replace the bolts if they're corroded. Install new anti-rattle clips (**Photo 6**). Then grease the bolts and install new rubber boots (**Photo 7**).

Next, clean all the rust and debris from the wheel hub. Just .003 in. of rust or crud on the hub can cause brake pedal pulsation and ruin a perfectly good brake job. So take this part seriously. Chuck a mildly abrasive polishing pad into your drill and clean the wheel hub (**Photo 8**).

Now clean the new rotors. Use aerosol brake cleaner to remove the rust preventive coating. Then wash the rotors in hot soapy water (**Photo 9**). It's a pain, but don't skip this step.

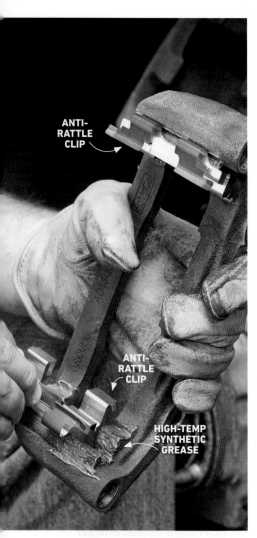

ANTI-RATTLE CLIP

ANTI-RATTLE CLIP

HIGH-TEMP SYNTHETIC GREASE

GREASED CALIPER BOLT

CALIPER BOOT

7 LUBE AND INSTALL NEW BOOTS

Apply a coat of high-temperature synthetic brake grease to the bolt and the bores in the caliper bracket. Seat new boots into the caliper bracket and slide in the greased caliper bolts until the boots seat on the bolt recess.

6 ADD THE HARDWARE

Apply a very light coat of high-temperature synthetic brake grease to the caliper bracket. Then snap in the new anti-rattle clips.

8 POLISH THE HUB

Spin the polishing pad around the face of the wheel hub. Then clean the rust off the center of the hub. Wipe off the debris and apply a light coat of nickel anti-seize to the face to minimize future rust buildup. (Don't get anti-seize on the wheel studs.)

REASSEMBLE

Slide the rotor onto the hub, aligning the rotor retention screw hole with the threaded hole in the hub. Tighten the screw to specs. Next, apply the correct thread locker to the caliper bracket bolts and reinstall the caliper bracket. Apply a thin film of brake grease to the back side of the noise reduction shims, slide them into the caliper bracket and install the springs **(Photo 10)**. Reinstall the caliper.

INSTALL THE WHEEL, TORQUE THE LUG NUTS, AND TEST THE BRAKES

Don't wreck all your careful cleaning and greasing work by using an impact wrench or ratchet to tighten the lug nuts. They must be tightened to the same torque to maintain the critical rotor-to-hub fit **(Photo 11)**. If they're torqued unevenly, the rotor will cock slightly and you'll get pedal pulsation.

Caution! You won't have immediate braking at this point, so don't start the engine or put the car in gear until you perform this next step.

Depress the brake pedal several times with the engine off until you get a firm pedal. Then go for a test drive at slow speed to be sure the brake pads work. Finally, perform the "bedding" procedure recommended by the brake pad manufacturer (see "How to Break In Brake Pads").

9 WASH THE ROTOR

Dunk the rotor into a tub of hot soapy water and scrub the entire surface with a stiff brush. Rinse with clear water and dry with paper towels.

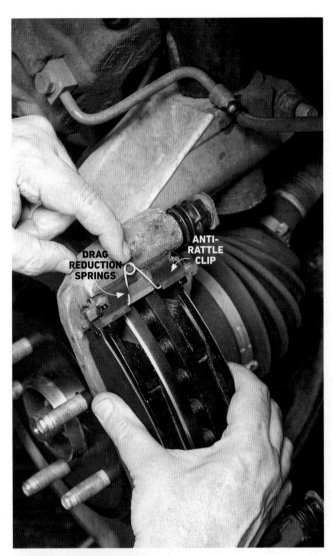

DRAG REDUCTION SPRINGS

ANTI-RATTLE CLIP

10 ADD THE SPRINGS

Slide the pads into the anti-rattle clips. Squeeze the pads together as you install the drag reduction springs. Make sure they go back in the same way they came out. Continue squeezing the pads and slide the caliper over the pads.

11 TORQUE THE LUG NUTS

Remove the jack stand and lower the vehicle until the tire just touches the ground. Set the torque wrench to one-half the specified torque and tighten the lug nuts in a star pattern. Then set the wrench to the full torque and tighten again in the same star pattern. Lower the vehicle the rest of the way and remove the floor jack.

HOW TO BREAK IN BRAKE PADS

Brake pads must be correctly "burnished," or "bedded," for proper operation. This step transfers a thin film of friction material onto the rotor and polishes the face of the brake pad. Consult the brake pad package insert for the recommended procedure. Most manufacturers recommend this 30-30-30 method: You accelerate to 30 mph and gently brake to a complete stop. Wait 30 seconds for the brakes to cool. Then repeat the procedure 30 times. (Perform the break-in procedure in a quiet parking lot or on a traffic-free road!) If you skip this critical break-in step, you might experience shorter brake pad life, along with noise and vibration.

REPLACE A SERPENTINE BELT

//
DO THE JOB YOURSELF IN LESS THAN AN HOUR

In the past, carmakers used several belts to drive alternators, water pumps, power steering pumps and A/C. But now those components are all driven by the serpentine belt. If that single belt fails, you're stranded. That said, if a mechanic wants to install a new belt, resist the sales pitch for now. You may be able to do the job yourself for a fraction of the cost.

Before you begin, pop the hood and take a good look. You'll see the belt at the front or side of the engine, running around all the pulleys. If the belt is exposed and looks like it'll slip free relatively easily, and you can access the belt tensioner bolt without disconnecting anything, you can do this job yourself. If access is blocked, you may want to hire this one out.

DO YOU NEED A NEW SERPENTINE BELT?

First-generation serpentine belts were made from a nitrile compound that cracked with use. If your belt has cracks in three or more adjacent ribs within a 1-in. span, or has four or more cracks per inch on a single rib, it's time to replace it. You also need a new belt if you notice chunks missing from the rib area, torn or frayed fabric, glazing on the belt's back side or debris trapped in the ribs.

Starting with the 2000 models, carmakers switched from nitrile to ethylene propylene diene monomer (EPDM) belts. EPDM belts last much longer and don't crack or lose chunks the way nitrile belts do. But they do wear. Because the damage is difficult to see, some pros measure this wear using a specialized belt wear gauge.

CHECK THE TENSIONER FIRST

If your tensioner is bad and it's one of the more difficult styles to replace, you won't want to waste your time changing the belt. The shop would just have to remove the belt again to replace the tensioner. So check the tensioner first with these three tests.

The first test is a visual inspection with the engine running to assess the dampening feature of the tensioner. Pop the hood, start the engine and turn on the A/C. Then shine a light on the belt tensioner and observe the tensioner arm roller for excessive movement **(Photo 1)**. If it passes the visual test, move on to the "crank" test **(Photo 2)**. The tensioner arm should rotate smoothly during crank and release with no binding. If the travel isn't smooth, replace the entire tensioner. Next, check the condition of the tensioner arm pulley/roller **(Photo 3)**. If the pulley or roller exhibits any roughness, binding or noise, that is also cause to replace the entire tensioner.

HOW TO REPLACE THE TENSIONER

Many tensioners are readily accessible and attach to the engine with a single bolt. To replace that style, simply remove the belt and then the retaining bolt. Pull off the old tensioner, noting the location of the locking pin on the back. Then slide the new unit into place, lining up the locking pin with the hole in the engine. Hand-tighten the bolt and then tighten it with a torque wrench to the factory specifications shown in your shop manual.

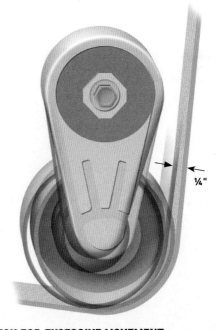

¼"

1 CHECK FOR EXCESSIVE MOVEMENT
A "good" tensioner arm should exhibit just a slight vibration with about $\frac{1}{32}$ in. or less of arm movement. And the belt should run smoothly with no visible vibration. If the tensioner arm exhibits a jerky vibrating motion, the belt vibrates, or the tensioning arm moves ¼ in., the tensioner is bad.

2 CHECK FOR SMOOTH ROTATION
Snap a long-handled ratchet into the square ½-in.-drive or ⅜-in.-drive opening. Or use a socket on the hex-shaped protruding nut. Slowly rotate the tensioner arm as far as it will turn. Then release the tension. Feel for binding and creaking in both directions.

WORN NEW

3 CHECK THE PULLEY/ROLLER
Rotate the tensioner and slide the belt off the pulley/roller. Then turn the pulley/roller and feel for resistance, binding and roughness. Then spin it and listen for rumbling. If the pulley/roller doesn't spin smoothly or has a rough surface, replace it.

REPLACING THE SERPENTINE BELT

Before you even think about removing the old belt, find the belt-routing diagram **(Photo 4)**. If the diagram is missing, sketch one yourself. Trust us, if you don't have a diagram, you'll spend far more time trying to figure out how the new one installs than it takes to make a sketch ahead of time.

Remove the belt by releasing the tension and sliding the belt off any smooth roller **(Photo 5)**. Then release the belt tensioner and remove the old belt. To install the new belt, wrap the belt onto the pulleys as far as you can and then rotate the tensioner to allow the rest of the belt to go on **(Photo 6)**. If you can't get the belt onto the last pulley, that's a sign it isn't seated properly on a preceding pulley. Don't force it on. Recheck your work to make sure all the ribs are properly seated on each grooved pulley.

4 FIND THE UNDER-HOOD DIAGRAM
Search for the factory belt-routing diagram. It's located near the serpentine belt, on the radiator support or strut tower or on a label affixed to the underside of the hood.

5 REMOVE THE OLD BELT
Rotate the tensioner and slide the belt off any smooth pulley. Then release the tensioner and finish removing the old belt.

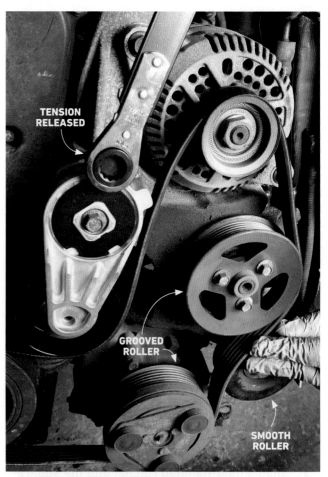

TENSION RELEASED

GROOVED ROLLER

SMOOTH ROLLER

6 BEGIN WITH THE GROOVED PULLEYS
Wrap the new belt around the crankshaft pulley, then around the grooved pulleys. Finish the job by sliding the belt onto a rounded, non-grooved roller.

REPLACE A PICKUP BUMPER

DON'T LEAVE YOUR PICKUP AT THE SHOP—INSTALL A NEW BUMPER YOURSELF AND SAVE

A rusty or dented bumper can drag down the whole appearance of a pickup that's in otherwise good shape. Having it replaced by a pro can set you back upwards of $1,000, but you can save $500 or more in labor and parts by doing the job yourself. It takes only a few hours.

To make sense of all the bumper buying options and various prices for the "same" part, we contacted parts expert Tom Taylor, owner of *rockauto.com*. Tom walked us through the options and offered buying advice for owners of new and old trucks.

We put our truck up on a hoist to replace the bumper, which makes things a bit easier. Don't be afraid to do the job with the truck on the garage floor, though it's a good idea to have a floor jack and stands available just in case you can't reach the upper bolts. An air impact wrench speeds things up, but you can do the job by hand with sockets, a

ratchet and a breaker bar. You'll also need spray rust penetrant, screwdrivers and eye protection.

We'll walk you through the steps to replace a chrome step bumper on a 2002 Dodge Ram. It's representative of most pickup truck bumpers, but the number of bolts and their location may be different on your truck.

FIRST, ASSESS THE DAMAGE

Before you order any parts, inspect the condition of the bumper step pad, license plate lights, trailer light socket, and any other accessories that might have been damaged by the impact. Next, get your creeper and take a look behind the bumper. Check the condition of the bumper brackets to see if they're bent or rusted. If so, invest in some new ones—trust us, you don't want to try to bend them back into shape.

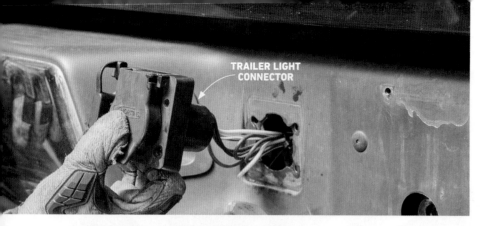

TRAILER LIGHT CONNECTOR

1 REMOVE THE TRAILER LIGHT CONNECTOR

Reach behind the bumper and hold each nut as you unscrew the trailer light screws. Place the small parts in a magnetic tray or zip-top bag so you don't lose them.

BACKUP LIGHT

BULB AND SOCKET

2 TWIST AND REMOVE THE BULB SOCKETS

Twist each license plate bulb socket a quarter turn and pull them straight out of the light assembly. Set them aside.

3 REMOVE THE SMALLER BOLTS

Remove the license plate to reveal the bolts that hold the bumper to the trailer hitch. Use a socket and ratchet to remove them.

BUMPER BRACKET

FRAME BRACKET

4 DISCONNECT THE BRACKET BOLTS

Use a deep socket and ratchet to remove the bottom nut connecting the bumper bracket to the frame bracket. Repeat on both sides. Then loosen the top nuts on the same brackets, but don't remove them until you're out from under the vehicle.

BUMPER BUYING TIPS

Replacement bumpers are available from retail auto parts stores, truck and trailer hitch upgrade shops, local bumper reconditioning shops, and online retailers (rockauto.com and autoanything.com are two examples). Auto recycling yards are also an option, but we found we could buy a brand-new factory-quality bumper with new brackets and bolts for just a few bucks more than a used part from the local yards.

Low-price bumpers are usually economy-grade units. They're bare-bones products (no brackets or bolts) with minimal chrome plating and a short rust-through warranty (if any). An economy bumper for our Ram truck cost us about $170 online, including shipping. Tom says those units are perfectly fine for an old truck that you plan to keep only a short time or just want to get into good enough shape to sell or trade.

However, if you need brackets or want a longer-lasting bumper that matches factory quality, he recommends buying a premium version that includes those extra parts. That winds up being cheaper than buying an economy bumper and paying a la carte prices for the brackets. A premium unit for our truck cost about $450 including shipping and came with new brackets and bolts and two complete license plate light assemblies.

GREASE THE SKIDS WITH RUST PENETRANT

Removing the rusted fasteners is the hardest part of a bumper replacement job. To make removal easier, pretreat all the fasteners with spray rust penetrant. Shoot a liberal dose on each nut and bolt a few days before you plan to do the swap, then drive the vehicle to create the vibrations that will make the penetrant work faster. Reapply when you get home so that the penetrant can soak overnight. Repeat.

REMOVE THE ACCESSORIES FIRST

If your bumper has a built-in trailer light connector, remove the fasteners that hold it to the bumper. Next, disconnect and remove the trailer light connector and harness **(Photo 1)**. Then remove the license plate bulb sockets **(Photo 2)**.

THEN REMOVE THE BUMPER BOLTS AND BRACKETS

Our bumper was attached to the trailer hitch and bed, bumper brackets and frame brackets. Start by removing the license plate and the bolts behind it **(Photo 3)**. Next, reach behind the bumper and remove the bolts that connect the bumper to the truck bed. The frame brackets can be difficult to remove and can make bumper removal more cumbersome. So it's best to remove the bumper first to give yourself more room to access the frame brackets (if necessary). To do that, remove the bolts that connect the left and right bumper brackets to the frame brackets **(Photo 4)**. Then lift off the entire bumper **(Photo 5)**.

INSTALL THE NEW BUMPER

Place the new bumper on cardboard to prevent scratches, then install the new license plate light assemblies **(Photo 6)**. Then install the new bumper **(Photo 7)**. Reinstall the trailer light connector and harness.

5 LIFT OFF THE OLD BUMPER
Remove the remaining brackets, nuts and bolts and lift the bumper up and off the truck.

BACKUP LIGHT RETAINER

6 SNAP IN THE LICENSE PLATE LIGHTS
Slide the license plate light into the new bumper. Then align the legs of the U-shaped spring retainer with the slots on the light. Push the retainer onto the light until it snaps into place.

7 INSTALL THE BUMPER
Lift the new bumper into place and loosely attach the bumper brackets to the frame brackets. Align the bumper with the bolt holes in the bed and insert all the bolts. Then tighten all the bolts to the manufacturer's specifications.

FIX DENTS THE RIGHT WAY

DON'T LIVE WITH AN UGLY DENT—REPAIR IT WITH PROFESSIONAL TECHNIQUES

Our editors have patched quite a few vehicle dents over the years, but that doesn't mean their techniques are flawless. One used to patch vehicle dents the same way he tapes drywall: by applying 5 lbs. of body filler and then sanding off about 4.9 lbs. But then he went to "boot camp" at 3M and learned there's an easier way (as in, the correct way) to do dent repairs.

We asked 3M expert Jenn Cook to walk you through the same dent repair process. If you follow these steps, you can patch a dent yourself in just an afternoon and save a few hundred bucks over body shop prices. Once the dent is patched, you just spray on a primer coat and matching paint from the dealer or an auto

parts store. The repair won't be completely invisible, but at least it won't stand out like a sore thumb.

PICK UP SUPPLIES

Stop at any auto parts store and buy a 24-grit sanding wheel and sheets of 80-, 180- and 320-grit sandpaper. Also buy a bottle of wax remover, a tack cloth, a mixing board, several plastic spreaders and a tube of finishing glaze. Finally, you'll need body filler. Professional-grade filler is creamier and easier to spread and sand than bargain-priced products, so it's worth the extra cost. One choice is Bondo Professional Fast-Dry Filler. Expect to pay about $20 per quart.

PREP AND CLEAN BEFORE FILLING

Start by removing the paint inside and around the dent with 24-grit paper (**Photo 1**). Switch to 80-grit sandpaper and hand-sand the entire dent. Use the same sandpaper to rough up and feather the paint around the edges of the dent. Clean the entire area with wax remover and a clean rag. Then wipe with a tack cloth.

MIX THE FILLER

Don't mix body filler on a scrap piece of cardboard. Instead, use a mixing board or an old, clean cookie sheet that you're willing to toss.

Scoop filler onto the mixing board and apply the hardener according to the manufacturer's directions. Then mix it using a spread-and-fold motion (**Photo 2**). The spreading and folding technique is crucial because it fully mixes the hardener into the filler and prevents air bubbles from forming. Never stir the mixture.

APPLY THE FILLER

Spread the filler to form a "tight" coat (**Photo 3**). That will burp air out of the scratches and wet the bare metal. Then apply a fill coat (**Photo 4**).

SAND TO SHAPE AND GLAZE

Sand the filler to match the contours of the car body using 80- and 180-grit sandpaper. Then feather the edges of the filler right up to the painted edge.

Next, apply finishing glaze to the entire patch and then sand the area with 180-grit and then 320-grit sandpaper (**Photo 5**). Spray the patch with primer, and then paint it.

1 REMOVE THE PAINT
Chuck the 24-grit disc into your drill and spin it deep into the dent, getting all the way down to the metal. Then work your way out to the edges.

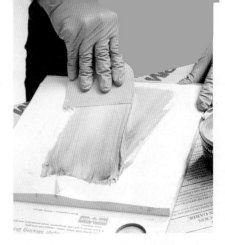

2 SPREAD, SCOOP AND FOLD
Spread the filler down the mixing board in an S-shaped curve. Then scoop it up and fold it over. Repeat until the filler has a consistent color.

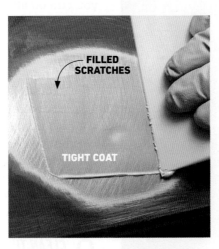

FILLED SCRATCHES

TIGHT COAT

3 APPLY A "TIGHT" FIRST COAT
Scoop up some filler and press it hard into the rough metal.

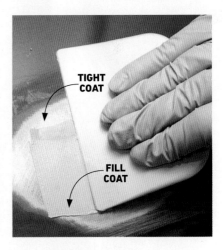

TIGHT COAT

FILL COAT

4 ADD MORE FILLER
Wipe on a thicker layer of filler to completely fill the dent.

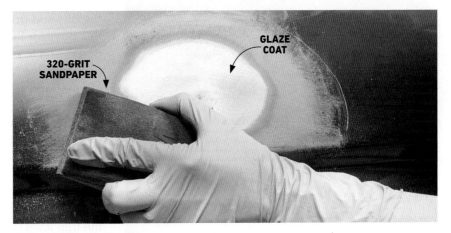

320-GRIT SANDPAPER

GLAZE COAT

5 SAND THE GLAZE
Hand-sand the glaze coat with 180-grit and then 320-grit sandpaper to get a smooth finish. Then prime and paint.

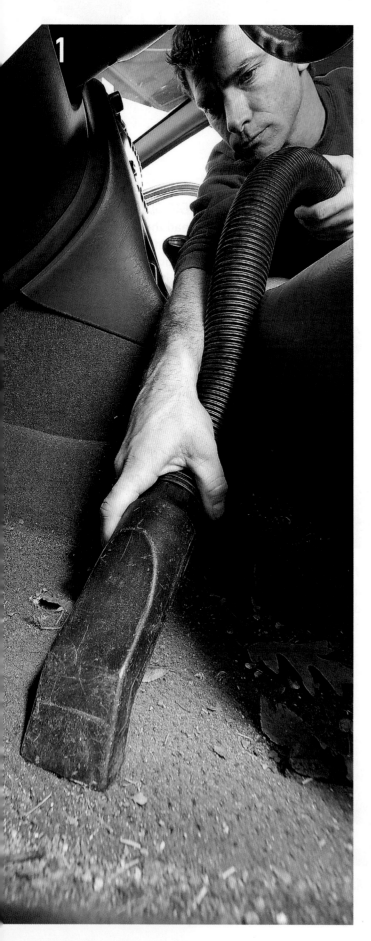

RENEW YOUR AUTO INTERIOR

WHEN CLEANING A CAR, THE DEVIL'S IN THE DETAILS

Unless you're fastidious about your car's interior, it's usually the last thing on your cleaning list. As the months roll by, grime, wrappers, dust and junk can just pile up. Unfortunately, most of us finally get around to the deep cleaning when we tape the "For Sale" sign on the windshield. But why wait when you can easily get your car looking its best with these tips from professional detailers? Your efforts will be rewarded with a car that looks and feels brand new.

1 VACUUM LIKE YOU MEAN IT

Slide the seat all the way forward and clean out all the junk underneath. You'll be surprised by what you find. Vacuum the seats, remove the mats and vacuum the carpet. Use a brush attachment for the dash and door panels. Don't forget to clean out and vacuum those handy door pockets (another source of buried treasure).

2 CLEAN THE CARPET

Deep-clean the carpeting and upholstery. Use a carpet cleaning machine to get the dirt that settles deep into the fibers of the carpet. (Clean cloth seats this way as well.) It sprays the carpet with a solution of water and cleaner and then sucks the dirt and grime into a reservoir. A machine like this pays for itself after just a few uses, but if you don't want to make the up-front investment, you can also rent one from a rental center or use a spray-on cleaner and a scrub brush instead.

3 REMEMBER THE RECESSES

Detailing means just that—remembering every detail, including cleaning all the trim lines and recesses. Wrap a cloth around a worn screwdriver (no sharp edges) and spray it with Simple Green or another all-purpose cleaner. Move it gently along the trim lines to pick up dirt, using fresh sections of cloth as you go. Then clean around the buttons and controls, and follow up with a rejuvenator such as Armor All.

4 CLEAN & CONDITION THE SEATS

After a few years, you'll notice that the color of the leather or vinyl seats no longer matches that of the rest of the interior. It's not enough just to condition the leather. First spray on leather cleaner and rub vigorously with a clean terry cloth towel. To avoid rubbing the grime back into the seats, keep flipping the cloth to expose a fresh surface. Let the seats dry for an hour and then rub in a leather conditioner such as Lexol to keep the leather supple. It's available at discount stores and auto stores.

5 WASH THE WINDOWS

Don't forget the top edges. Ever notice that line of grime on the tops of windows when they're partially rolled down? Most people overlook this detail when giving their vehicle a quick wash. A few minutes with Windex and a clean rag is all it takes.

6 BRUSH OUT THE AIR VENTS

These louvers are a real magnet for dust, and a vacuum with a brush attachment just won't get it all. Take an inexpensive paintbrush and give it a light shot of Endust or Pledge furniture polish. Work the brush into the crevices to collect the dust. Wipe the brush off with a rag and move on to the next vent.

7 SCRAPE OFF OLD WINDOW STICKERS

While all of your national and state park stickers may call to mind great memories, they can be a visual hazard as they accumulate. The high-quality stickers will pull off if you can get under a corner and carefully pull them free at a 90-degree angle. Others will leave a gummy residue and require a bit more attention. Cover your dash with an old towel and dab on Goo Gone. Then scrape and wipe it off.

A LANDSCAPER OR EXTERIOR CONTRACTOR

**PRO TIP: LEAVE A PATH
TO THE BACKYARD**
If there's an addition or new
patio in your future, leave a path
for machinery. You don't want to
tear out shrubs or a retaining
wall later so a skid steer can
reach the backyard.

DESIGN A LANDSCAPE

///

DOING IT YOURSELF CAN SAVE MONEY AND BOOST CURB APPEAL

For many homeowners, improving the landscape is high on the to-do list. Settling on and implementing a design, however, isn't always straightforward, and achieving a great look requires a little nuance. The stakes are also high: If you get it wrong, you might end up with dead plants and an ugly yard for all your hard work. Still, DIYers can save roughly 40% to 60% of the cost of a professional landscaper and dramatically boost their house's curb appeal. To help you get it right, we spoke with a landscaping expert, who shared these quick tips.

1 DEVISE A MASTER PLAN

Most people jump into landscaping without thinking of the big picture. They end up with a jumble of plants that don't look right with the house or one another. Start with the end goal in mind for better results. If you want help with the design, a landscape architect will typically charge $600 to $3,500 to visit your home and create a plan; costs vary by the size of the property and the work to be done. Many garden centers offer free design services if you buy your materials from them.

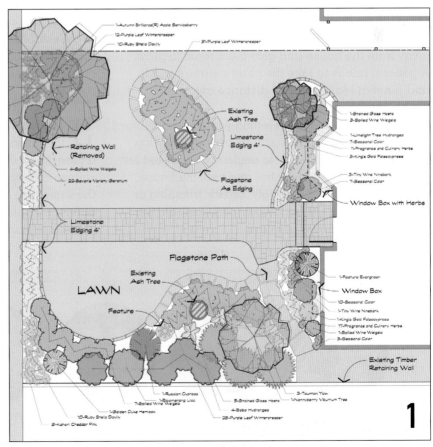

3 CHOOSE WHITE AND YELLOW FOR DRAMA

Red and purple are vivid colors, but in a landscape, yellow and white flowers are the real attention grabbers. They stand out more against green foliage while others tend to disappear. So, if you want an eye-catching landscape, use yellow and white flowers.

2 AVOID COMMON SHRUB MISTAKES

It's common for homeowners to plant large shrubs and other plants too close to their house's foundation and siding. Then the owner prunes them back and they eventually become half a plant. For a better look, plant shrubs farther away from the house and give them room to grow. A general rule is to take the plant's mature width and put it at least half that distance away from the house.

Another common error is letting your shrubs grow unchecked. Because shrubs are relatively low maintenance, they're easy to neglect. Overlooked for years, they grow out of control and hide the house, crowd doorways and look ugly. Drastic trimming or removing them might be the best and easiest thing you could do for your front yard.

4 START PLANTING EARLY IF YOU PLAN TO SELL

Improving your landscaping is a great way to boost the curb appeal—and selling price—of a home. But remember that most plants take time to get established and look their best. If you hope to sell in midsummer, get started in early spring, or better yet, the year before you plan to sell.

5 PLAN FOR ALL-SEASON COLOR

You want your plants to bloom throughout the growing season. When you're developing a plan, know the bloom time for each plant, and choose coordinating colors for plants blossoming at the same time. Design your landscape to highlight different plants during each season. It's fun to see individual plants have their day in the sunlight.

SPRING TO EARLY SUMMER BLOOMS — LATE SUMMER TO FALL BLOOMS

5

NINEBARK "TINY WINE"

WEIGELA "SPILLED WINE"

HOSTA "STAINED GLASS"

HYDRANGEA "BOBO"

REBLOOMING LILAC "BLOOMERANG"

6

MAP OUT YOUR COLORS

Our pro recommends repeating your chosen colors in different sections of your landscape. For example, if you use red at your walkway, use red at the side of your house as well. This technique gives your design continuity and balance. Remember, foliage is color too!

7 PREVENT WEEDS WITH MASS PLANTING

Weeds will pop up wherever light reaches the soil. To make your landscaping low maintenance, place plants tightly together so weeds can't get started.

8 TEST YOUR SOIL

Good soil is the key to healthy plants. A simple test will tell you whether you need to add lime, nitrogen, phosphorus or potassium to the soil. Dig 6 in. and scoop samples from five to 10 areas in your yard and mix them in a bucket. You can purchase an at-home soil testing kit at most home centers, but for best results, send your soil sample to a state-certified soil-testing lab or university extension service. To find yours, enter "university extension service" and your state in a search engine. Testing fees are usually about $20, and results take one to two weeks.

9 DON'T PUT POLY UNDER WOOD MULCH

Putting poly under wood mulch prevents the decomposing mulch from enriching the soil. Instead, place a 4-in. layer of wood mulch on the soil to block sunlight from reaching it. Like poly, this prevents weeds. But unlike poly, it will naturally decompose, providing nutrients to your plants. You'll have to add mulch as needed.

10

10 MIX UP TEXTURES

Plant texture refers to the size and shape of the leaves. Don't make the mistake of choosing all the same textures for your landscape; it's dull and monotonous. For an appealing landscape, use plants with varying leaf shapes and sizes.

11 PLAN FOR GROWTH

Before buying a plant, check the tag for its mature size. Keep in mind that many plants grow larger than the tag indicates. Knowing the maximum size—and allowing a little extra space—helps you avoid a crowded, overgrown look later.

11

12 PLANT IN RANDOM PATTERNS

In a formal garden, you may see plants all lined up, but most residential landscapes look best with a more casual design like the one shown at right. Planting in random or zigzag patterns provides good ground coverage with fewer plants, and these arrangements are visually interesting too.

12

INSTALL OUTDOOR LIGHTING

LOW-VOLTAGE SYSTEMS MAKE IT EASY—EVEN IF YOU HAVE NO ELECTRICAL EXPERIENCE

Imagine a relaxing afternoon out on your deck or patio. The weather's perfect, the cooler's stocked and you've got steaks sizzling on the grill. Everybody's happy—until the sun goes down and an old 100-watt flood light turns itself on, blasting its blinding, bright light into the eyes of all your guests.

It doesn't have to be that way, you know. There are lots of great outdoor lighting options available. And because most are low voltage, any DIYer can install them. A little planning and the right advice are all you need, so here are some tips for lighting your path back to backyard bliss.

1

2

HOW IT ALL FITS TOGETHER
A low-voltage system has three parts:

LOW-VOLTAGE
CABLE

TRANSFORMER

LIGHT
FIXTURES

- The **TRANSFORMER** plugs into a nearby GFCI-protected outlet and reduces a 120-volt current to 12 volts.
- The **LOW-VOLTAGE CABLE** carries the current between the transformer and the light fixtures.
- The **LIGHT FIXTURES** get connected to the cable with wire connectors made specifically for outdoor use (see "Skip the Quick Connectors," p. 120).

1 *DON'T BE INTIMIDATED*
Since most outdoor lighting is low voltage, it's safe and easy enough for any DIYer to install—there's no electrical experience necessary. In fact, the only special tool you'll need is a wire stripper.

2 *INSTALL UNDERGROUND WIRING AFTER PLANTING*
To prevent accidental cutting of wiring for ground-level fixtures, install wiring after your landscape has been planted. That way you won't accidentally chop through it with a shovel. Also, don't install wiring in digging areas such as garden beds, which are likely to be disturbed, and be sure to bury low-voltage wire at least 6 in. below the surface.

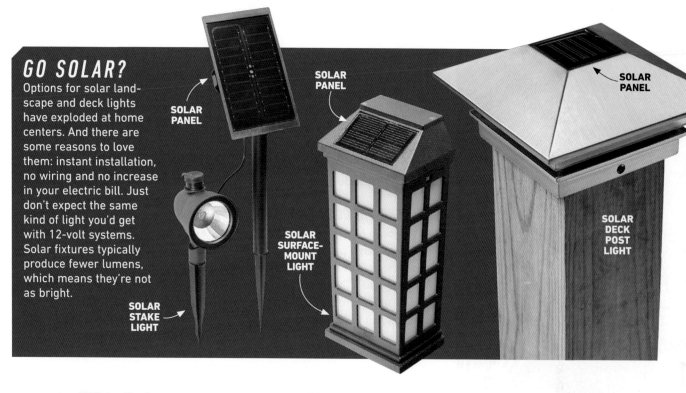

GO SOLAR?

Options for solar landscape and deck lights have exploded at home centers. And there are some reasons to love them: instant installation, no wiring and no increase in your electric bill. Just don't expect the same kind of light you'd get with 12-volt systems. Solar fixtures typically produce fewer lumens, which means they're not as bright.

SOLAR PANEL

SOLAR PANEL

SOLAR PANEL

SOLAR SURFACE-MOUNT LIGHT

SOLAR DECK POST LIGHT

SOLAR STAKE LIGHT

3 KEEP YOUR FIXTURES; UPGRADE YOUR BULBS

For decades, halogen lights reigned supreme in low-voltage outdoor lighting systems, but LEDs have all but replaced them because they cost less to operate and last much longer. But you don't have to tear out all your old halogen fixtures to enjoy the benefits of LEDs—retrofit bulbs are available. Just be sure to replace each halogen bulb with equivalent wattage and the same base type.

LED bulbs cost more per bulb, but they use less energy and you'll get up to 20 years of life from a single LED bulb compared with only two or three years from a halogen one.

4 DON'T OVERLAP POOLS OF LIGHT

The purpose of most deck lighting is ambience, and professional outdoor lighting designers say it's best not to create overlapping "pools" of light on decks and patios. So avoid mounting fixtures too close together. For decks, choose fixtures that cast a 4- to 5-ft. pool of light. Keep them 30 in. up off the deck's floor and space them up to 10 ft. apart. Overlapping lights on deck stairs and walkways, however, can be key in providing enough light to help people avoid tripping.

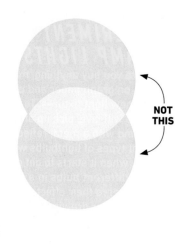

DO THIS

NOT THIS

MR16 HALOGEN BULB

3

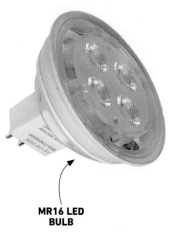

MR16 LED BULB

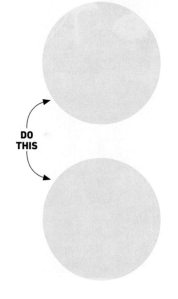

4

5 CONSIDER INDIRECT LIGHTING FOR PATIOS

Instead of focusing lights directly onto a patio, try lighting objects around it, such as boulders and trees. This eliminates glare and creates attractive shadow effects.

6 SKIP THE QUICK CONNECTORS

Some landscape lighting kits have preinstalled quick connectors, but they aren't what the pros use. Cheap connectors buried underground will work for a while, but they can corrode over time and fail. Cut off the factory-installed connectors and make splice connections using gel-filled wire connectors made specifically for outdoor use.

7 RESEARCH STORE-BOUGHT KITS

You can buy complete ground-level landscape lighting kits at a home center for $40 to $200. Kits are convenient and adequate if you need only a few fixtures. But the transformer—sometimes called a power pack—will be too small if you decide to add more fixtures down the road, and style options for fixtures will be much more limited with a kit. For a deck lighting system, plan to buy individual components.

5

6

QUICK CONNECTOR

OUTDOOR WIRE CONNECTORS

EXPERIMENT WITH CLAMP LIGHTS

Before you buy anything, make a sketch of your deck or patio on graph paper and plan the location for each of your new light fixtures. To get an idea of the effect a fixture will give, pick up an inexpensive clamp light—the kind with a metal reflector shade—and a few different types of lightbulbs with different brightnesses. Then, when it starts to get dark, try out the clamp light using different bulbs in a few different spots so you can observe their effect. Mark the most desirable locations on your drawing, and pay particular attention to lighting areas such as stairs and transitions to different levels for safety.

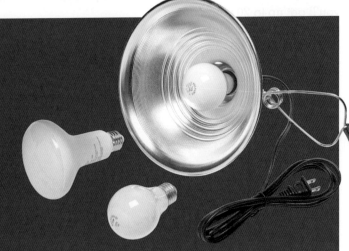

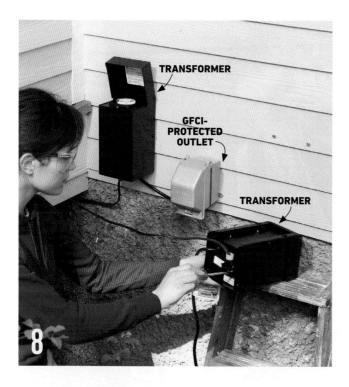

TRANSFORMER

GFCI-
PROTECTED
OUTLET

TRANSFORMER

8

300-WATT
TRANSFORMER

45-WATT
TRANSFORMER

9

AVOID THE RUNWAY EFFECT

To prevent making your walkway look like an airport runway, stagger lights so they're not perfectly parallel.

DO THIS

WALKWAY

NOT THIS

WALKWAY

8 KNOW WHEN TO KEEP YOUR OLD TRANSFORMER

Any older low-voltage transformer can be used to power both halogen and LED lights—even if they're mixed on the same circuit—as long as you have enough wattage to spare in your old transformer. If your transformer isn't big enough to handle the additional load, add a second transformer or upsize your existing one.

9 BUY THE RIGHT NEW TRANSFORMER

A "low-voltage" lighting system starts with a transformer plugged into a GFCI-protected receptacle. The transformer's job is to convert a 120-volt household current to 12 volts before sending it through special outdoor cable to light your fixtures. Just a few years ago, you would have needed a 600- to 1,200-watt transformer to light a yard full of halogen lamps. But because LEDs use fewer watts than their halogen predecessors, smaller transformers—45 to

300 watts—are usually all that is needed.

So how big should you go? Simply add up the wattage for all the light fixtures you're planning to install, and use that number to pick the right transformer. Buy one slightly bigger than you need in case you decide to add fixtures in the future.

10 RUN WIRE UNDER WALKWAYS

If you need to run wiring under an existing walkway, try this trick: Dig a small trench on both sides. Next, flatten the end of a piece of rigid metal conduit and use a sledgehammer to drive the conduit, flattened end first, horizontally under the walkway. Then cut off the ends of the conduit with a hacksaw, file off the sharp edges and feed your wire through the conduit. You can buy a 10-ft. stick of rigid steel conduit (the thick, heavy-duty stuff) from your local home center.

10

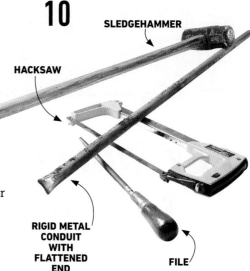

SLEDGEHAMMER

HACKSAW

RIGID METAL
CONDUIT
WITH
FLATTENED
END

FILE

LAY SOD LIKE A PRO

LAYING SOD IN A NEW YARD IS EASIER WITH ADVICE FROM LANDSCAPING EXPERTS

Recently we shadowed a pro sod crew from Wagner Sod, Landscaping and Irrigation Co., located in Inver Grove Heights, Minnesota, to get the lowdown on how experts lay sod in a new yard. We learned a lot from the Wagner crew, and believe it or not, there's much more to laying sod than "green side up."

We got some great installation tips, including what needs to be done before the sod arrives and how to care for the sod after it's down. Armed with this helpful information, you'll be able to lay sod like a pro—without needing to hire one—and the grass will always be greener on your side of the fence.

1 USE IT OR LOSE IT

Be ready to start laying the sod the minute it arrives. Sod is usually harvested and shipped directly from the fields because it has a very short shelf life. It's not a lack of water that wreaks havoc (though sod does dry out fast); the real killer is heat.

Sod starts decomposing as soon as it's stacked up, and the decomposition process generates heat, a lot of it—enough heat that the rolls in the center of the pile could be lost in as little as 24 hours. Watering won't help, and covering the pallets with a tarp compounds the problem. So if you need just a roll or two for a repair and want to shop at the local nursery, wiggle your arm down into the pile and check for heat. If it's smokin' hot down there, you may want to consider buying elsewhere.

2 DRESS FOR THE OCCASION

Laying sod is a messy business; there's no way to do it without getting dirty. Wear a junky shirt so you can carry the rolls right up against your belly. One surefire way to break your back is to try to carry sod out away from your body. Tight-fitting gloves work best; loose gloves pull off your hands when they get pinched under the rolls. Don't wear shorts without wearing kneepads, and don't forget the sunscreen.

3 LOWER THE GRADE NEAR CURBS AND SIDEWALKS

Use a flat shovel to lower the grade about an inch near curbs, driveways, edging, etc. Start raking the rest of the yard smooth starting at those places. Grass that sits too high next to sidewalks and driveways tends to dry out and will get scalped by the lawn mower. The pros at Wagner prefer standard garden rakes for grading by hand.

4 FERTILIZE THE SOIL FIRST

Starter fertilizers are formulated to provide the nutrients a new lawn needs. But if you want the greenest grass in the neighborhood, take a soil sample and send it in for analysis. Many universities have extension services that will do soil tests for about $20. Some garden centers will also do testing, or you can search online for companies as well. The test results will tell you precisely which nutrients your soil is lacking, so you can buy the exact fertilizer mix to make up any deficiencies. Starter fertilizers often contain phosphorus, which can pollute waterways and is banned in some states for use other than on new lawns.

CONSIDER ADDING TOPSOIL

Sod will grow in most soil types as long as it has water and nutrients, but adding a topsoil mixed with compost will improve your chances of maintaining a healthy green lawn. If you decide to go this route (the owners of the yard featured in this story did not), you'll want to hire a skid steer to spread it out for you if you have a large yard. You could rent a skid steer yourself, but if you've never run one before, there is a learning curve. Existing compacted soils should be loosened up with harrows on a skid steer or with a tiller.

HEADER ROWS

5

6

7

5 LAY DOWN A HEADER ROW

Picture-frame the entire yard with a "header" row, as well as the perimeter of the house. A header row hides all the cut ends, which results in smoother, more unified edges.

6 AVOID GAPS

Pull the sod tight together without overlapping. Exposed edges are the first to dry out, and the more gaps you have between pieces of sod, the more exposed edges there are. Small crowns (uplifted sections) are preferable to gaps because they will be flattened with a roller. Also, if the rolls have been sitting on the pallets too long, the end that's in the center of the rolls may stay curled (another reason to lay it right away). If that's the case, straighten it out with your hands before butting the next one into it.

7 CUT FROM THE UNDERSIDE

Cut the sod to size from the bottom, or the "dark side," as the Wagner crew refers to it. It's easier to see where to make the cut from the top, but it's much, much harder to do. If you cut your pieces on the dark side, all you need is a standard utility knife. Fancy, quick-change knives get all gummed up with dirt, so sod pros prefer a basic retractable knife. Whichever knife you use, make sure it's a bright color; grays and silvers are sure to get misplaced and buried under the sod.

8

8 STAGGER THE SEAMS

Stagger the seams by at least one-third the length of a roll. If you don't, you'll end up with a few long, super-noticeable seams that dry out faster.

9 DRIVE STAKES ON HILLS AND SWALES

Sod on hills needs to be held in place with stakes. Our experts prefer simple stakes made from wood lath, which is available in cheap bundles at home centers. Metal staples and biodegradable stakes are less conspicuous, but they may stick up far enough to injure a bare foot. Install two stakes about 1 ft. in from each end.

Whenever possible, start laying sod at the bottom of hills to keep the sod pieces from separating and creating gaps. Sod can actually float away during heavy downpours, so make sure to stake down sod that's in swales designed to divert water. Also stake sod that's directly in front of gutter downspouts that dump a high volume of water.

9

DIVIDE THE YARD INTO LONG, NARROW SECTIONS

There's no reason the sod in side yards has to be laid the same direction as in the front or back yard. To make things easier on yourself, divide the yards into long, narrow strips. Laying sod the long way goes a lot faster because there are fewer cuts to make.

For purely aesthetic reasons, if you're dealing with a square area, lay the rows of sod perpendicular to where they will be most visible, like from the street or living room windows. The lawn will seem more full that way because the long, continuous edge seams are much less noticeable when they run perpendicular to the viewer.

10

CUT OUT PIE-SHAPE PIECES ON CURVES

Full rolls of sod can be bent around gradual curves. Bending sod around tighter bends requires the removal of one or more pie-shape pieces. Start by bending the sod in place. Let it fold up in the middle. Slice down the top of the fold (one of the few times you'll have to cut through the top side). Lay down the two folds and remove the section that overlaps.

11

USE UP THE SMALL CHUNKS

When we asked one of our experts how much extra sod to order to account for the waste, he said, "What waste? There's no reason not to use up just about every bit of sod. Even small chunks will grow when properly watered and not left out on the edge." If the idea of not having extra sod makes you nervous, order 5% more, but remember, picking up an extra roll or two later is much easier and cheaper than disposing of many rolls of excess sod.

MAKE STRAIGHT LINES WITH A STRING

12 Your sod will look better if you start the first row perfectly straight. Stretch a string along property lines and use it as a guide for the starter row.

FLATTEN WITH A ROLLER

13 Rolling freshly laid sod is extremely important—**do not skip this step**! A roller will remove any crowns and press the roots down in contact with the soil. Sod will eventually settle on its own, but until it does, those areas with space underneath will dry out fast and require much, much more water to stay alive. Rollers are available at rental centers.

PROPERTY LINE STAKE

MOTORIZED ROLLER

WATER, WATER, WATER!

Water until runoff begins. Dry spots indicate the need for more water; dial it back if you start growing mushrooms. Adjust according to weather and season: Water more frequently during warm, dry or windy weather.

- **WEEK 1:** Water three times a day—morning, noon and evening.
- **WEEK 2:** Water twice a day—morning and evening.
- **WEEK 3:** Water once a day in the morning.
- **SUBSEQUENT WEEKS:** Water once every other day in the morning.
- Mow at the end of Week 2 or if the height exceeds 3½ in. Fertilize per instructions from the sod farm.

CHOOSE A WALK-BEHIND LAWN MOWER

NAVIGATING THE MAZE OF MODELS AND FEATURES CAN BE DAUNTING—USE THESE TIPS TO HELP NARROW DOWN YOUR CHOICES

1 ***SPEND MORE UP FRONT TO SAVE IN THE LONG RUN***
Residential, walk-behind lawn mowers range in price from less than $200 to well over $600. And you may be wondering if it's worth spending top dollar on a mower. In addition to the extra features available on more expensive mowers, high-end mowers have better-quality components.

You'll find easy-rolling ball bearing wheels, long-lasting composite or aluminum decks, and top-quality engines. And most high-end mowers include a longer warranty. This adds up to a mower that will last longer and need fewer repairs. So you may save money by not having to replace or repair your old mower.

start. A built-in battery and starter motor eliminate the need to pull-start your mower. This is great for people with shoulder or strength problems. The electric start feature is also handy when you need to stop to empty the grass-catcher bag or pick up a stick that's in the way. Just turn off the engine. Restarting is a button-push away. Honda even makes a mower that charges the battery while you mow, so you don't ever have to plug in the mower to recharge the battery. You'll spend a bit more for the electric start feature.

5 CHECK ONLINE REVIEWS TO AVOID BUYING A LEMON

Even a top-brand mower will occasionally have a quirky problem. One good way to discover whether the mower you're considering has a hidden flaw is to check online reviews. You'll find user reviews on manufacturer websites, Amazon and other websites where lawn mowers are sold. There will always be a few users who have had a bad experience, but multiple complaints about the same problem should stand out as a red flag.

2 DON'T FORGET YOUR LOCAL DEALER

You may be able to save a little money by purchasing a lawn mower from a department store or home center. But buying from a local servicing dealer has advantages that might outweigh any cost savings. First, you're more likely to get better purchasing advice from the more knowledgeable staff at a dealer showroom. And when it comes time for a tune-up or warranty repairs, you'll know right where to go for convenient, personal service. Most dealers have at least two or three top-quality brands to choose from and will display the most popular models on the showroom floor.

3 CONSIDER AN ELECTRIC MOWER

If you don't have a huge lawn, a battery-powered mower may be perfect. Cordless mowers are quieter, require less

maintenance, and of course, run without gas or oil. Best of all, you'll never have to start a gas engine—just push a button or lever and go.

As lithium-ion battery technology has improved, most manufacturers have included cordless mowers in their lineup, so you'll have plenty of choices. Many of these mowers can cut an average suburban yard (about one-fifth of an acre) on a single charge. Prices for battery-powered mowers are similar to those of their gas-powered rivals, and you'll find most of the same features, too.

4 GET ELECTRIC START AND STOP PULLING

If pulling a starter rope is difficult for you or anyone else who will be using the mower, look for a mower with an electric

option since it works great on hills and with a bag. All-wheel drive is needed only for severely sloping terrain.

If you buy a self-propelled mower, consider upgrading to variable speed for more flexibility in matching your mowing speed to the lawn conditions and your walking speed.

7 GET A GOOD MULCHER

If you mulch your grass, look for features such as special mulching blades or an aluminum or composite deck that resists grass buildup on the underside better than steel. If you prefer to bag your grass, make sure the bag is easy to remove and reinstall. And for the greatest versatility, look for a mower that also has a side discharge chute for times when you've let your grass grow too long for mulching or bagging.

Some mowers have features like Toro's "Bag On Demand" that simplify the changeover from bagging to mulching. Honda makes a mower with a feature

called Versamow that allows you to mulch and bag at the same time, as well as adjust the percentage of clippings that go into the bag.

8 MAKE SURE IT'S EASY TO ADJUST THE CUTTING HEIGHT

Try out the height adjusters on the mower you intend to buy to make sure they work smoothly and easily. On some mowers, a single lever adjusts a pair of wheels or even all four wheels at once.

9 STOP WITHOUT RESTARTING

If you collect your clippings and need to empty the bag frequently, or if you have to stop often to pick up sticks or move toys out of the way, you know what a hassle it can be to restart the lawn mower every time. You can avoid this problem by shopping for a mower with a blade brake clutch (BBC) or Toro's Blade Override System (BOS). Mowers with either feature allow you to stop the blade but leave the engine running. Expect to pay about $100 more.

6 MATCH THE DRIVE SYSTEM TO YOUR TERRAIN AND YARD SIZE

If your lawn is relatively flat and not huge, chances are you will be perfectly happy with a push mower—that is, a mower that's not self-propelled. In addition to being more affordable, mowers without power to the wheels are lighter, have fewer mechanical parts to wear out, and are usually easier to maneuver.

If you have hills or a large yard, a self-propelled mower is a better choice. Front-wheel drive mowers pull the mower along but may lose traction on hills, where you tend to push down on the handle. And if you bag your grass, the weight of the bag will reduce the traction on the front wheels, making the drive wheels less effective. In most cases, rear-wheel drive is the best

FIX YOUR WELL YOURSELF

A LITTLE KNOW-HOW CAN SAVE YOU TIME, EFFORT AND MONEY

If you own a home with a well, you know that trouble can hit at the worst possible time, like at the start of a holiday weekend, and off-hours repairs can be very expensive.

We spoke with Steve McCullough, owner of Lauren McCullough Well Drilling, to get his advice on how DIYers can address well problems. If you're comfortable replacing electrical and plumbing components, you can save at least $150 on the service call as well as money on the parts. All the parts that can be replaced by a DIYer are located inside the house. You'll still need to make a call to a professional for outside electrical, piping, pump and check-valve failures.

Most of the time you'll find the parts you need at home centers. But home centers may not carry the highest-quality parts. If you want to get long-lasting parts, shop at a plumbing supplier.

THREE COMMON PROBLEMS

The most common symptoms of well trouble are no water at all, pulsing water pressure and a pump that runs constantly. We show you how to address each of these issues on the following pages.

PROBLEM 1: NO WATER AT ALL

BE SURE THE POWER IS ON

Start by checking that the well switch located near your pressure tank hasn't been switched off. Then check the well's double-pole circuit breaker to see that it hasn't tripped. If it has, reset it. A breaker that keeps tripping likely means a problem with the well pump, and you'll need to call a pro for that.

CHECK THE PRESSURE SWITCH

You'll find the pressure switch mounted on a ¼-in. tube near the pressure tank. It's what senses when water pressure has dropped to the point where the pressure tank requires more water. The switch then powers up the well pump.

   If the switch is bad, it won't start the pump and you won't have water, so testing the switch is your first step. Remove the cover and bang a screwdriver handle sharply against the tube below the switch to jar the electrical contacts. If you see a spark and the pump starts, the pressure switch is the problem, and you'll need to replace it. A new switch is about $25. If there's still no spark, you'll have to replace the controller.

IF THE SWITCH IS BAD, REPLACE IT

If you find the pressure switch is bad, test the pressure tank to make sure it isn't waterlogged (see "Problem: Pulsing Water"). To replace the switch, start by removing the wires to the old switch (be sure to label them) and unscrew the switch **(photo at right)**. Coat the tubing threads with pipe dope or Teflon tape and screw on the new switch so it sits in the same orientation. Then reconnect the wires.

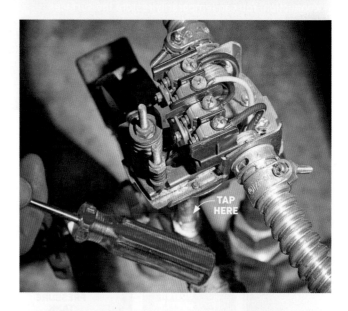

TAP HERE

PRESSURE SWITCH

DRAIN OPEN

VALVE OFF

NON-CONTACT VOLTAGE TESTER

Figure A Anatomy of a Well

Rural homes usually have a "deep well" with a submersible pump situated at the bottom of the well casing.

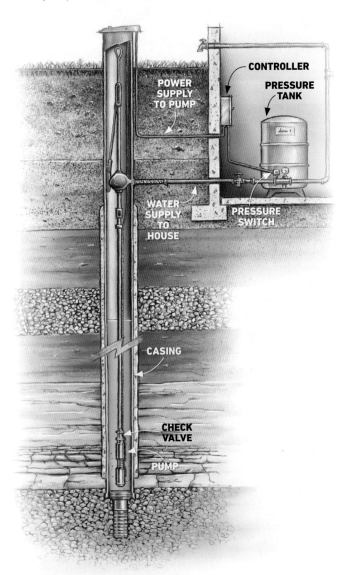

IF ALL ELSE FAILS, REPLACE THE CONTROLLER

The pump controller houses a capacitor to help start the pump. Most pump controls are mounted in the house near the pressure tank, but others are mounted inside the well pump itself and the fix requires a pro. If you don't have the box shown below, this fix isn't for you.

There's no way to test the controller, so you either have to risk blowing about $75 by replacing a good one, or throw in the towel and call a pro. Replacing the pump controller as shown here is easy, and it's your last, best shot at avoiding a service call. If you've replaced the pressure switch and the pump still won't start, we think it's worth the risk to replace the pump controller.

REPLACE THE PUMP CONTROLLER

Remove the screw at the bottom of the pump controller cover and lift it off the box to disconnect it. Take it to the store and buy an exact replacement. Snap the new cover onto the old box (no need to rewire if you buy the same brand). Then start the pump.

PROBLEM 2: PULSING WATER

CHECK THE PRESSURE TANK

When water "pulses" at the spigot, it usually means you have a waterlogged tank. Replacement is your only option. A new tank costs about $200 and up. At right are two methods for diagnosing a bad tank: checking for water at the air valve and shaking the tank.

A typical pressure tank stores about 6 to 10 gallons of water inside a balloonlike bladder on the bottom half of the tank. The top portion is filled with air. As the pump fills the tank, the water compresses the air above the bladder. The compressed air is what powers water through your house when you open a faucet. When the bladder fails, water seeps into the top half, reducing the tank's ability to force out more than 2 or 3 gallons of water. The water also rusts the tank from the inside.

These are the symptoms of a bad pressure tank:

- Water pressure in one faucet drops dramatically when someone opens another faucet or flushes a toilet—because the tank has lost its capacity to store and pressurize water.
- Water pressure fluctuates while taking a shower or filling a tub—the tank can only pressurize a few gallons of water, forcing the pump to cycle on and off.
- Water leaks onto the floor around the tank, or water starts to look rusty.
- Your electrical bill jumps for no apparent reason—because the pump has to start so many times, and frequent starting takes more power than longer run-times.

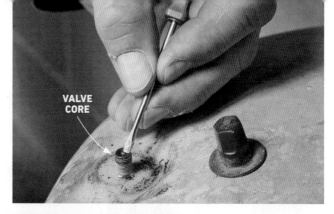

TEST FOR WATER AT THE AIR VALVE
Unscrew the plastic cover from the air valve on the top of the tank. Use a small screwdriver to depress the air valve to see if water comes out.

ROCK THE TANK
Push against the top of the tank to rock it slightly. If you can't rock it or it feels top heavy, it's bad. Drain it and replace it.

PROBLEM 3: PUMP RUNS NONSTOP

KNOW WHEN TO CALL A PRO

When a pump turns on, you'll hear the clicking of the pressure switch opening and closing. If you hear frequent clicking when no water is flowing, you have problems outside the house and you'll need to hire a pro. It could be a broken water line from the well to the house (usually you'll have a wet area between the well head and the house), a bad check valve just above the submersible pump at the bottom of the well, a bad connector leaving the well casing or even a broken water line inside the well casing. Each of those problems requires a pro.

TANK REPLACEMENT TIPS

- **BUY A LARGER PRESSURE TANK.** Frequent starts wear out well pumps, controllers and pressure switches much faster than longer run-times. The larger the pressure tank, the fewer times your well pump must start. Since well pumps are much more expensive, the longer pump life more than offsets the higher tank cost. This is particularly good advice if your home uses more water than average (for example, you run a business with high water needs, irrigate a large area or raise animals that require large amounts of water).
- **DON'T BUY A TANK BASED ON PRICE ALONE.** Cheap tanks cost far more in the long run because of shorter bladder life and accelerated tank rust-out. The pro we consulted swears by the Well-X-Trol brand, but it may not be available at your local store.

OLD CONCRETE

NEW CONCRETE

BEFORE

AFTER

RESURFACE A SIDEWALK

A FRESH COAT CAN COVER OLD CONCRETE OR HIDE REPAIRS

Replacing a damaged section of sidewalk is a great way to get rid of obvious eyesores and dangerous tripping hazards, but next to new concrete, the old sidewalk can end up looking kind of shabby—pitted, flaking and worn. Plus, the color of the old concrete may be different. We solved those problems at one home by coating the entire walk with concrete resurfacer, a cement-based powder that mixes with water. We used Sakrete Flo-Coat, but there are several other brands. Here's how it went.

1 TRENCH ALONG THE EDGES

To prep, we power-washed the old concrete and the new (the new section had cured for a month). The next day, we edged along the sidewalk with a shovel to clear away overhanging grass and create a small trench. A deeper, wider trench would have been better (see "Lessons Learned," p. 137).

2 PROTECT AGAINST SLOP-OVER

To protect areas that we didn't want to coat, we masked the adjoining concrete surfaces with duct tape. Duct tape adheres well to concrete. Masking tape doesn't.

3 DAMPEN THE CONCRETE

Dry surfaces quickly steal water from the mix and inhibit easy spreading. We misted the entire sidewalk to dampen it before applying the product. We made sure it was thoroughly damp but not puddling. This is critical.

4 MAKE A GIANT MEASURING CUP

We marked a bucket to indicate the exact amount of water recommended per bag of resurfacer. This allowed us to get a consistent mix without wasting time.

5 MIX IT UP

We poured about three-quarters of the required water into the bucket, poured in a little resurfacer and mixed with a heavy-duty drill. Then we gradually added more resurfacer, mixing each time. Finally, we poured in the last of the water and blended the mix thoroughly. After letting the mix sit for a few minutes, we mixed one last time.

6 POUR IT ON
We poured resurfacer across the first section, making sure to distribute it evenly.

7 SPREAD IT OUT
We used a squeegee to spread the mix across the entire surface to a depth of just over ⅛ in. We used the squeegee to both push and pull the mix across the section, always finishing by pulling across the sidewalk in the same direction.

8 HURRY UP!
We continued this process until we'd coated the entire walk. Since resurfacer has limited working time, we had one person mix additional buckets while another poured and spread. Wear a respirator when you mix, pour or cut concrete.

9 CUT A GROOVE
As the coating began to harden, we used a mortar rake to re-form the existing joints in the concrete. If you leave a joint filled, you risk cracks in the future.

10 ADD TEXTURE

We applied a broom finish for better traction using a soft-bristle push broom. We found that brooming within 15 minutes of the initial pour worked best, but this depends on temperature and humidity. We watched the surface and broomed when the sheen evaporated. We had to keep moving because once the resurfacer begins to harden, it becomes difficult to broom.

11 SCRAPE THE EDGES

When the mix had become firm but not hard, we used a trowel to scrape away any excess along the edge of the concrete.

12 COVER UP AND CORDON OFF

We covered the sidewalk with plastic to keep the resurfacer damp. Slower drying means better bonding and a tougher surface. To keep traffic off the resurfacer, we strung warning tape.

LESSONS LEARNED

■ **TRENCH ALONG THE EDGES.** Our trenches weren't wide enough. We had to spread the resurfacer carefully along the edges to avoid dragging soil in with the squeegee. Make your trenches at least 4 in. wide and a couple inches deep.

■ **GOOD PREPARATION IS KEY.** Resurfacer hardens fast—you have about 10 minutes to spread it. We were well pre-pared, though, and had one person mix while another applied the coating.

■ **A REDO IS EASY.** The first coat took us two hours and wasn't quite perfect. The areas we had troweled were evident and the broom finish was inconsistent. We opted for a second coat, which took just over an hour, and the result was perfect.

FIX DRIVEWAY CRACKS

MAKE YOUR ASPHALT LAST LONGER WITH MELT-IN FILLER

Every asphalt driveway develops cracks. They're more than just an eyesore; they actually speed up the demise of your driveway if you ignore them. Plus, in cold climates, water seeps in and destroys the asphalt when it expands during freezing. If you plan to topcoat your driveway, you'll need to fix the cracks first.

Squeeze bottle and caulk tube–style crack filler products are quick and easy to apply, but they shrink and crack and don't last very long. However, there's another way to fill asphalt cracks: with melt-in filler that doesn't shrink—the same type used by pro highway crews.

It'll take almost a full day to repair several cracks if they're 20 ft. long or so, but the repairs will last much longer than other quick fixes. In addition to the melt-in and trowel mix products, you'll need a propane torch with an extension hose, and a compressed air gun or leaf blower. Use an angle grinder fitted with a diamond wheel to widen hairline cracks and to quickly remove old crack fillers.

BUY THE SUPPLIES AND TOOLS

We used melt-in ½-in.-diameter Latex-ite Pli-Stix Crack and Joint Filler and Latex-ite Trowel Patch for this project. Our driveway had several 25-ft.-long cracks, so we bought four 30-ft. packages of the crack filler and four 2-gallon pails of the trowel patch. We already had a propane torch, but we bought an extension hose to eliminate the flame-outs that occur when you tip a propane cylinder upside down (WH0159 Bernzomatic Universal Torch Extension Hose, 5 ft.).

CHECK THE WEATHER AND PREP THE CRACKS

Choose a sunny day with no rain in the forecast for at least 24 hours. Start by rolling the crack filler rope onto a sunny section of the driveway so it warms and softens. While it's warming, remove all the dirt, weeds and old crack filler from the cracks using a flat-blade screwdriver or 5-in-1 paint tool. It's a painstaking process, but it's critical to getting a successful repair, so don't take shortcuts. Cleaning and filling hairline cracks are more time consuming, and the fix won't last unless you widen them with an angle grinder and diamond wheel **(Photo 1)**.

Once you finish digging out all the cracks, blow the dust and debris out of the cracks and off the driveway using a compressed air gun or leaf blower.

ADD THE FILLER AND MELT IT

Push the melt-in filler deep into the cracks **(Photo 2)**. If any filler bulges above the surface of the driveway, cut off the excess with a knife or compress it so it sits below the surface **(Photo 3)**.

Then screw the extension hose onto your propane tank and mount the torch to the other end and fire it up. The melt-in filler burns easily, so don't try to melt it in one fell swoop. Using just the tip of the flame, slowly melt the filler **(Photo 4)**. If the filler starts to burn, blow out the flames and use a faster sweeping motion or move the flame farther from the crack.

Let the filler cool to the touch (at least 20 minutes) before covering it with the trowel patch material. Then lay down a bead of trowel patch and smooth it **(Photo 5)**. Let the trowel patch dry overnight. If a depression remains the next day, apply a second coat.

PREVIOUSLY FILLED HAIRLINE CRACK

WIDER, CLEAN CRACK

1/16" BELOW DRIVEWAY SURFACE

1 WIDEN HAIRLINE CRACKS
Plunge the diamond wheel into one end of the crack and drag backward to dig out any old filler and widen the crack.

2 STUFF THE CRACK WITH FILLER
Jam the filler deep into the crack using a flat-blade screwdriver. Add a second layer to fill deeper or wider cracks.

3 COMPRESS THE FILLER
Hammer the filler so it sits at least 1/16 in. below the surface of the driveway. Don't overfill the crack.

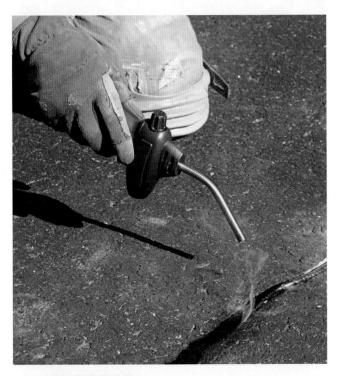

4 MELT THE FILLER
Sweep the torch flame side to side slowly over a 12-in. section until the filler begins to melt. Then move on to the next section. Return to the previous section and heat again until the filler levels out and seeps into the crack.

5 ADD TROWEL MIX AND THEN SMOOTH IT
After the filler has cooled, scoop up the trowel patch and tap it onto the crack filler to create a small mound. Smooth it with a trowel and let dry overnight. Apply a second coat if you see a depression where the crack was filled.

PATCH PITTED ASPHALT

///
A WEEKEND FIX CAN RID YOUR DRIVEWAY OF UNSIGHTLY PITTED AREAS

Asphalt driveways can develop pitted areas from things such as motor oil and coolant contamination and repeated freeze/thaw cycles. If the pits are ½ in. or less, you can fill them with a spreadable filler product (Latex-ite Trowel Patch is one choice available at a variety of home centers).

To get started, clean any oil stains and prime the asphalt with oil stain primer. Then coat the entire pitted area with patch material and let it dry overnight **(Photo 1)**. Apply a second coat to top off any partially filled pits **(Photo 2)** and smooth the surface. Let dry.

1 FILL THE PITS
Force the filler material into the cracks and pits with a trowel. Then smooth the streaks with an old broom.

2 ENLARGE THE AREA AND SMOOTH
The next day, pour more filler material onto the pitted area and spread it with a floor squeegee to smooth the surface.

PREP A DECK FOR STAIN

THE RIGHT TECHNIQUES WILL BRING A DISMAL DECK BACK TO LIFE

Preparing an old deck for stain is easy; chemicals do most of the work for you. But it's not a job that allows for shortcuts. If you break a few basic rules, your finish will fail fast and you'll be back where you started (minus your investment of time and money). Here's how to do the job right.

1 TEST THE EXISTING STAIN

Water-based (acrylic) stains must be stripped off before you apply a new finish, while oil-based stains can be recoated after you use a deck cleaner. So, your first step is to determine which type of stain is on the deck. Apply a small amount of deck stripper to an inconspicuous spot. Let it sit for about 15 minutes, then wipe it off. If the stain comes off, the stain is a water-based product and you'll have to strip it off. If the stain doesn't come off, it's an oil-based product that can be recoated with an oil-based deck stain once properly cleaned. If you have a deck that's never been stained, just go right to the steps shown in **Photos 8** and **9**.

2 PROTECT PLANTS AND SIDING

Deck stripper and cleaner can kill grass and plants. Protect vegetation with a fabric drop cloth or light-colored tarp. (Clear plastic sheeting will trap heat from the sun and fry your plants.) Then wet down the siding near the deck using your garden hose. Wet surfaces are less likely to be damaged by splashes of stripper. Clean off all loose deck debris with a push broom or leaf blower.

PICK UP A DECK STRIPPER AND A CLEANER

To prepare your wooden deck for restaining, you'll need to pick up these two types of products from a hardware store or home center:

- **DECK STRIPPER** removes the old stain. An average-size deck will require about 2 gallons at around $20 each.
- **DECK CLEANER** gets rid of stripping residue, refreshes the surface of the wood and opens the wood pores to better receive the new stain.

CAUTION:

The two types of products used to prep a deck contain hazardous chemicals. Deck stripper contains a caustic chemical that will burn your skin, and the cleaner is actually an acid. Wear long pants, eye protection and rubber gloves. Above all, avoid skin and eye contact.

3 **APPLY THE STRIPPER**
Shake the deck stripper and pour it into a paint tray. Working in small sections, roll on a thick coating using a ½-in. or ¾-in. nap roller and an extension pole. Use a paintbrush to get stripper on areas that can't be reached with the roller. If you splash stripper onto your siding, wash it off right away.

4 **KEEP THE STRIPPER DAMP**
Let the stripper work its magic for 15 minutes. If the stripper starts to dry during this period, keep it damp with water from a pump-up sprayer.

5 **SCRUB AWAY THE DISSOLVED STAIN**
Scrub with a stiff-bristle broom. If you have thick layers of stain, you may need to scrape off the residue with a floor scraper first. If that's the case, you'll likely have to reapply more stripper for the scrubbing step.

6 POWER-WASH THE STRIPPER

Rinse off the stripper and dissolved stain using a stiff stream from a garden hose nozzle, or a pressure washer on the lowest setting. A pressure washer makes the job much easier. If you only have a garden hose, you'll have to scrub more as you rinse.

7 SAND THE STUBBORN SPOTS

Let the deck dry. Areas that need additional treatment will be obvious. Repeat the stripping/scrubbing routine on those spots. If there's no improvement after a few rounds, sand those areas with a random orbital sander.

8 CLEAN AND NEUTRALIZE THE DECK

Clean the deck with a deck cleaner. Mix a 50/50 solution of water and cleaner if your wood is reasonably clean. For extremely weathered boards, try the cleaner at full strength. Experiment with a small area to determine which is better. Wet the wood with your garden hose and apply a liberal coating of the cleaner using a pump sprayer. Let the cleaner sit for 10 to 15 minutes and keep it damp before scrubbing with a stiff-bristle broom. Then rinse the entire deck and let it dry.

9 SAND AWAY THE BURRS

The cleaning step will raise lots of small fibers. After the deck dries to the touch, lightly sand the deck with a drywall sanding pad and 100-grit sanding screen. That'll knock down any raised wood fibers and give your deck a much smoother finish. Blow the sanding dust off with a leaf blower, and after a couple of days of dry weather, you'll be ready to stain.

10 MAKE THE STAIN LAST!

Follow the directions on the can. Typically, the surface of the wood should be completely dry, and the stain should be applied in temperatures between 40 and 90 degrees F. Check the forecast and don't apply stain if rain is expected within 24 hours.

SANDING DOWN THE DECK MAY BE THE BEST OPTION

If you have a tired-looking deck with an oil-based finish, your best option may be to sand. That's a slow job if you use belt sanders and orbital sanders. Most pros use a large electric drum floor sander instead, and edge sanders for areas the drum sander won't reach.

You can rent a drum floor sander and an edge sander for a few hours without spending an arm and a leg. However, it takes some practice to run a drum sander without gouging the wood. If you've never run one before, we recommend hiring a deck refinishing pro to do the sanding for you.

PROTECT EXTERIOR STONEWORK

//

A FEW SIMPLE STEPS CAN EXTEND THE LIFE OF STONE AND MORTAR

MASKED HOUSE NUMBER

MASKED SIDING

PUMP SPRAYER

PROTECTED PLANTS

1 PROTECT TRIM AND PLANTS
Mask off surfaces, such as trim boards, siding, house numbers and mailboxes. Cover plants and grass with tarps to prevent kill-off from the spray.

Exterior stone, including manufactured stone, can be damaged when it absorbs water and freezes. Applying a waterproofing sealer to the stone and mortar extends their life and reduces stone chipping and mortar cracks.

A silane/siloxane product is best for this— it works without changing the color of your stone or mortar and allows the mortar to breathe. Buy a pump sprayer and silane/ siloxane waterproofing product (about $30 to $65 per gallon at home centers and paint stores). To determine how much to buy, check the label for the product's coverage and measure the square footage of your stonework.

Mask off the surrounding area (**Photo 1**), then use the pump sprayer to apply a first coat followed by a "curtain" coat (**Photo 2**).

2 APPLY IN TWO STEPS
Spray the stonework with the first coat of waterproofer. Then immediately apply a liberal, wet-on-wet "curtain coat" so that the solution drips down 6 to 8 in. over the entire surface.

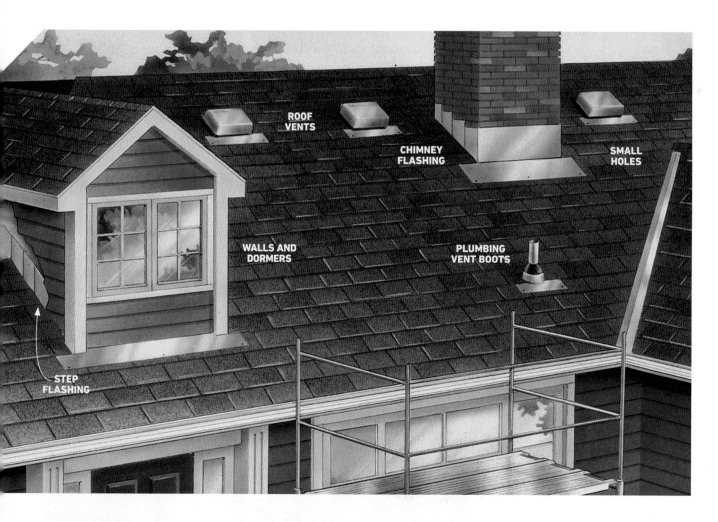

ROOF
VENTS

CHIMNEY
FLASHING

SMALL
HOLES

WALLS AND
DORMERS

PLUMBING
VENT BOOTS

STEP
FLASHING

FIND & FIX ROOF LEAKS

//
TRACK DOWN THE PROBLEM TO PREVENT FURTHER DAMAGE

If you have water stains that extend across ceilings or run down walls, the cause is likely a roof leak. Over time, even small leaks can lead to big problems, such as mold, rotted framing and sheathing, destroyed insulation and damaged ceilings. While tracking down the leak can be hard, the fixes are usually pretty easy. We'll show you simple tricks for finding and repairing the most common types of roof leaks.

FIND THE LEAKS

Start by looking at the roof uphill from the stains. Roof penetrations are the first thing to look for. Items that penetrate the roof—plumbing and roof vents, chimneys, dormers and more—are by far the most common source of leaks. They can be several feet above the leak or to either side of it.

If you have attic access, head up there with a flashlight and look for water stains, black marks or mold. But if access is a problem or you have a vaulted ceiling, you'll have to go up onto the roof. The photos in this story will show you what to look for.

If the problem still isn't obvious, enlist a helper and go up onto the roof with a garden hose. Start low, soaking the area just above where the leak appears in the house. Isolate areas when you run the hose. For example, soak the downhill side of a chimney first, then each side, then the top on both sides. Have your helper stay inside waiting for the drip to appear.

Let the hose run for several minutes in one area before moving it up the roof a little farther. Tell your helper to yell when a drip becomes visible. You'll be in the neighborhood of the leak. This process can take well over an hour, so be patient and don't move the hose too soon. Be sure to buy your helper dinner!

PROBLEM: Water that sneaks behind walls and dormers dribbles down into your house just like a roof leak.

1 LEAKY WALLS & DORMERS

Water doesn't always come in at the shingled surface. Often, wind-driven rain comes in from above the roof, especially around windows, between corner boards and siding, and through cracks and knotholes in siding. Dormer walls provide lots of spots where water can dribble down and enter the roof. Caulk can be old, cracked or even missing between the corner boards and between window edges and siding. Water penetrates these cracks and works its way behind the flashing and into the house.

Even caulk that looks intact may not be sealing against the adjoining surfaces. Dig around with a putty knife to see if the area is sealed. Dig out any suspect caulk and replace it with a high-quality caulk. Also check the siding above the step flashing. Replace any cracked, rotted or missing siding, making sure the new piece overlaps the step flashing by at least 2 in. If you still have a leak, pull the corner boards free and check the overlapping flashing at the corner. Often, there's old, hardened caulk where the two pieces overlap at the inside corner.

SOLUTION: Recaulk the corner flashing. Lift the overlapping section, clean it thoroughly and add a generous bead of fresh caulk underneath. Make sure the gap at the corner is filled with caulk.

PROBLEM: Plastic roof vents can crack and leak. Duct tape is not the solution this time!

2 ROOF VENTS

Check for cracked housings on plastic roof vents and broken seams on metal ones. You might want to throw caulk at the problem, but there's really no fix other than replacing the damaged vents. Also look for pulled or missing nails at the base's bottom edge. Replace them with rubber-washered screws.

In most cases, you can remove nails under the shingles on both sides of the vent to pull it free. There will be nails across the top of the vent too. Usually you can also work those loose without removing shingles. Screw the bottom into place with rubber-washered screws. Squeeze out a bead of caulk beneath the shingles on both sides of the vent to hold the shingles down and to add a water barrier.

SOLUTION: Replace the old vent. If you're careful, you won't have to remove any shingles to slip out the old one and slide the new one into place.

PROBLEM: When the source of a leak is gasket-type vent flashing, the culprit is usually a cracked gasket or missing or loose nails.

3 PLUMBING VENT BOOTS

Plumbing vent boots can be all plastic, plastic and metal, or even two-piece metal units. Check plastic bases for cracks and metal bases for broken seams. Then examine the rubber boot surrounding the pipe. That can be rotted away or torn, allowing water to work its way into the house along the pipe. With any of these problems, you should buy a new vent boot to replace the old one.

However, if the nails at the base are missing or pulled free and the boot is in good shape, replace them with the rubber-washered screws used for metal roofing systems. You'll find them at any home center with the rest of the screws. You'll have to work neighboring shingles free on both sides. If you don't have extra shingles, be careful when you remove shingles so they can be reused. Use a flat bar to separate the sealant between the layers. Then you'll be able to drive the flat bar under the nail heads to pop out the nails.

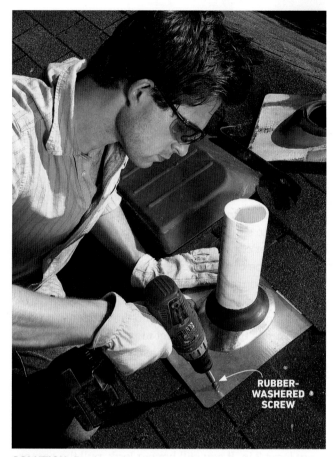

RUBBER-WASHERED SCREW

SOLUTION: Replace the old boot. Screw the base to the roof with rubber-washered screws. Don't use nails. They'll just work loose over time.

PROBLEM: Leftover mounting holes can let in vast amounts of water.

4 SMALL HOLES

Tiny holes in shingles are sneaky because they can cause rot and other damage for years before you notice the obvious signs of a leak. You might find holes left over from satellite dish or antenna mounting brackets or just about anything. And exposed, misplaced roofing nails should be pulled and the holes patched. Small holes are simple to fix, but the fix isn't to inject caulk in the hole. You'll fix this one with flashing as shown at right.

SOLUTION: Seal nail holes forever. Slip flashing under the shingle and add a bead of caulk under and over the flashing to hold it in place.

5 STEP FLASHING

Step flashing is used along walls that intersect the roof. Each short section of flashing channels water over the shingle downhill from it.

But if the flashing rusts through, or a piece comes loose, water will run right behind it, and into the house it goes. Rusted flashing needs to be replaced. That means removing shingles, prying siding loose, and then removing and replacing the step flashing. It's that simple. But occasionally a roofer forgets to nail one into place and it eventually slips down to expose the wall.

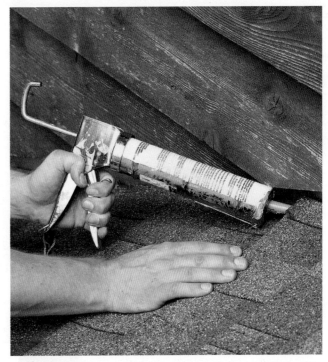

SOLUTION: Push a loose piece of step flashing right back into place and then secure it with caulk above and below.

BRICK CHIMNEYS

All kinds of bad things can happen around brick chimneys. In fact, there are far too many to cover in this story. Flashing around chimneys can rust through if it's galvanized steel, especially at the 90-degree bend at the bottom. A quick but fairly long-term fix is to simply slip new flashing under the old rusted stuff. That way any water that seeps through will be diverted.

The best fix, though, is to cut a saw kerf into the mortar and install new flashing. If you want to see what's involved, go to *familyhandyman.com* and search for "chimney flashing."

WET CEILINGS AREN'T ALWAYS FROM ROOF LEAKS!

Water stains on the ceiling don't always indicate a leak up on the roof. Many times the stains come from, or are caused by, problems up in the attic. Here are three of the main culprits:

■ **ATTIC-MOUNTED A/C COMPRESSORS** Clogged condensate tubes will cause collection trays to overflow. And improperly sealed or insulated ducts can cause condensation to form and drip into the house. A quick look around the attic will help you track down this problem.

■ **BATH AND KITCHEN VENTS** These vents are often vented directly into the attic (or become detached from roof vents). They can pour gallons of water vapor into the attic, where it'll freeze or condense and drip back into the house. Again, a visit to the attic will locate it. Even an uninsulated exhaust vent that is vented through the roof can create condensation on the duct. That moisture then leaks back into the house, usually around vent grilles. Those ducts should be replaced with insulated ones.

■ **ICE DAMS** Ice buildup on eaves, coupled with water coming in along outside walls, is a sure sign of ice dams. They're usually caused by some combination of improper attic venting, attic bypasses and inadequate attic insulation. To learn more, search for "attic bypasses" and "ice dams" at *familyhandyman.com*.

A PAINTING, DRYWALL OR FLOORING PRO

A strip of 3" masking paper stuck to the underside of the tape shields the trim from paint spatters and drips.

PAINT EDGES PERFECTLY

GET CLEAN, STRAIGHT LINES WITH THESE MASKING TAPE TIPS

Masking off baseboards and other trim is a fantastic way to get a professional-looking paint job. You'll get crisp, clean paint lines where the walls meet the trim. And the job will go quicker because you'll avoid the time-consuming "cutting in" with the paintbrush and cleaning up of paint spatters from your woodwork. Of course, the masking process itself requires a little patience and skill. Wavy tape will result in wavy paint lines. Poor adhesion will allow "paint creep." And ragged tape in corners will leave blotches. Here are some techniques that will solve these problems and make your masking job go quickly and smoothly.

TIGHT TO WALL

1 PULL THE TAPE DIRECTLY FROM THE ROLL
Position the end of the tape precisely and stick it down. Hold it in place while you pull about 8 to 10 in. of tape from the roll.

PULL FROM THE ROLL TO GET THE TAPE PERFECTLY STRAIGHT

One of the trickiest parts of masking is getting the tape on straight and tight against the wall. There are many techniques, but here's one we know works great: Strip 8 to 10 in. of tape from the roll and use the roll itself, held tightly against the wall, to pull the tape straight **(Photos 1 and 2)**. It's a little awkward at first, and it may seem slow, but the results are nearly perfect every time. Use this technique wherever you're masking at a right angle to another surface.

SEAL THE EDGE TO PREVENT BLEEDING PAINT

Seal the tape to the surface by pressing it down firmly with the edge of a flexible putty knife **(Photo 3)**. This is the most important step in good masking, and it takes only a few moments. If you skip it, you risk a loose seal that will allow paint to seep underneath. Then you'll have to scrape off the seeped paint later and touch up the trim.

Keep in mind that you don't have to press down the entire width of the tape. Sealing about 1/32 in. along the edge is all that's needed. Hold the putty knife at an angle as shown. This puts pressure along the critical wall edge of the tape.

PRESS DOWN

2 PLACE THE ROLL TIGHTLY AGAINST THE WALL
Lay the tape roll flat against the wall and rotate the roll to tighten and straighten it. Slide your finger across the tape to press it down.

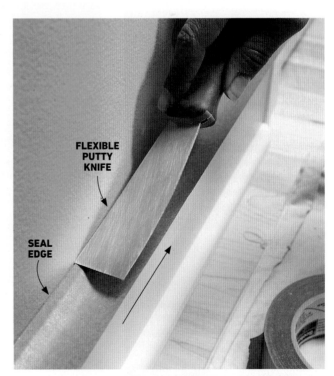

FLEXIBLE PUTTY KNIFE

SEAL EDGE

3 SEAL THE TAPE WITH A FLEXIBLE PUTTY KNIFE
Run the blade of a flexible putty knife along the edge of the tape. Apply firm pressure but avoid wrinkling or tearing the tape.

USE EXTRA TAPE TO MAKE PERFECT INSIDE CORNERS

Getting two long pieces of tape to meet exactly in the corner is difficult, so don't even try. Instead, start the pieces of tape about ¾ in. from the corner and run them using the method shown on p. 155. Then go back and finish the corner with small lengths of tape using the technique shown in **Photos 1 and 2**.

1 USE A SMALL PIECE OF TAPE FOR THE CORNER
Press a short section of tape into the corner with the blade of a flexible 2-in. putty knife.

PULL AT 45° ANGLE

TIPS FOR REMOVING MASKING TAPE

A couple of things can go wrong when you remove masking tape. If you wait too long, the adhesive will harden and remain stuck to the woodwork. Or if the paint sets but isn't completely dry, some of the wall paint may peel off along with the tape. Here are solutions to these problems:

■ If you're a procrastinator, check the label and choose tape that's designed to be left on for several days.

■ To avoid peeling paint, pull the tape off immediately or wait at least overnight for the paint to dry completely. Remove tape at a 45-degree angle to the painted surface. If the paint still peels with the tape, use a utility knife to cut the seal between the wall and the tape before you remove the tape.

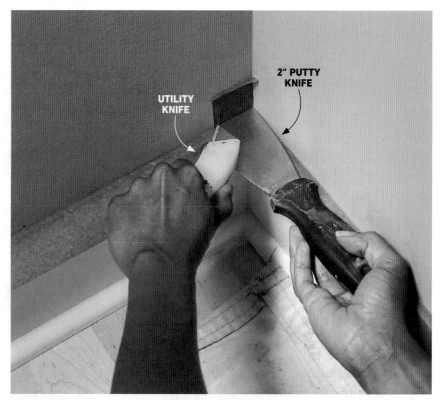

UTILITY KNIFE

2" PUTTY KNIFE

2 TRIM THE TAPE WITH A UTILITY KNIFE
Cut the tape using the putty knife as a guide. Peel off the extra tape to create a perfect corner.

PRIME BEFORE YOU PAINT

HARNESS THE POWER OF PRIMER FOR BETTER RESULTS

One of the most powerful tools in any pro painter's arsenal is what goes underneath the paint—primer. Primer is an excellent problem-solver that's less like paint and more like glue. It sticks to whatever you're prepping and turns it into a smooth, uniform surface that's ready for paint.

But if you've ever walked down the primer aisle at a home center, you know the primer choices are mind-boggling. To cut through the clutter, we asked three professional painters, each with 20-plus years of experience, to recommend the best primers to use for common painting challenges. Their expertise will

help you choose the best primer for your job, so the paint will look better and last longer.

PRO TIP
Use primer and paint from the same manufacturer. Many primers are formulated to work best with certain paints.

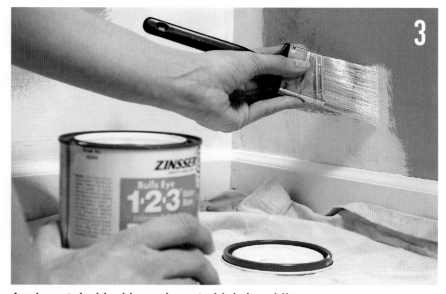

Apply a stain-blocking primer to high-humidity areas to prevent mildew and peeling on interior walls and blistering on exterior walls.

1 NEW DRYWALL

The mud used on drywall seams absorbs paint differently than the rest of the drywall. This difference in porosity can cause blotchy, dull areas under the paint (a problem called flashing) and an inconsistent sheen. Prevent this problem by using a drywall primer-sealer.

If you're an ace drywall finisher and your walls are perfectly smooth, you can use a standard drywall primer-sealer. But if you're like most of us, your finished drywall probably has some tiny pockmarks, fine ridges and scuffed paper from sanding. The solution is a "high-build" drywall primer-sealer. This heavier-bodied primer-sealer is a little more expensive than standard primer-sealer, but it does a better job of leveling and filling in rough or uneven drywall construction. (But not even a high-build drywall primer can hide a bad tape job.)

Alternatively, if your drywall is relatively smooth and the topcoat is going to be a flat paint, you can skip the primer and use two coats of high-quality self-priming water-based flat paint. This thick, high-build paint provides a dense, hard, durable paint film that resists moisture and mildew, without a separate prime coat. Self-priming paints seal the surface and fill imperfections (which are less visible in flat paint anyway).

2 INTERIOR STAINS AND ODORS

Some stains will bleed right through most primers and paints no matter how many coats you apply. The same goes for severe odors such as smoke from fires and cigarettes.

The solution is stain-blocking primer, available in oil-based (alkyd) and water-based (acrylic-latex) versions. Oil-based versions give off a nasty smell and require paint thinner for cleanup, but they're more reliable for blocking water-based odors and stains such as rust, nicotine, smoke, wood tannins and, of course, water (see "Shellac: The Original Primer" on p. 159 for dealing with severe stains and odors).

Water-based stain-blocking primers offer easy cleanup and less odor, and they come in low- and no-VOC (volatile organic compounds) formulations. These work best to block solvent-based stains such as crayon, grease, ink and scuff marks. Both versions are white, so tint them gray or close to your topcoat color if they'll be covered by dark-colored paint.

3 MOISTURE-PRONE AREAS

The high moisture in areas such as kitchens, bathrooms and laundry rooms can cause paints to mildew, flake or peel. Interior moisture moving outward through a wall can cause peeling, bubbling or blistering on exterior walls too. Use a vapor barrier primer to seal the surface and minimize the passage of moisture through walls to the outside. If mildew is a big concern, use a stain-blocking primer to prevent any stains from bleeding through the topcoat; then use a topcoat that specifically resists mildew (check the label). Kill mildew with a 1 part bleach and 3 parts water mix before priming.

For quicker priming, use a roller on the door and a 2-in. brush on interior trim such as casings, base and doorjambs. For a smooth paint job, sand lightly after the primer dries.

5 MDF (MEDIUM-DENSITY FIBERBOARD)

Use an oil-based primer unless the MDF is already preprimed. Don't use a water-based primer, which can soak into the surface and cause it to swell. Before priming, sand the surface smooth and make sure it's dust-free. Prime all surfaces, including the board edges.

6 REPAIRED WALLS

Like new drywall mud, wall patches absorb paint differently than the rest of the wall. To prevent flashing, cover everything from dabs of filler to broad patches of joint compound with a good-quality drywall primer-sealer.

However, if you have plaster rather than drywall, any repairs will need a coat of oil-based stain-blocking primer. Without it, lime stains will form around the repairs and bleed through the topcoat. This applies to tiny caulking and spackling touch-ups as well as major repairs with joint compound.

7 NEW INTERIOR BARE WOOD

It's important to prime bare wood to seal the thirsty surface, hide imperfections and bind the wood fibers to make the surface more uniform. Slower-drying oil-based primers, such as an enamel undercoat primer, provide better adhesion and are easier to sand than water-based primers. If you use a water-based primer, it's likely to raise the wood grain, so the wood will require more sanding before you apply the topcoat.

4 PREVIOUSLY PAINTED INTERIOR WOODWORK

If the old paint is in good shape, there's no need to prime. But if the paint is chalking or is chipped, use an oil-based enamel undercoat primer after properly prepping the surface. An enamel undercoat primer bonds well to previously painted surfaces and improves the topcoat by flowing out to a dense, smooth uniform foundation without laps or brush marks. Fast-drying primers, such as shellac, and many water-based products dry too quickly and become brittle. This can cause lap marks and makes it harder to sand and get a smooth base for the topcoat. Oil-based primers sand well but dry more slowly (some can take 48 hours or longer). If you want to use a water-based product, look for a high-build acrylic-latex enamel undercoat that's specifically designed to be sanded.

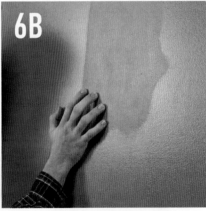

A drywall primer-sealer (Photo 6A) seals the porous surface so paint won't sink in and look dull or blotchy (Photo 6B).

SHELLAC: THE ORIGINAL PRIMER

Shellac has been used for centuries and is still the best primer for a few situations. It's an excellent choice if you need a fast-drying spot primer to prevent wood knots, rusty nail heads, and the most severe water-based stains and odors—such as smoke, soot, urine and nicotine—from bleeding through the topcoat. Shellac (a common brand is BIN) can soften in direct sunlight and by itself isn't durable enough for exterior use. If you use it for exterior spot priming, prime over it with a water-based exterior primer before applying the topcoat. Shellac requires denatured alcohol for thinning and cleanup. For the best results, make sure the surface is completely clean and dust-free before applying.

8 DRASTIC PAINT COLOR CHANGE

When you change from a light color to dark, or vice versa, it can take many coats of paint to hide the existing paint color. Tinting your primer gray or a color similar to your finish paint reduces the number of topcoats you need to apply to get good results. Not all primers can be tinted darker colors, so make sure to choose one that can be. Even without a drastic color change, tinting your primer gray will help enhance the color of most dark-colored interior paints and improve a primer's "hide" (how well it covers the imperfections and color of your wall surface).

9 OLD EXTERIOR PAINT

If exterior paint is in great shape, there's no need to prime. But that's hardly ever the case. At the very least, you'll have to spot-prime any bare wood where the paint has peeled away. Use a high-quality acrylic/latex exterior primer. And if the paint is "chalking," prime the entire surface. To detect chalking, just wipe the paint with a rag. If the rag picks up colored dust, you've got chalking. Before you prime, thoroughly scrub and power-wash the siding. Any peeling areas with dirt and mildew must be cleaned, scraped or sanded. Preparation is key to a long-lasting paint job. If it's not done correctly, the paint will peel again within a year or two.

10 EXTERIOR WOOD

Exterior wood paint takes a beating. One of the best ways to extend the life of your paint job is to splurge on a top-quality acrylic/latex exterior primer. Look for "100% acrylic" on the label, and make sure the wood surface is clean, dry and dull (no sheen). On properly prepared wood, a high-quality primer can double the life of exterior paint.

However, some exterior woods, such as cedar, redwood and less common ones, contain lots of pigments, called tannins, that will bleed through standard primer and paint. To stop the bleeding, use an oil-based stain-blocking exterior primer for larger areas and top with an acrylic/latex finish coat.

DO I ALWAYS NEED TO PRIME BEFORE PAINTING?

You don't have to prime previously painted surfaces if the paint is in good shape—no chipping or peeling. Interior walls usually don't need priming except in the cases of stains, repairs or a paint color that's drastically different. Interior painted woodwork usually needs spot priming at a minimum. Exterior paint takes such a beating that it almost always needs priming.

Pressure-washing removes loose paint and built-up grime and improves paint adhesion. Keep the nozzle at least 16 in. away from the wood.

BUY BETTER TRIM PAINT

SEE THE RESULTS OF A QUEST TO FIND THE BEST

When *Family Handyman* editor Mike Berner replaced all the doors and windows in his house a few years ago, he also installed new trim. Unfortunately, he didn't get around to painting it and recently decided it was time to finish the job. The first step was to determine the paint that would perform best regardless of brand, sheen or color. To research the options, he picked up 12 trim paints to try. After running tests and conferring with pro painters and industry experts, he singled out a few top performers.

SIX FACTORS THAT MATTER

1 COST

One thing the experts emphasized was that quality paint starts with expensive raw materials, which means cost is a pretty good predictor of the results. Using inexpensive paint could save a few bucks on the front end but cost you down the road. The paints Mike tested ranged in price from $45 to $110 per gallon.

2 ODOR

Mike skipped any oil-based paints because of their smell, but some of the new acrylic-alkyd formulas (see p. 164) still use solvent. These are a lot less stinky than pure oil-based paints, but some may bother sensitive noses.

3 CLEANUP

With two kids under age 2 running and crawling around, Mike didn't want to mess with any solvent cleanup, and with so many great water-cleanup options, you shouldn't either.

4 TOUGHNESS

It's no fun sanding and repainting the trim when it gets dinged up by kids. Mike tested the toughness of the finish by dragging a piece of 80-grit sandpaper weighted with 1-lb. boxes of screws across it. The toughest paints took the offense with only light scuffing.

5 WORKABILITY

A good trim paint can be applied in tight areas such as corners and curved profiles, then smoothed before it starts to dry. Painting an intricate profile at a mitered corner showed which paints were more workable.

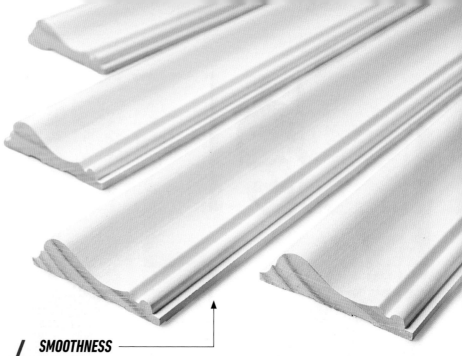

6 SMOOTHNESS

Smoothness is king when it comes to a trim paint job. If you've worked hard to make your trim look great, you don't want to ruin it with brush marks, drips or roller ridges. A good trim paint should flatten and become smooth as it cures. Not all the paints tested did this well.

FIVE PAINTS THAT STOOD OUT

1 SHERWIN-WILLIAMS EMERALD URETHANE TRIM ENAMEL (ABOUT $110)

This represents a new category of paint; it reminded Mike of a pigmented, water-based polyurethane—even its smell. This stuff produced the toughest coating of all the paints tested. Even when Mike dragged a piece of 80-grit sandpaper—weighted with five 1-lb. boxes of screws—over the painted surface, the paper just glided right along.

Emerald enamel brushed on well, had a long enough open time to work into the corners and leveled out nicely. It had less sheen than other paints—the semigloss tested was more like a satin. If you want a super-hard finish and have over $100 to spend on a gallon, this is right up your alley. It would be Mike's choice if cost didn't matter.

2 BEHR PREMIUM ALKYD ENAMEL (ABOUT $45)

This acrylic-alkyd hybrid may not be as tough as other hybrid trim paints, but it's still pretty tough, and because it's a great value, it made the list of standouts. It's thicker than other hybrids and brushes on really well. It also has great leveling characteristics and could get into the tough-to-reach areas in the mitered corners of the trim-painting test.

3 PPG BREAK-THROUGH! (ABOUT $50)

This is one of the non-hybrid paints Mike tested. It's a low-VOC (volatile organic compound) formula with a strong ammonia odor, but it leveled out better than any other paint. According to the manufacturer, it is used to coat warehouse floors. If it can stand up to forklifts, it ought to be able to take on Matchbox cars. It dries in 15 to 20 minutes, so lay and smooth it quickly. It won't fill in dings or scratches, even small ones, so sand well before painting.

4 BENJAMIN MOORE ADVANCE (ABOUT $70)

With a longer drying time, this acrylic-alkyd hybrid was the most workable of all the paints Berner tested, and it was also the runner-up in the toughness test. The downside is that you have to wait at least 16 hours between coats, compared with four to six hours for the other options. It also takes about 30 days to cure, so be careful reassembling parts or using the things you paint.

5 SHERWIN-WILLIAMS SNAPDRY (ABOUT $95)

This acrylic latex ultra fast-drying paint has great resistance to "blocking"—the tendency of two painted surfaces to stick together. The paint's fast drying time was worrisome, but Mike was able to apply it and spread it before it became tacky. It leveled out fairly well and was one of the tougher paints tested. It's tricky to work with, but the fast drying time enables you to close a freshly painted door.

MIKE'S CHOICE

Ultimately, the winning primer was Advance by Benjamin Moore. Mike had worked hard to make his trim look nice, and he wanted the paint to look as if it'd been sprayed on. The base trim also had to stand up to vacuum cleaners and toys. Advance offered a good balance of price and performance, and it hung with the top performers in the tests. It did require sacrifice in recoat and cure times—someone really should add an extra day to the weekend!

PRO TIP
Always ask specialty paint stores about possible discounts. They're often running some sort of unadvertised sale or may have the freedom to give discounts.

THE TWO MOST COMMON OPTIONS FOR TRIM PAINT

■ **ACRYLIC LATEX** Most of the cans you see as you walk through the paint aisle will be labeled "acrylic." These vary drastically in both price and performance. Some gallons cost as little as $15, but steer clear of them. Paints made of 100% acrylic are more expensive but will cure harder and are less porous, making them durable and easy to clean. Acrylic latex paint can be a great choice for interior trim, but it won't match the toughness of an oil-based paint.

■ **ACRYLIC-ALKYD HYBRID** Acrylic-alkyd hybrid paints have been available to contractors for a while but are still fairly unknown to most homeowners. These paints have all the good qualities of an oil-based paint (leveling, hardness, flow and open time) while still providing easy soap-and-water cleanup and resistance to yellowing over time. Most brands have a version of these paints, and they're definitely worth checking out.

PICK THE BEST PAINT COLORS

CHOOSE WISELY NOW FOR HAPPINESS LATER

Selecting paint colors can be a very subjective (and difficult!) process. But aside from what's fashionable at the moment, some practical considerations can make the decision easier. Here are our top suggestions to help you pick paint colors and sheens that you'll be happy with for years to come.

1 USE ACTUAL PAINT SAMPLES, NOT CHIPS

It's difficult to tell what a color is going to look like on your wall from a small paint chip, so many manufacturers offer sample containers of their colors. Depending on the manufacturer, you can buy sample containers in quarts, pints or even smaller sizes, and they are usually inexpensive. They're a wise investment that will prevent you from wasting money on a color that isn't right. And because colors can change dramatically under different lighting conditions, instead of rolling the sample onto the wall, roll it onto white tagboard. You'll be able to move the sample around **(Photo 1B)** and view it under all the different lighting conditions in your home.

1A

1B

SHUTTER AND DOOR COLOR COMPLEMENT EXISTING ROOF AND BRICKWORK

2

2 START WITH THE PERMANENT COLORS

Base your color choice on the permanent furnishings in the room or the features on the exterior of your home. Inside, the flooring, rugs, artwork, blinds and upholstery will suggest a color direction. Outside, factory-finished materials such as the roof, gutters, fascia, soffits and brickwork are existing elements whose colors rarely change but should play a role in determining paint colors. The landscaping is another important factor. Select colors that fit in with the surrounding palette. If you have brilliant-colored spring-blooming trees or a sea of green foundation plantings, choose colors that will complement them.

3 LOOK FOR PAINT FAMILY COLOR COLLECTIONS

Paint companies have gone to a lot of trouble (and spent a lot of money) grouping colors into "families" and "collections" and "concepts" and "schemes." Basically, these are combinations of complementary colors that may not occur to you until you see how well they work together. There are specific room-by-room collections, white-only collections, color combinations for kids' rooms, exterior paint collections designed for specific areas of the country and so many more.

Take advantage of all the research already done for you by color experts. Find brochures at paint stores and go online to paint manufacturer websites, *houzz.com* or Pinterest, where you'll find hundreds of examples of interior and exterior paint color combinations.

4 CONSIDER THE NEIGHBORS

A clashing color choice is a lose-lose situation. You might think a purple house with red trim would be really groovy, but your neighbors might not. You'll not only drag down your resale value but affect theirs as well. Inside you may aim to please only yourself and your family. But remember this: If you plan on selling, bizarre colors or schemes will likely turn off potential buyers.

3

5 LIGHTEN THE CEILING COLOR

Because ceilings are seen in shadow, the same paint color often appears darker there than on the walls. If you want the ceiling to match the wall color, buy ceiling paint one or two shades lighter than the wall color. Or instead of buying another gallon of a lighter shade, save money by diluting the wall color you have with 50% white paint.

6 CHOOSE THE RIGHT SHEEN

When you choose a color, you have to choose its sheen too. Most paint companies offer flat, eggshell, satin, semigloss and gloss as options. Glossier finishes offer greater durability and are easier to clean, but they will emphasize any wall imperfections.

Flat paint will do a much better job of hiding any imperfections, but it's easier to damage than high-gloss. Flat finishes are generally best for ceilings and low-traffic areas such as dining rooms, where all you'll need to do is wipe the walls with a damp sponge. If they do get scuffed, they're easy to touch up.

Glossier finishes—including satin and semigloss—can withstand moisture and grease, so they're good for trim, cabinets and high-traffic rooms such as kitchens and bathrooms. If you love the way flat wall paint looks but wish it were more durable, try mixing it 50/50 with eggshell paint. The paint will still offer a nonreflective look, but the eggshell will add some durability to the finish.

7 SKIM-COAT BAD WALLS—ESPECIALLY FOR DARKER COLORS

Lighter colors are more forgiving in terms of showing wall imperfections; darker colors show more detail. If you're set on using a darker color (or a glossy sheen) and your walls are in rough shape, you should really skim-coat your walls with a thin layer of drywall compound before painting (for more information, see "Skim-Coat Large Areas" on p. 177). However, even skim-coating the walls won't make dark colors look good in every room.

Very dark colors don't handle the moisture in a bathroom particularly well; they can look blotchy and chalky. As such, you might want to stick with lighter colors when choosing a paint for the bathroom. If you're planning to use a dark color, reduce the number of coats necessary by using a high-hide gray-tinted primer. For more information about primers, see "Prime Before You Paint" on p.157.

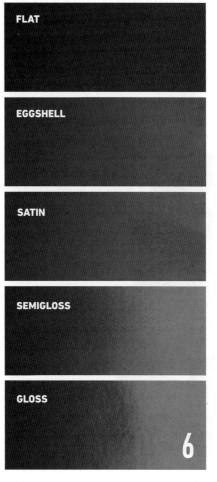

FLAT

EGGSHELL

SATIN

SEMIGLOSS

GLOSS

8

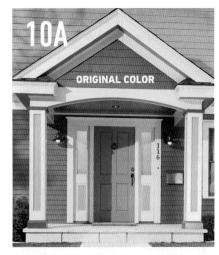

10A ORIGINAL COLOR

DON'T BUY CHEAP PAINT

For the best results, spend at least $40 to $60 per gallon of paint. Better-quality paint will be more concentrated with finer pigments and higher-grade resins, so the final product will have a more even color and durable finish. It's tempting to try to save money up front, but better coverage means less paint to buy—you could easily wind up spending just as much for two coats of a less expensive formula. Reputable brands have a range of paint qualities within their product lines. Do homework and buy the best you can afford.

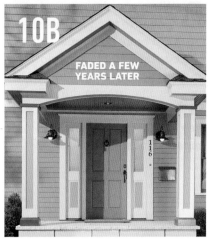

10B FADED A FEW YEARS LATER

8 DON'T JUST PAINT THE WALLS

Just as paint accentuates features, you can use it to hide unappealing elements too. Paint conduit, radiators, gutters and other utilitarian components the same color as the walls to make them blend in. You can also do that with light fixtures, switches, outlets and just about anything else. There are now spray paints for all different types of material.

9 VIRTUALLY PAINT YOUR HOUSE

Many manufacturers offer opportunities to "paint" your home virtually—just upload a photo of your home or a room to try out different colors and painting schemes. You can also search for homes similar to your own and try "painting" with various combinations and products. There are also apps that allow you to take a photo of a color you like and have it matched with a manufacturer's color or suggested palette. Just be aware that your computer monitor, cellphone or tablet screen will affect the color of the paint you see, so don't skip Tip 1!

10 CHOOSE LIGHTER COLORS FOR GREATER LONGEVITY

Dark colors can give your house an air of dignity or drama, but the more intense or dark a color is, the more likely it is to fade and show dirt. After a few years, vivid blues and deep reds become subdued, and you may see streaks and splotches of dirt more readily. Dark colors can also absorb heat and sustain more moisture problems than lighter shades. And because dark paint fades, it can be difficult to match when you do small touch-ups.

Generally, colors such as red, blue, green and yellow tend to fade more quickly than earth tones such as beiges, tans and browns, which are considered more stable.

9

UP YOUR DRYWALL GAME

GET FLAWLESS RESULTS—FASTER!

Putting up drywall may be intimidating, but it doesn't have to be. With a better understanding of the tools and materials used to perform the task, you can confidently transform heavy sheets and mud into lovely walls. We reviewed some fundamentals with our resident drywall expert and discovered some new tips and methods along the way.

UNDERSTANDING JOINT COMPOUND

DRYING TYPE

Most folks are familiar with drying compounds—they come in a bucket or a box, and they dry as the water content evaporates.

- **ALL-PURPOSE** All-purpose compound **(1)** is the strongest type of drying compound, with the highest glue content. Use as a first coat to embed paper tape.
- **DUST CONTROL** A relative newcomer, dust control compound **(2)** is aimed at DIYers. Perfect for repairs, it greatly reduces the mess involved with sanding any drywall compound.
- **PLUS 3 LIGHTWEIGHT** Use this lightweight all-purpose joint compound **(3)** for second coats and as a topping compound. It has good open time and sands easily.

SETTING TYPE

Think of setting-type compounds like cement—just add water and they set. Unlike the drying type, these set through a chemical reaction. The setting times vary and are called out in the names: DuraBond 90 or Easy Sand 45, for example.

- **REGULAR SETTING COMPOUND** This compound **(4)** dries fast and hard. It's difficult to sand, too, so this is where your skill with a blade can make a big difference. Get it on right and leave it alone. It's not the best choice for beginners, but skilled drywall pros appreciate the rapid drying time so they can quickly apply a second coat.
- **LIGHTWEIGHT** Trading a little toughness for sandability, lightweight setting compound **(5)** is perfect for DIYers.

USE THE RIGHT FASTENERS

Always use drywall screws, not nails. Drywall screws typically come in two sizes—No. 6 and No. 8. Choose the smaller No. 6 screws; they won't blow out the edge of the drywall. Length is determined by sheet thickness plus ¾ in. Use coarse-thread screws for wood stud walls and fine-thread for metal studs.

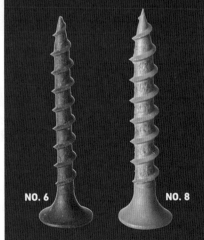

NO. 6   NO. 8

½"

FIRE
RESISTANT

¼"

THE TOP TAPE TYPES

PAPER TAPE
Paper drywall tape is the most common type, yet it's not the easiest to use and you need practice to become proficient. But paper tape does offer advantages: It's inexpensive; it's actually stronger than fiberglass mesh; and most paper tape comes creased so you can easily bend it into a corner. Some paper tapes have micro perforations to help prevent blistering.

FIBERGLASS MESH
Fiberglass mesh might be the easiest drywall tape to use. Simply stick it to the wall and trowel on your mud. The ease of use, however, comes with a caveat: The first coat of mud must be a setting type—its higher glue content will create a strong base. Drying-type compound is prone to cracking when used as a first coat over mesh tape.

CORNER TAPE
Designed for inside corners and wall-to-ceiling joints, corner tape has plastic or metal strips on the back. This doesn't make the joint stronger, but it provides a stiff guide for your knife to make a straight corner joint.

TYPES OF DRYWALL SHEETS

■ **½-IN. SHEETS** Half-inch drywall is the standard thickness for most applications. When possible, choose lightweight or "ultralight" drywall. It's about 25% lighter than standard ½-in. sheets, easier to handle and stiffer too. It can even span ceiling joists 24 in. on center.

■ **FIRE-RESISTANT SHEETS** Standard gypsum board is naturally fire resistant, but Type X is actually fire rated. The core includes additives designed to slow the spread of fire. It's often required on garage ceilings and walls that adjoin living areas.

■ **¼-IN. SHEETS** You won't often need ¼-in. drywall, but it's great for arches and curved walls. Our expert suggested skipping the screws with this thin material. Use construction adhesive instead. Tack it with a few nails until the glue sets and apply one more layer to reach ½-in. thickness.

CONCAVE CUT

MAKE SPACE FOR THE TAPE AND MUD

1

2

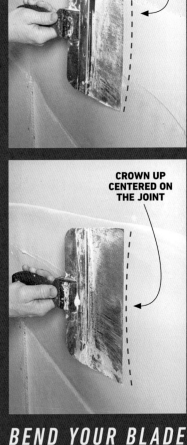

CROWN DOWN TO FEATHER INTO THE JOINT

CROWN UP CENTERED ON THE JOINT

1 CREATE BUTT JOINTS EASILY

Drywall sheets have depressed edges that account for the thicknesses of tape and mud. When you cut a sheet, you lose that edge. Our expert cuts a concave shape on one side of a piece of pine with a table saw blade set to 2 degrees. This helps pull the edges of drywall in, forming a valley for tape and mud. Do this to create seamless joints between studs.

2 MIX THE COMPOUND

You've got a brand new bucket of joint compound and you are ready to start mudding, right? Wrong. Before you start, remove enough compound to make room for 2 to 3 cups of water. Mix the water and compound thoroughly using a paddle mixer and a ½-in. drill until you have the consistency of yogurt. Now you are ready to go!

BEND YOUR BLADE

You don't want your blade to be perfectly flat. Bend your blade so it has a slight curve, and mark the concave side so you always know which side is which. Our expert uses the convex side to feather out the edge of the joint and the concave side to float over the joint.

MUD UP TO THE TAB

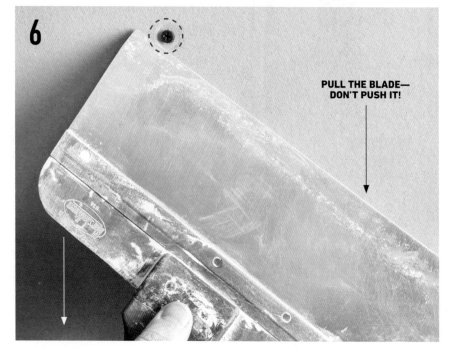

PULL THE BLADE— DON'T PUSH IT!

3 STAPLE YOUR CORNER BEAD

Attach corner bead in a better way that's easy, strong and won't mess up the profile—with staples. A pneumatic stapler is faster than screws, easier than nails and much less likely to push the corner bead out of shape—something that's easy to do with other methods.

4 USE TEARAWAY BEAD FOR EXPOSED EDGES

Whenever drywall meets another surface such as stone, brick or paneling, you need a way to neatly finish the edge.

Tearaway bead gets you pro results with minimal effort. It attaches just like corner bead, but the compound is applied just up to the back edge. Once the compound dries, the tearaway strip easily pulls off, leaving a nice, finished edge.

5 TAPE YOUR METAL CORNER BEAD

Strengthen corners by taping your corner bead. It will take a little extra time,

but you will thank yourself later. A taped corner joint will last a lifetime.

6 CHECK FOR CLICKERS

Before spreading an ounce of mud, check your wall for "clickers." These are the screws you didn't sink quite deep enough. It is best to find all of these now, before you have a hawk full of mud in one hand and a blade in the other.

AN EXPERT'S TOOLBOX

Here are some essential tools for doing drywall.

MUD MIXER
Use this with a power drill to mix compound. It's about $15 at home centers.

6- AND 10-IN. BLADES
These sizes will cover most every need.

MUD HAWK
Load this with mud as you work. A 12-in. hawk will cost about $15.

PNEUMATIC STAPLER
Attaching corner bead with a hand-powered stapler is hard work. A pneumatic stapler makes this job easy.

UTILITY KNIFE
Used to score gypsum board and tape alike, you can't drywall without one!

AUTOMATIC DRYWALL DRILL
With automatic depth setting and a continuous feed of screws, an automatic drywall drill takes your drywall game to a whole new level. Fast and accurate, this drill is often longer than a regular cordless drill so it can reach the ceiling with less effort on your part.

CORDLESS DRILL
A lightweight cordless drill makes screwing drywall sheets much easier than by hand.

PREP DRYWALL FOR PAINTING

FIX THE 8 MOST COMMON FLAWS

Let's face it—no wall is perfect. If you want to rejuvenate a room with fresh paint, first repair and smooth beat-up walls. Some flaws, such as shoddy taping work, have been around since day one. Others, such as cracks and nail pops, start showing up as the house ages. Still others are just insults from day-to-day living: holes from doorknobs, dents from furniture, or holes from shelving and picture hangers. The good news is that you can fix all these problems with only a few inexpensive tools and a bit of finesse. With some patience, a keen eye and our tips—for the most common and easiest flaws to the ones that are less common but more challenging—even beginners can get good results.

To find the problems, inspect the entire wall surface by holding a light close to the wall and "raking" across the surface. The light will highlight flaws not obvious to the unaided eye. Circle each problem area with a pencil (not a pen or marker) to mark it for repair.

1 FILL NAIL POPS AND SMALL HOLES

Small holes from brads or picture hangers are simple to fix. Gently tap on the wall with the handle of your putty knife to drive any standing drywall facing paper below the surface and create a tiny crater, and then fill it with wall filler.

Nail pops are usually caused by fasteners driven through the drywall paper during installation, or by gaps between the drywall and the stud. Vibration and seasonal wood swelling and shrinkage then cause the overlying filler to pop out from the wall. Drive in another 1¼-in. drywall screw near the nail pop so the head penetrates just below but not through the drywall paper. Next, remove the old screw by pushing the screw gun tip through the middle of the nail pop and backing out the screw. If it's a drywall nail, drive it into the stud with a nail set and leave it. Then dimple the old hole **(Photo 1A)**, and fill it and the new screw head with two coats of filler **(Photo 1B)**.

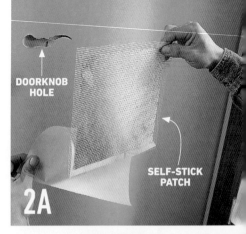

DOORKNOB HOLE

SELF-STICK PATCH

2A

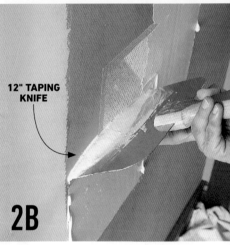

12" TAPING KNIFE

2B

2 PATCH MEDIUM-SIZE HOLES

Large holes require fixes that include cutting out a square chunk of drywall around the hole, installing backing, adding a drywall patch and taping the wound. But holes under 6 in. in diameter can be more easily repaired with a self-adhesive drywall patch. Find 4 x 4-in. or 8 x 8-in. squares at home centers and paint stores. Select a size that'll overlap the sides of the hole by at least 1 in. Pick away any loose chunks of paper or gypsum that protrude above the surface. Then peel off the backing and stick the patch in place **(Photo 2A)**.

Spread a wide, thin layer of mud over the patch and surrounding wall **(Photo 2B)**. The patch is perforated so mud can penetrate and lock it in place. After the first coat dries, spread a second layer of mud to fill in imperfections and low spots, then sand.

DIMPLE

NEW SCREW

1A

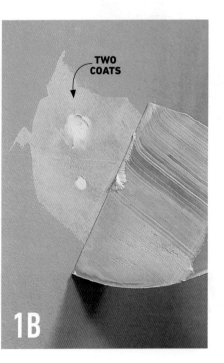

TWO COATS

1B

3 CAULK CRACKS AT INSIDE CORNERS

Hairline cracks at inside corners usually signal slight movement between adjoining walls. Choose any type of latex caulk and cut the tip just short enough to leave a ⅛-in. hole in the end. Squeeze a narrow line of caulk directly over the crack **(Photo 3A)**. Then mold the wet caulk into the corner with a moistened finger **(Photo 3B)**. The caulk will stay flexible and keep the crack from reappearing. Avoid thick layers of caulk that may look too rounded in a square corner.

4 SKIM-COAT LARGE AREAS

If a large area of drywall has significant damage, the only answer is to "skim-coat," which means covering the surface with a thin layer of joint compound to bury the damage. Tackle one area at a time, preferably areas no larger than 4 x 4 ft., until you get the hang of it.

Prepare the wall by picking away any loose edges of drywall facing paper. Prime the leftover raw paper with any type of priming paint to seal the raw paper. (Kilz is a great product to use for this step because it seals well and dries fast.) Dab at the wet paint with a foam brush or rag to saturate the paper and wipe away any runs. Let the paint dry and lightly sand away any standing paper nubs. If you sand through the paint and expose fresh paper, paint it again or the paper will absorb moisture from the taping compound and paint and show through later.

Trowel on the compound with overlapping vertical strokes as we show in Fix 7. Then make a series of overlapping vertical strokes with a knockdown knife to smooth out tool marks and fill in low spots **(Photo 4A)**. Next, make a series of overlapping horizontal strokes, again with the knockdown knife **(Photo 4B)**. Work quickly so the thin coat of mud doesn't begin to dry. If after sanding the wall you find some uneven areas, trowel on more taping compound wherever it's needed to fill in problem spots and sand again.

MUD BASICS

Most of the fixes in this story require at least two coats of taping compound. Compound is too thick to use right out of the bucket, so mix in small amounts of water until you get a smooth, mashed potato–like consistency. Use a slightly runnier mix for embedding paper tape. Let each coat dry completely (usually overnight) before applying another coat. If you have leftover ridges from tools, let them dry and scrape them off with a putty knife before adding the next coat. With the first coat, don't worry about craters, scratches or other small flaws. Just try to avoid large humps and make sure any patches are covered. The second coat is to fill in and smooth out any voids or low spots.

Generally, larger patches call for wider coats of drywall compound to mask them. That way, higher areas from patches or existing humps can be feathered out over wide areas so the wall will appear flatter. The most common mistake is to use narrow rather than wide swaths of compound over patches and humps. Strive for a thickness of ⅛ in. or so over the fix and feather the edges flush with the drywall. Sand all the fixes with 120-grit drywall sandpaper. Use a handheld sander for small jobs and a pole sander for big jobs. Check your work with the light again after sanding to look for areas that need more work. You can always add a third or even fourth coat of joint compound to fix any remaining problems.

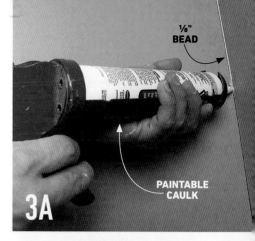

⅛" BEAD

PAINTABLE CAULK

3A

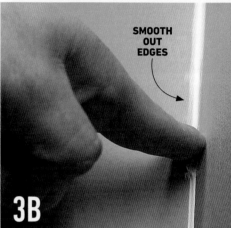

SMOOTH OUT EDGES

3B

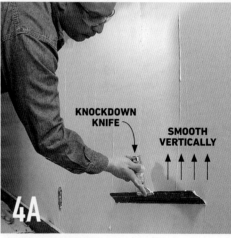

KNOCKDOWN KNIFE

SMOOTH VERTICALLY

4A

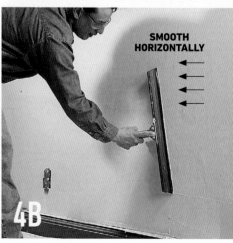

SMOOTH HORIZONTALLY

4B

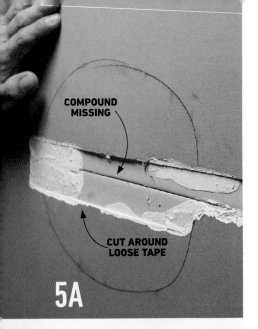

COMPOUND MISSING

CUT AROUND LOOSE TAPE

5A

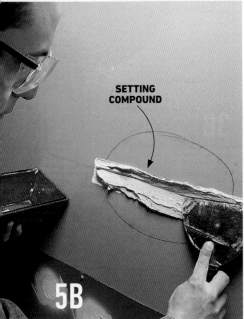

SETTING COMPOUND

5B

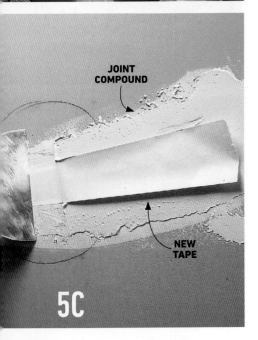

JOINT COMPOUND

NEW TAPE

5C

5 CUT OUT AND REPLACE LOOSE TAPE

If tape is blistering or lifting away from the wall, there wasn't enough joint compound under the tape to anchor it to the drywall. The solution is to cut through the paint and joint compound and then peel every bit of loose tape away from the wall to expose the surface behind **(Photo 5A)**. Be aggressive with this step, even cutting and peeling tape beyond the evident crack. There's bound to be more poorly anchored tape that just hasn't come loose yet—you can tell just by looking at the lack of compound on the drywall surface behind. After cutting loose material away, fill the hole with setting compound **(Photo 5B)**. When that hardens, embed a strip of paper tape in taping compound a few inches beyond and directly over the patch. Then overlay two wide swaths of taping compound to blend the patch into the wall **(Photo 5C)**.

6 NAIL, RETAPE AND MUD CRACKED CORNERS

If a metal corner bead is badly dented or damaged, your only option is to pry it off and replace it. That's a big job because you'll have to remove and reinstall the base trim as part of the project. But if only the edges are popping through the surface or there's a hairline crack along the flange, you can fix it. (Chances are the flange of the corner bead wasn't nailed securely or the taper neglected to tape the edges.)

Drive 1¼-in. drywall nails through any corner bead edges that are loose, using as many nails as needed to hold the flange flat to the wall **(Photo 6A)**. Center fiberglass mesh tape over the flange for the entire length of the corner bead **(Photo 6B)**. Spread

two coats of joint compound over the mesh tape, using the corner of the bead as a guide for the taping knife. If you have a corner that's in a vulnerable spot and constantly gets bumped, use setting compound for the first coat and regular joint compound for the second one. Setting compound is much tougher and won't crack nearly as easily. But be careful to apply even coats that don't project beyond the corner or leave humps or tool marks. Setting compound is very hard to sand.

NAIL LOOSE FLANGE

6A

FIBERGLASS TAPE

6B

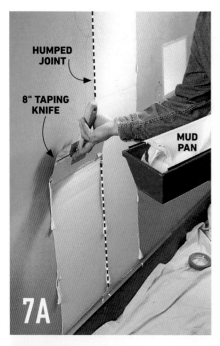

HUMPED JOINT

8" TAPING KNIFE

MUD PAN

7A

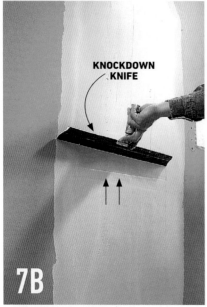

KNOCKDOWN KNIFE

7B

bottom to the top of the hump (most of the time these will be vertical joints; **Photo 7A**). Use a little more pressure on the knife edges on both sides of the hump to help feather (taper) the edges. Strive for an overall width of at least 2 ft. for the patch. Immediately after applying the first coat, drag a knockdown knife over the wet compound, smoothing the edges flat against the drywall **(Photo 7B)**. (A knockdown knife, about $30, has a 22-in.-long rubber blade.) Wait too long with this step, even a few minutes, and the rubber blade will drag in the mud and you'll have poor results. Let the first coat dry and apply a second slightly wider and thinner coat with the same techniques. Check out your patch with a raking light while sanding, and add more coats if needed to fill in low spots, craters or grooves.

8 CARVE OUT AND FILL JOINT CRACKS

Midwall cracks are tricky to fix and may crack again, so there are no promises here. The cracks usually occur at the corners of windows, doors and other openings, which are the weakest points in the framing. Seasonal movement or foundation shifting shows up in these spots, especially if joints are there. If this is the case, the only sure fix is to tear off the drywall and seam new pieces near the center of the openings.

However, try this fix first. Carve a ½-in.-wide by ½-in.-deep "V" with a utility knife in the center of the crack **(Photo 8A)**. Fill the crack with setting compound and let it harden **(Photo 8B)**. Then embed paper tape in taping compound directly over the patch **(Photo 8C)** and overlay it with two or more wide layers of taping compound.

7 TAPER HUMPED JOINTS

Butt joints (where drywall joins at the ends) often have unsightly humps left from built-up or poorly feathered edges when the walls were originally taped. (These really show up with the raking light.) Fix them by overlaying a wider layer of compound to blend the hump in with the surrounding wall. Apply the first layer of compound with a taping knife, working from the

CUT NOTCH AT CRACK

8A

SETTING COMPOUND

8B

PAPER TAPE

TAPING COMPOUND

8C

REMOVE CEILING TEXTURE

SCRAPE OFF UNSIGHTLY POPCORN FASTER AND EASIER

Popcorn ceilings were all the rage back in the '60s and '70s. Applying the texture to drywall and plaster ceilings was a quick and easy way to hide imperfections and didn't require any painting afterward. But the rough texture catches lots of dust and cobwebs, and it can be a real pain to match if you have cracks or holes in need of patching. Removing popcorn texture from a ceiling is a messy chore but worth the effort if the substrate underneath is in good shape. Here are tips to take some of the pain out of scraping the popcorn texture off your ceiling.

1 PREP FOR A BIG MESS

Cover floors and walls with plastic drop cloths. Don't use canvas drop cloths—water can soak through. Cleanup is easier with plastic because you can just ball it all up when you're done working and throw it in the trash. But leave the plastic in place after scraping to catch the mess you'll make later while repairing and sanding the ceiling.

2 DO A SCRAPE TEST

Before you go to all the trouble of prepping the room, try scraping a small area. Try it dry first, then dampen the texture with water (see p. 182) and try again. Some texture comes off easily without water, but in most cases wetting is best. If the water doesn't soak in and soften the texture, the ceiling has probably been painted or paint was added to the texture mix. In that case, wetting the ceiling may not help, and you'll have to decide whether you want to tackle a really tough scraping job or choose another way to hide your popcorn ceiling.

3 REMOVE CEILING FIXTURES AND FANS

You might think it's easier to leave light fixtures and ceiling fans in place, but they'll just be in your way and get covered with wet popcorn. Plus, you don't want to accidentally spray water into an electrical fixture.

4 GET THE FURNITURE OUT

If possible, remove all furniture from the room you'll be working in. Scraping popcorn is messy work, and you won't want furniture in your way every time you move the ladder around. If moving everything out of the room isn't possible, cluster it and cover it with drop cloths.

TEST FOR ASBESTOS!

Any popcorn ceiling installed before 1980 might contain asbestos—a known cause of lung cancer. Before trying to scrape off any popcorn texture, contact your local health department and ask about getting a sample tested. If the test comes back positive, cover the popcorn with new drywall or tongue-and-groove planks, or hire an asbestos abatement contractor to remove the popcorn.

5 PROTECT CAN LIGHTS FROM WATER SPRAY

If you have recessed can lights, stuff newspaper or rosin paper inside them to keep them dry. Also, make sure the power to those fixtures is turned off at the circuit breaker panel or fuse box.

6 COVER ELECTRICAL BOXES

Shut off the power to any electrical junction boxes in the ceiling and cover them with painter's tape to keep the wiring dry when spraying water on the popcorn. Overlap the sides of the junction box with the tape, and then trim around the perimeter with a utility knife, being careful not to nick the wires.

7 WET THE CEILING WITH A PUMP SPRAYER

For easier scraping and practically no dust, use a garden pump sprayer to mist the ceiling; let it soak in for about 15 minutes before scraping. Give it only a light misting—too much water could damage the drywall or loosen the joint tape. If the texture hasn't softened after 15 minutes or so, spray it again and wait another 10 to 15 minutes.

If the texture still hasn't softened, it might be painted or paint might have been mixed into the texture before application. In either case, water won't easily penetrate it. If the texture is painted, you may be able to dry-scrape it first to expose some of the unpainted texture, then follow up with wet scraping. If the texture has paint mixed in, you might have to dry-scrape the whole ceiling or cover it up with drywall or tongue-and-groove boards.

8 WORK IN SMALL SECTIONS

Only spray and scrape a small area at a time—about 4 x 4 ft. If you work too large of an area at once, the popcorn might dry before you have time to scrape it off. If that happens, respray the area and wait another 10 to 15 minutes before scraping.

9 TAME THE MESS WITH A MUD PAN

Use a mud pan—the kind for holding joint compound—to catch the wet popcorn before it hits the floor. That way, you're not tracking it all over the place when you walk and move the ladder around. Also, use the edge of the pan to clean off your scraper when it gets loaded up with wet popcorn. A mud pan costs about $6 to $20 at home centers.

10 PREVENT GOUGING

Round off the corners of your scraper—whether it's a wide putty knife or drywall taping knife—so it won't gouge the ceiling and leave you with dozens of ceiling wounds to repair. Use a file, a sander or an electric grinder to do this.

PRO TIP: GET TWO SCRAPERS

A stiff 6-in. putty knife (about $15) works great for smaller areas, and a 12-in. drywall taping knife (also about $15) helps you get a wide area done faster.

9B

9A

10

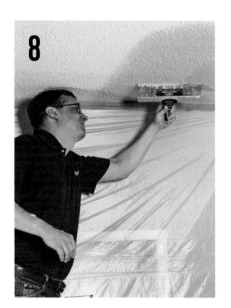

8

AFTER SCRAPING

Scraping alone won't leave you with a paint-ready ceiling. You'll probably have small dings and gouges to fix. At a minimum, you'll have to sand the ceiling to get it perfectly smooth before painting.

INSTALL THE EASIEST FLOORING EVER

MAKE YOUR LUXURY VINYL INSTALLATION FAST, SIMPLE AND FLAWLESS

Luxury vinyl is a beautiful, tough alternative to tile or hardwood flooring. Luxury vinyl tile (LVT) resembles stone or ceramic tile, while luxury vinyl plank (LVP) mimics hardwood boards. Both can be installed over many types of flooring, so you may not have to deal with the cost and hassle of removing your old floor at all. With these tips from our expert, you can install luxury vinyl over an existing floor at a fraction of the cost in just a few hours.

LUXURY VINYL TILE BASICS

TONGUE

GROOVE

1

1 INTERLOCKING TILES

The tongue-and-groove design makes it easy to snap these tiles into place. Working from left to right, the short ends angle in first. Then you will tip the opposite end downward, lift and angle the long edge into the previous tiles, and push them together.

WEAR LAYER

The wear layer on luxury vinyl is 8 to 28 mils thick. This layer protects the decorative layer from scratches to keep it looking like new. Thicker is generally better, but your lifestyle matters more. If you wear socks around the house, 8-mil will be plenty; if you have three kids and two dogs, go for a thicker wear layer.

DECORATIVE LAYER

From modern tile and stone to rustic wood designs, LVP and LVT come in many styles to fit any room.

RIGID CORE

Some luxury vinyl has a rigid core to provide extra durability and better sound blocking. A thicker rigid core, however, requires a flatter surface to avoid bridging low spots.

INTEGRATED PAD

Some vinyl tiles come with a built-in pad attached to the bottom of each tile to provide cushion underfoot. This eliminates the need for a separate underlayment.

2 UNDERLAYMENT

If a tile doesn't come with a built-in pad, the manufacturer may recommend a cushion of underlayment. It acts as a pad for a softer landing, provides a vapor barrier and may reduce sound. It can also prevent some imperfections in the existing floor from telegraphing through the tile. Without underlayment, things such as screw head holes, uneven seams, small high spots and even tiny grains of sand can lead to wear marks.

2

COVER ALMOST ANYTHING

CONCRETE If it's flat and smooth, you're good to go. If the surface is pitted or rough, either grind it smooth or cover it with self-leveling compound.

OSB/PLYWOOD Fill any gaps and screw holes with a patching compound and sand down high spots.

SHEET VINYL Make sure seams are sound. If they're not, adhere them to the subfloor before moving on.

TILE Avoid installing luxury vinyl over grouted tile. If removing the tile isn't an option, your best bet is to pour a self-leveling compound.

PREP AND PLANS

1 SPREAD SAMPLES ALL OVER THE ROOM

The samples will look different throughout the day. Before you buy your flooring, place samples around the room to see how they look in different light conditions.

2 BUY ALL THE TILE AT ONCE

Tile is produced in large batches, or lots. Within the lots, all the tiles will be consistent, but each lot may vary slightly in size and color. Buying all the tile you need at one time will give you a better shot at getting tiles in the same lot. Double-check the batch, lot or dye number, and make sure all the boxes match.

3 ACCLIMATE THE TILES

Vinyl shrinks and expands slightly as the temperature changes, so let the tiles assume room temperature before install. With the tiles packed together, that can take several hours. To speed up acclimation, get them out of the box.

4 SHUFFLE THE TILES

Each style consists of a limited number of unique designs. To get a good random pattern, mix tiles from several different boxes. Open your boxes and pull from the top of each to make new stacks. You can cross two things off your list by doing this when you unpack the tiles.

5 CLEAN THE OLD FLOOR

Don't leave even a tiny grain of sand on the old floor before you install the new one. It might "telegraph" through the vinyl and cause a wear mark, especially with thinner luxury vinyl.

MAX023/311843	SQ.FT 27.39
Meridian	SQ.MT 2.54
Carbon	LBS 45.89
6X48	Pieces / Box 14
20181013	Quality 1
Protected by USFL patent US 9,234,357	

BATCH NUMBER

6

7

LEAVE FIRST ROW OUT TO ALLOW SHIFTING

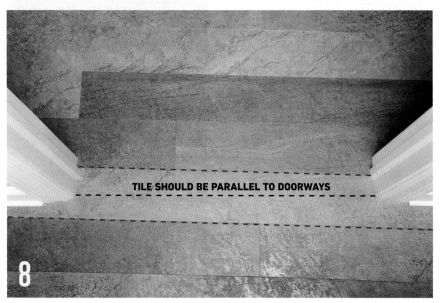

TILE SHOULD BE PARALLEL TO DOORWAYS

8

CHECK YOUR SUBSTRATE

6 Use a level or straightedge to find out how flat your substrate is. Check several areas in different directions for low spots. Measure the biggest gap between the floor and the straightedge and check it against the manufacturer's specifications. For this tile, the manufacturer says the floor should be flat to within ³⁄₁₆ in. over 10 ft. If the gap is bigger than what the manufacturer recommends, you'll need to address this before moving on. See "Pro Tip: Dealing with High Spots and Low Spots" for options.

PLAN THE LAYOUT

7 To avoid skinny rows along walls or cabinets, connect tiles to span the room until a full-width tile can't fit. If the distance between the last row of tile and the wall is less than half the width of a tile, you'll want to shift the first row. You could measure the width of the space and figure out how the tiles will land along the walls, but it's best to trust your eyes.

EXPECT OUT-OF-SQUARE ROOMS

8 Many rooms aren't perfectly square, and it's easy to notice planks or tiles cut with a taper (wider at one end than the other), especially if the wall is particularly long. Crooked flooring is obvious at doorways. Shift the layout so it's crooked somewhere less visible.

INSTALLATION TIPS

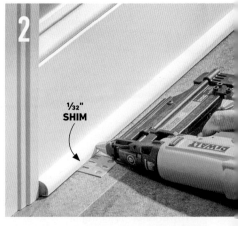

1/32" SHIM

1 STAGGER THE SEAMS

There's no set rule for staggering seams in vinyl planks, but if you lay your planks down and the seams end up creating a pattern, you'll notice it every time you walk on the floor. Avoid forming H and stair-step patterns. If you make sure seams don't line up for four or five rows, it's unlikely you'll spot a pattern.

2 LEAVE A GAP UNDER SHOE MOLDING

Pinching the flooring down with shoe mold won't allow for expansion and contraction and could cause buckling or separation at the seams. Use a 1/32-in. tile spacer or shim under the shoe to create a small gap. Be sure to nail the shoe into the baseboard, not down through the vinyl.

3 START ROWS WITH CUTOFFS

You'll end each row by cutting the last tile to fit. Instead of wasting the leftover cutoff, make it the beginning of the next row.

4 HEAT AND BEND

If you run into a situation where you need to bend the tile to get it to fit under a doorjamb or toe-kick, make the tile more flexible with a heat gun. Be careful not to scorch the face of the tile.

CHANGE LEVELS WITH TRANSITION MOLDING

Transition molding is used to cover the cut ends of vinyl and to make up for height differences when meeting a different type of flooring. There are three common options:

- **REDUCER STRIP** For transitioning vinyl floor to another floor of a different height

- **T-MOLDING** For a smooth transition between floor surfaces that are about the same height

- **END CAP** For transitioning from vinyl floor to carpet; also used to terminate vinyl flooring into an exterior door

5 LEAVE A GAP AT THE EDGES

It's surprising how much vinyl can expand or shrink with changing temperatures. A gap at the edges will ensure you won't ever come home to a buckled floor. Check with the manufacturer to see what it recommends for your tile.

6 INSTALL PLANKS IN REVERSE

Being able to install vinyl tile backward is a real time-saver and makes going through doorways and installing tile under cabinets a snap. Assemble the row first, then tip the tongue underneath the groove on the previous row and pull them tight.

7 MARK WITH A SCRAP

Instead of using a tape measure to transfer measurements to the tile, use some scrap. Align the tile you want to cut where it will snap in, placing it on top of the previous row. Use a full-width scrap (with the tongue removed) against the wall and scribe the tile.

QUICK, CLEAN CUTS

■ **CUT WITH A CARPET KNIFE**
A carpet blade, which is much stiffer than a normal utility blade, makes it easier to score a straight line across a tile with a square as a guide. Then bend the tile backward until it snaps. If the tile has built-in padding, you'll have to finish the cut with the carpet blade.

■ **USE A WHEEL FOR NOTCHES**
With notch cuts, you can't just score and snap. Make these tricky cuts a whole lot easier by using a rotary tool equipped with an abrasive wheel for cutting plastic.

■ **SLICE FASTER** A slicing-style laminate cutter (about $65) is great for cutting vinyl tile. Its blunt slicer punches out a ¼-in. strip with a clean-cut edge. If you have a lot of cutting to do, invest in this tool to make your job go faster.

■ **MAKE LONG CUTS WITH A TABLE SAW** The fastest and easiest way to cut a full tile lengthwise is to use a table saw. Using a straightedge and a carpet blade is much slower.

FIX HARDWOOD FLOORS

REPLACE THAT "ONE BAD BOARD" IN 12 EASY STEPS

Repairing tongue-and-groove hardwood floorboards is easy with the right tools and a little know-how. Many common problems can be fixed in a day to make your floor look like new again.

Over the years, all of us have seen our share of damaged hardwood floors. Sometimes the flaw can be repaired with wood putty and a quick touch-up—other times surgery is required. Here are some tips to help you repair your own flooring trouble spots.

STAIN AND FINISH TO MATCH

It is good to do this first. Test some stain colors on new floorboards and apply some urethane. Once you find a good match, repeat that process for the actual repair.

1 TAPE THE BOUNDARY

Inspect the damaged flooring plank and decide how much length to remove. Stagger the ends of the repair about 5 in. from the butt joints of the adjacent floorboards. Then place masking tape to define the boundary, using the replacement board as a guide.

REPLACEMENT BOARD

2 DRILL RELIEF HOLES

Drill three ½-in. holes close to each end of the board you're removing. Don't try to get the holes perfectly on the butt joint—about ⅛ in. away is fine.

½" FORSTNER BIT

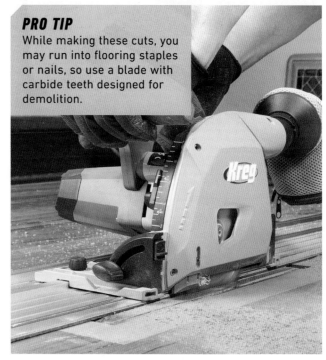

3 CHISEL THE BUTT JOINT

With a sharp chisel, clean the space between the holes and the end of the repair. First, make a vertical cut to cleanly sever the wood fibers, then come in at a slight angle to remove waste. Repeat this process until you reach the subfloor.

CHISEL

4 MAKE RELIEF CUTS

Saw two parallel relief cuts an inch apart down the center of the floorboard to be removed. To avoid cutting through the subfloor, set the saw blade no more than 1/16 in. deeper than the thickness of the flooring.

PRO TIP
While making these cuts, you may run into flooring staples or nails, so use a blade with carbide teeth designed for demolition.

NARROW WOOD-CUTTING BLADE

5 FINISH THE CUTS
You can get only so close to the ends of the repair with the circular saw. Finish the relief cuts using an oscillating multitool and a narrow wood-cutting blade.

6 REMOVE THE DAMAGED BOARD
With a small pry bar, remove the strip of flooring between the relief cuts. Next, pull out the tongue-and-groove edges of the damaged board. Completely clean out the open section of flooring with a shop vac.

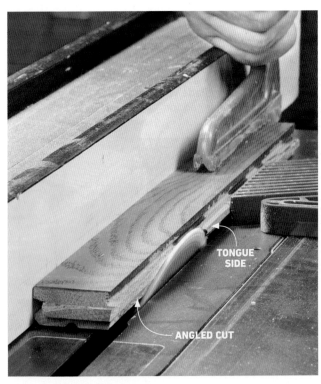

TONGUE SIDE

ANGLED CUT

GROOVE SIDE

BOTTOM LIP

7 TRIM THE TONGUE
To make it easier for the tongue on the replacement board to slip into the existing floorboards, trim it at a slight angle. Angle the blade on the table saw to about 7 degrees, and set the fence so the blade just trims the tongue.

8 TRIM THE GROOVE SIDE
Cut off the bottom lip of the grooved edge of the replacement board. Be sure to set your blade depth so that it cuts off only the bottom lip and doesn't cut into the top lip.

9 CUT TO LENGTH

Cut the replacement piece to length using a miter saw. Make the cuts with a slight bevel so the piece will drop into place easier, creating a cleaner, tighter butt joint.

BEVELED CUT

10 GLUE THE BOARDS

Spread glue on the tongues of both the replacement piece and the adjacent board. Any wood glue will work for this purpose.

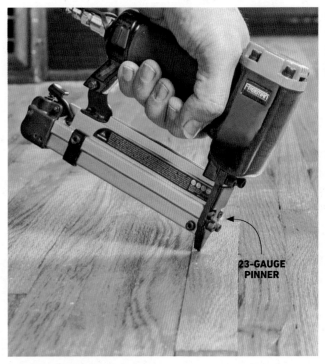

11 INSTALL THE NEW BOARD

Tap the repair board into place with a rubber mallet. If you don't have a rubber mallet, a hammer will work, but use a piece of scrap wood under it to protect the repair. Wipe off any excess glue with a damp cloth.

12 SECURE THE REPAIR

After gluing in the replacement board, add 23-gauge pins for peace of mind. Angle the gun slightly, and drive in a pin about every 4 in.

23-GAUGE PINNER

A REAL ESTATE AGENT OR MOVER

1

CREATE INSTANT IMPACT

EASY UPGRADES CAN BOOST YOUR HOME'S APPEAL—WHETHER YOU'RE BUYING, SELLING OR STAYING PUT

We recently sat down with home-staging expert Melanie Zaelich of Happy Place Interiors. She flooded us with great home-selling tips—we could hardly write them down fast enough. Then it struck us: This would be great advice for everyone. We all want our homes to "show" better, whether we're selling a house, moving into a new home or apartment, or staying in place for years.

1 GET RID OF RUGS—MAYBE

If you're staying in your home, you probably want the softness and silencing effect of area rugs. But if you're selling, remove them. They chop up the room in photographs and hide your nice flooring. Melanie tells her clients, "You're selling the floor, not the rug." There is an exception to this rule: In a large open layout, rugs help to define the space. For example, a rug can make a seating area distinct from an adjoining dining area.

2 UPGRADE LIGHT FIXTURES

In many homes, this is the most powerful, effective thing you can do: Replace dated lights with more stylish fixtures, especially in "public" rooms such as the living room and kitchen. It doesn't have to be expensive since home centers carry up-to-date fixtures starting at about $50. And it isn't difficult, even if you have no experience with electrical work. To see how, search for "light fixture" at *familyhandyman.com*.

3 INSTALL AN INSTANT BACKSPLASH

An attractive kitchen backsplash can transform a kitchen. Melanie recommends a peel-and-stick backsplash as an easy DIY solution. Just peel off the backing from the sheet of tile and stick the tile to the wall. These are available in all types of materials, from natural stone to gel, and cost about $3 and up per sheet.

4 REPLACE A DOORBELL BUTTON

If the first thing buyers notice as they approach a house is a stuck, broken or ugly doorbell button, it will affect their impression as they check out the rest of the house. Replacement is easy; there are just two low-voltage wires to connect. To solve other doorbell problems, go to *familyhandyman.com* and search for "doorbell."

5 TRIM TREES THAT BLOCK VIEWS OR LIGHT

Natural light is something everyone craves, especially during the shorter days of the year. To let in as much light as possible, trim trees or shrubs that are creating shade. If the branches are within arm's reach, use a lopper or reciprocating saw with a pruning blade. Use a pole saw if the sun-blocking limb is higher.

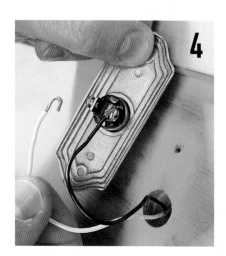

6

7

6 RESTORE GROUT

If the grout lines in your tile are dingy and dark from grime, you can easily get the grout to look like new again with a grout restorer. Some are kits that come with two solutions—a tile-and-grout cleaner and a color sealer. Other products consist of just a colorant. Either way, clean the grout and wipe it dry, apply colorant according to the manufacturer's directions, then wipe off the excess. Products range from about $15 to $30 and can be found at home centers.

7 REPLACE CABINET HARDWARE

Changing out old cabinet hardware for an updated style can drastically change the way the entire room looks. Updating the cabinet knobs and pulls can cost as little as $2 apiece, and each can be done in a matter of minutes. If the shape of the knob is up to date but the color or shade isn't, give it a few coats of spray paint.

8 BLOCK THE VIEW, NOT THE LIGHT

People like bright, sunlit spaces. So if you want to block your view of a neighbor's backyard junk collection, go with translucent window film rather than opaque window coverings. Window film is also ideal for bathroom privacy.

9 PRIORITIZE EYE-LEVEL PROJECTS

During showings, potential home buyers first notice things at eye level, then they look up and, lastly, they check near the floor. Keep that in mind when choosing the projects you want to prioritize.

WINDOW FILM

8

10 COVER CLAW MARKS

Claw marks from pets need to be fixed. If the door is painted, it's easy to fill the gouges with wood filler or patching compound and then repaint. On a stained door, try gel stain. Lightly sand the area and then, using a dry brush, start with a light stain and darken it to match the old finish. Keep the brush on the drier side by wiping excess stain off on a clean rag. When you're done, feather from the newly stained area into the surrounding area with a clear spray finish.

11 ADJUST CABINET DOORS

Make sure cabinet doors are aligned properly. This will make a huge difference and it's really easy. Euro hinges have two screws you can tighten and loosen to align the doors and make sure gaps between them are consistent.

12 MAKE SPRAY PAINT YOUR FRIEND

Any homeowner should get familiar with laying a nice coat of spray paint over all kinds of faded, rusty or outdated things around a home. The key to a good spray-paint job is a good cleaning with a degreaser followed by a starting coat of primer and several very light coats of paint. Spray-paint appliance handles, HVAC registers, bath fan covers and light fixtures to give them new life. If the material you are painting is plastic, use a paint formulated for plastic.

13 FOCUS ON THE FRONT

The front entry is first priority. Buyers typically know within 10 seconds whether or not they're interested.

12

14

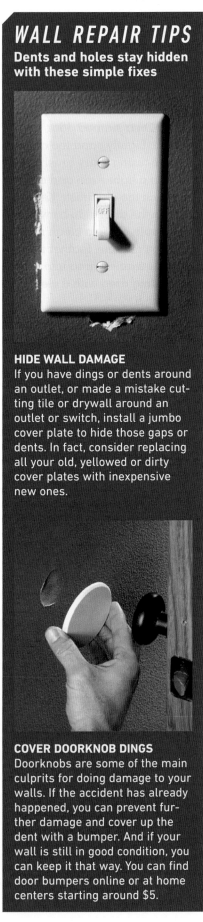

HIDE WALL DAMAGE

If you have dings or dents around an outlet, or made a mistake cutting tile or drywall around an outlet or switch, install a jumbo cover plate to hide those gaps or dents. In fact, consider replacing all your old, yellowed or dirty cover plates with inexpensive new ones.

14 FIX DOORS

If you've lived in your home for a while, you've learned to tolerate your sticking, stubborn doors. But to other people, they're a frustration and a turnoff. The good news is that you can solve most door problems in less than an hour. *Familyhandyman.com* has how-to help for any type of door trouble. Search for "door repair."

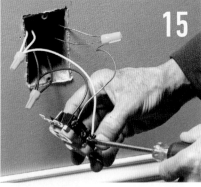

15

15 REPLACE OUTLETS AND SWITCHES

Switches, outlets and cover plates get dirty, damaged and discolored, giving your home a worn look. New ones give your home a remodeled feel. Replacing them is usually easy and inexpensive.

16 CHOOSE THE RIGHT LIGHTS

Make sure lights match in color and brightness from room to room. The bulbs in recessed lights should be the same, and the bulbs in fixtures should all match as well. Melanie suggests using GE Crystal Clear incandescent bulbs because they show off a room's interior best.

COVER DOORKNOB DINGS

Doorknobs are some of the main culprits for doing damage to your walls. If the accident has already happened, you can prevent further damage and cover up the dent with a bumper. And if your wall is still in good condition, you can keep it that way. You can find door bumpers online or at home centers starting around $5.

17 REPLACE TORN SCREENS

This is an easy DIY project that involves a special screen roller and just a few basic tools. You start by removing the old spline and the stringy rubber piece that holds the screen in the groove. Then you'll be able to take off the old screen. Place the new screen over the frame and use the screen roller to press in a new spline. After cutting away the excess screen, you'll have it back in the opening in half an hour.

18 FIX IT BEFORE YOU LIST IT

Be sure to repair any torn window and storm door screens, doorbells, and bifold and sliding doors before you attempt to sell your house.

19 MASK CEILING STAINS

If you want to cover up an ugly water-stained ceiling, a stain-blocking primer is mandatory to prevent the stain from bleeding through a fresh coat of paint. Zinsser Covers Up and Kilz Upshot are both stain-blocking primers, and both have nozzles that shoot upward for a convenient application process. These primers attempt to match aged ceilings, so you may be able to get away without repainting the ceiling. You can pick up a can of stain-blocking primer at any home center for about $10.

PAINT YOUR HOME TO SELL

A FRESH COAT PROVIDES THE PERFECT UPDATE

"There are several reasons to paint a home prior to selling," says Shaun Larson, a real estate broker and general contractor with Parks Real Estate near Nashville, Tennessee. "One is to refresh the home's condition from it being worn, resulting in dirty, scratched or chipped walls and trim. Another is to make it appear newer and more marketable, leading to a quicker sale at a higher price."

But before you pick up the paintbrush, you'll need to spend some time choosing appropriate paint colors. Larson suggests considering these factors:

■ The region where the home is and what design trends are popular there
■ The style of the home — contemporary, traditional, coastal, etc.
■ The size of the home and individual rooms
■ Landscaping conditions and whether they reduce light levels in the home
■ Architectural elements of the home, like large overhangs that reduce interior light levels
■ The color of light entering the room: strong sun (warm light) or shade (cooler light)

With that in mind, here are the colors our real estate pros encourage their clients to paint their interiors for a quick sell.

WHITE

"Repeat this 10 times really fast: White, white or maybe white is the only interior paint color you need to sell your house well and quickly," says Baron Christopher Hanson with Coldwell Banker Realty in Florida. "Why? White makes your home look bigger and brighter inside, especially if you are staging."

White allows the buyer to envision their perfect color palette. "Trying to guess which paint colors your highest offer buyer will like is akin to winning the lottery," Hanson says. Choosing white might save you money, too, because it's a perfect primer for any color the new owner may want to paint—and may prevent a demand for a painting credit prior to closing.

Eli Pasternak, owner of Liberty House Buying Group in Miami, says one house that sold quickly was all white with navy blue accents. "This house was located in a neighborhood with very similar homes," Pasternak says. "I believe I was able to sell very fast due to the interior paint, which made it easier for the buyer to place their furniture. Other homes in the neighborhood had walls with bold colors, which weren't looked favorably upon."

Larson says some of the most popular interior wall colors are Sherwin-Williams Alabaster, Shoji White, Snowbound and White Flour. But be careful. "Consider whether you're painting walls or trim and ceiling as well," he says. "If you accidentally mix cool and warm tones, what may have been an attempt to brighten a room may have all of a sudden made something else look yellowish relative to the new paint."

Need a classic white? Realtor Eric Hegwer of Austin, Texas, says Benjamin Moore's Chantilly Lace is a good bet.

GRAY, BEIGE AND GREIGE

Light and airy should be your priority when choosing interior paint to help sell your home. Bill Gassett of Maximum Real Estate Exposure in Hopkinton, Massachusetts, loves Benjamin Moore's Stonington Gray, a light, soft hue he says pairs well with white trim. "Stonington Gray has looked good in so many homes that I decided to paint some of the rooms in my own home this color."

Larson says Sherwin-Williams Repose Gray and Amazing Gray are also popular gray shades.

Bill Samuel, a real estate developer and contractor for Blue Ladder Development, says he loves Behr's Water Chestnut in a flat finish. "It's a neutral beige shade that will appeal to a broad spectrum of buyers," he says. "The flat sheen does a better job of covering up prior blemishes and gives you a cleaner finished look."

He adds that it presents equally well in natural and artificial lighting.

LIGHT PASTELS

Our real estate pros generally agree: Some light color is OK if used properly.

"If you want to splash a little more color, the safe bet is to go with light and airy hues like pale pink, light blue, mint green and lavender," says Rinal Patel, Realtor and co-founder of We Buy Philly Home. "These tones can transform a room and make it feel warm and inviting."

PRO TIP
Give your front door some color. Brick red is the most common, followed by navy blue.

Light peach and pink can make a space feel luminous, warm and welcoming if done right. Blues are a universal favorite among buyers. Sage green is making a strong comeback. Just be careful—you want potential buyers to feel like the home is theirs, not yours.

FINAL TIPS

"I try to keep tabs on current trends on Instagram," Hegwer says. "I see a lot of influencers using dark, moody colors, but those haven't come to the suburbs of Austin where I'm working." Make sure your interior paint is in line with the tastes of people where you live.

A final word of advice, from Patel: "Uniformity is key. You want all of the rooms in your home to flow together, so choose a consistent color scheme. This doesn't mean every room should be the same color, but pick a few hues that complement each other. Then use them throughout your home to create a cohesive look that potential buyers will love."

UPGRADE YOUR GARAGE DOOR FOR A FASTER SALE

THESE WORTHWHILE REFRESH OPTIONS WILL TURN BUYERS' HEADS

A garage door is often your home's largest architectural element. According to a 2019 study done by *Remodeling* magazine, a garage door replacement returns on average nearly 100% of the project cost at resale. In 2018 a major garage door manufacturer partnered with an independent research firm to conduct a study to "gauge Realtor perceptions" to determine if the garage door's appearance was a key factor in a home's listing price. According to the study, if home shoppers don't like what they see from the street, they won't even go inside. Of the real estate agents surveyed, 70% agree that a new garage door sells a home faster, and more than 80% believe a new one boosts a home's value. Here are four options for maximizing the curb appeal of your garage door.

1 PAINT IT

This is the fastest, cheapest option if a door is attractive and in good condition. A clean, well-prepped surface is a must. The job can be done in a weekend. Be sure to choose the proper paint and primer for your door, whether it's wood, vinyl or metal.

2 GIVE IT A FACE-LIFT

If you have a metal door with a dull, aged finish, restore it with a Garage Door Renewal Kit from Everbrite (not shown). A one-car garage kit costs about $60.

You can also add magnetic decorative "hinges" **(Photo 2)**, as well as magnetic "windows" (not shown), which won't let in light but are quite realistic.

3 REPLACE IT

The cost of a new garage door ranges from a few hundred dollars to a few thousand, depending on the style, size and material. Adding windows will increase the natural light as well as the price. If you're not comfortable installing the door yourself, it is affordable to have installation done for you.

Learn how to install a garage door yourself by searching for "how to install a garage door" on *familyhandyman.com*. And before you buy a new door, search for "10 things to know before buying a garage door."

4 BUILD YOUR OWN

If you're a hardcore DIYer, you may want to build your own door. For a fraction of the cost of a manufactured door and a weekend of your time, you can build a carriage house–style door using a standard hardboard garage door as a base. Search for "garage door makeover" at *familyhandyman.com*.

2

3

4

KNOW WHAT A REAL ESTATE AGENT CAN DO FOR YOU

AN EXPERIENCED AGENT WILL MAKE MOVING EASIER

Whether you're buying or selling a house, remember that "the real estate agent you hire is there to negotiate for you," says Antoine Thompson, executive director of the National Association of Real Estate Brokers. When challenges arise, "you want a good advocate working on your behalf."

Here are some services you should expect:

LISTING AGENTS ...

■ **SET A FAIR PRICE, AND BOOST VALUE.** "Your agent should bring a deep understanding of the local market, including current economic conditions and new developments that could affect values, to help you set a reasonable price," Thompson says. The agent should also have a keen eye for modest improvements (say, a new coat of paint in a popular color) that could significantly improve your home's appeal to buyers.

■ **HAVE A CLEAR MARKETING STRATEGY.** "There should be a clear plan in place for publicizing your home, from professional photography and staging (setting up your house for showing) to getting the word out via social media and multiple websites," says Vicky Scarnuley, a licensed real estate agent in Trumbull, Connecticut. "The agent should help you evaluate offers and negotiate the best price," and help arrange ancillary services such as attorneys, title services and even moving companies.

■ **ORGANIZE OPEN HOUSES.** Open houses take time and money to arrange, and not all agents offer them, especially for mid-to lower-priced homes. Even so, "I encourage sellers to ask their agents to do open houses," Thompson says. "That gets traffic into the property, which reduces the amount of time it might be on the market."

BUYERS' AGENTS ...

■ **ACT AS PRICE ADVOCATES.** "A real estate agent should help you understand current market conditions for your area and the type of home you're looking for, and whether specific properties that catch your eye are priced fairly," Scarnuley says.

■ **HELP WITH INSPECTIONS.** Your agent should recommend qualified inspectors who will thoroughly examine any home you're thinking of buying. "The agent should attend every inspection and be with the buyer every step of the way," Scarnuley says.

■ **NEGOTIATE FIXES.** If the inspection reveals flaws, particularly safety or health risks such as structural problems, water damage, or mold, septic or asbestos issues, a buyer's agent "should have the client's best interest in mind," Scarnuley notes. That should include negotiating with the seller to ensure problems are fixed before you move in.

SHOP AROUND

Real estate is a relationship business, so interview potential agents. In addition to their experience and knowledge, consider whether you enjoy spending time with them. "You'll be working together through what can be a lengthy and stressful process," Scarnuley says. "If the personalities aren't a good match, you should be able to find a better fit with someone else."

SELL AT THE RIGHT TIME TO GET THE BEST PRICE

CONSIDER ALL OPTIONS AS THE SEASONS CHANGE

Real estate data may suggest an ideal time of year to sell your home, but the optimal time may not be the same in every place and for every person. There are other circumstances to consider:
- Do you need quick turnaround?
- Are you looking to hit the market while it's hottest?
- Is the "ideal time" convenient for family and work?

Each season comes with its own set of pros and cons.

- **SPRING IS THE OVERALL WINNER FOR SELLING.** In most places, homes sell the fastest and for the highest prices in the first two weeks of May. The months of April and June are typically strong as well. Warmer weather and longer daylight give buyers more opportunity to house hunt. Blooming flowers and lawns turning green maximize curb appeal.

- **SELLING IN THE SUMMER IS EASIER.** Longer daylight and flexible schedules make shopping easier, but buyers feel the pressure of time. Those with kids want to move in before school starts. Sellers benefit from this sense of urgency since it can drive up prices.

- **FALL IS AN IFFY TIME FOR HOME SALES.** Not every area of the country has pleasant fall weather, and people seem to turn their attention toward making necessary repairs before winter instead of selling. This reduces inventory as well as the number of potential buyers. That said, fall buyers are often serious, but picky. They may have looked all spring and summer without finding the perfect home.

- **WINTER IS BEST IN AREAS LIKE CALIFORNIA, FLORIDA, ARIZONA AND SKI RESORT TOWNS.** In other areas, curb appeal is low: Branches are bare, grass is brown and there are mounds of snow. It's also harder to schedule showings since days are shorter and people are busy with holidays. But winter buyers can be much more serious. They're often pressed for time, wanting to buy before the end of the year or to relocate for a job.

GET THE MOST FROM YOUR HOME INSPECTION

///

AN INSPECTION IS MORE THAN JUST A TO-DO LIST ITEM

You've chosen a home, made an offer and had it accepted. You are ready to charge ahead and are tempted to hire the first (or cheapest) home inspector you find so you can check that item off your list. But slow down. With a little extra time and knowledge, your home inspection can be much more than just a standard requirement in the buying process.

Aluminum wiring can be a fire hazard, and making it safe can cost thousands. If your inspector finds it, renegotiation is justified.

SEEKING AN INSPECTOR? READ A SAMPLE REPORT

When hiring an inspector, ask for recommendations from people you trust and read online reviews. But also go to the inspector's website and read a sample report. If there isn't one, look further. A good report contains these elements:

- Photos should accompany the items discussed in the report.
- The report should be written in plain English, understandable to anyone. You shouldn't need a degree in building science to understand it.
- The report should cover three aspects of each potential problem: what the issue is, why it's an issue and what should be done.
- Every report includes disclaimers. Like everyone else, inspectors don't want to be sued. But a good report keeps them to a minimum.
- Many reports are filled with recommendations for further testing or inspections. When this is the case, it's worth considering whether the inspector aims to avoid lawsuits more than to provide great service.
- Look for statements that mention an issue but also say it isn't a significant problem. Anyone can identify an issue and recommend further action. But it takes deep experience and knowledge to say an issue isn't worth worrying about. That's often the sign of a great inspector.

BIG PROBLEMS MIGHT MEAN RENEGOTIATION

If the inspection uncovers dangerous or expensive problems—such as aluminum wiring, a cracked heat exchanger or structural flaws—it's reasonable to rethink the agreement. There are four options:

- **LOWER THE PRICE:** This is often a fair way to compensate the buyer. But even though the home loan will decrease along with the sale price, the buyer will have to pay for the repairs. That's often burdensome on top of ordinary home-buying costs.
- **ASK THE SELLER TO MAKE THE REPAIRS:** This also can be fair—if the seller can afford to pay. But the buyer should keep this in mind: The seller will want the work done quickly and cheaply and may not be too concerned about the quality of the job.
- **CANCEL THE SALE:** This is usually the worst option. Both parties have invested time and money to

reach an agreement. Killing that agreement is a huge step backward for everyone.
- **DO NOTHING:** Since all the other options raise new complications, this is often the best response to problems—as long as those problems don't pose an immediate health threat.

THE REPORT IS NOT A NEGOTIATING WEAPON

Buyers sometimes use the inspection report as an excuse to renegotiate the price of the house. Unless the problems are dangerous or major, this is a bad idea. Defects like peeling paint, sidewalk cracks or wall damage are considered "known conditions." In other words, they were already obvious when you first toured the house. Asking for compensation after the agreement will poison your relationships with the seller and the real estate agents.

The same goes for old construction that doesn't meet newer building codes. If old stair balusters, for example, are spaced farther apart than current code allows, the report will note it. But that doesn't mean the seller should pay for correction.

This railing is unsafe and doesn't meet building codes. But since it's an obvious problem and one that was visible before the inspection, it's not a good reason to renegotiate the sale of the house.

A sewer inspection camera and a trained eye can spot cracks before they cost you big bucks.

GET A SEWER INSPECTION

For about $200, you can hire a sewer guru to run a camera through the waste pipe that runs from the house to the city sewer system. After seeing dozens of fractures in newer lines—and repairs that cost thousands—we suggest this for homes old and new.

ASBESTOS: SOMETIMES HAZARDOUS, SOMETIMES NOT

Asbestos does terrible damage to lungs, but only if it's inhaled. Asbestos in siding that's sealed under a good coat of paint, for example, can't get airborne and inhaled, so it's nothing to panic about. On the other hand, asbestos in vermiculite insulation can easily drift into a home through tiny air leaks in ceilings and walls; that's a serious risk. Most inspectors recognize materials that may contain asbestos and will note them on the report. But keep in mind that asbestos sampling and lab testing are not a standard part of a home inspection. Also keep this in mind: Asbestos was used to make more than 3,000 kinds of building materials. If a home was built before 1980, there's a good chance it contains asbestos somewhere.

Vermiculite itself isn't a problem. But some of it contains asbestos, which is definitely a health risk.

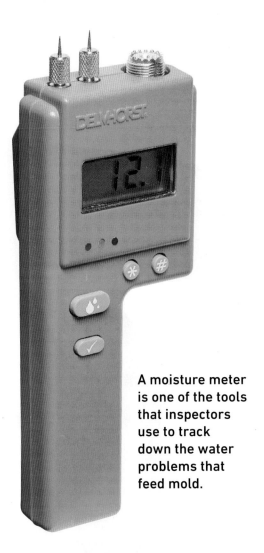

A moisture meter is one of the tools that inspectors use to track down the water problems that feed mold.

Plumbers sometimes forget to remove the plug in a rooftop vent. Some owners of new homes live for years with the results—slow, gurgling, stinky drains.

Keep in mind that the majority of foundation cracks will never become a structural problem. They might let in some groundwater, but that's usually an easy fix.

SKIP THE MOLD TEST

An inspector can provide mold testing, but it usually isn't necessary. Testing costs hundreds of dollars and rarely provides practical information. And since mold issues are caused by moisture problems, moisture testing is a better path to the root of any problems.

NEW HOMES NEED INSPECTIONS TOO

During construction, a house gets several inspections by city building inspectors, so it's reasonable to assume that a new house won't have problems. But you shouldn't assume that. We've seen hundreds of serious problems in new homes over the past few years—homes built by big, reputable builders.

FOUNDATION CRACKS? DON'T FREAK OUT

When the walls that support an entire building are cracked, it seems pretty scary. But here's the deal: All foundations have some cracks, and most will never become a problem, even in a hundred years. A good inspector will make note of cracks but will rarely recommend further inspection by an engineer.

SELLING? DON'T RISK AN INCOMPLETE INSPECTION

If you're selling, you'll want an inspector to complete the job. If an inspector labels it an "incomplete inspection," that may delay or even sink the sale. Good preparation is mostly about providing easy access. Keep in mind that it isn't the inspector's job to move barricades of boxes or stacks of paint cans.

- Make sure an inspector can get to and open the main electrical panel and any subpanels.
- Clear a path around the furnace and water heater.
- For a detached garage, leave keys or an opener.
- If you have crawl spaces, make sure the doors to them are accessible.
- Secure any pets that might escape through an open door—or worse, attack. An inspector is not a burglar!
- If the house has been unoccupied, make sure the water, gas and electricity are turned on.

MOVE HEAVY STUFF THE SMART WAY

//

MOVERS SHARE WISE TIPS (AND A FEW FUN QUIPS)

Need to move a boulder? Or maybe wrestle a refrigerator down a flight of stairs? Brute strength may have served you well back in high school. But growing older means using your mind more than your muscles when it comes to moving heavy or awkward things. Otherwise, you risk wrecking your back, your house and the item you're moving.

We asked veteran movers and *Family Handyman* field editors for their top moving tips—and were given some fun examples of what *not* to do as well. Their brains can make your next move faster and easier, even if you no longer have the brawn of a high school student.

1 TAKE THE BACK OFF A RECLINER

Find the back brackets on the outside or inside of the back frame. Lift the locking levers on both sides (you may need to use long-nose pliers) and slide the back straight up to remove it from the recliner. Always lift a recliner from the sides, not by the back or footrest. Tie the footrest in place so it doesn't spring open.

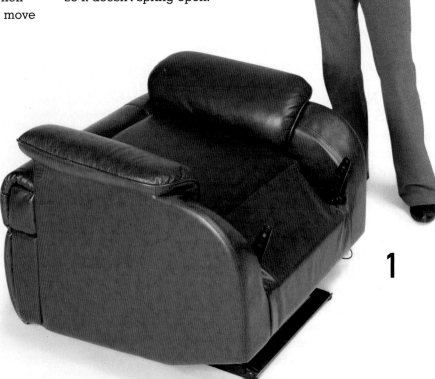

1

3

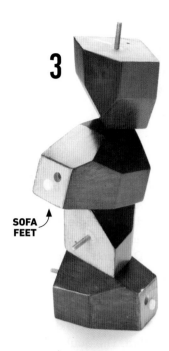

SOFA
FEET →

2 BE A SOFA MAGICIAN

One unlucky mover thought a large sofa could make it around the 90-degree angle of his basement stairs—and promptly got the sofa wedged in the stairwell. He had to climb under it just to escape. A bold strategy saved the day: He took out a trusty handsaw and sawed the thing in half! Once it was downstairs, he was able to quickly fasten it back together with some screws and scraps of wood. Because the rips in the fabric were at the back and bottom, nobody was the wiser.

3 TAKE APART WHAT YOU CAN

If you'd rather not break out the handsaw when you're lugging a sofa through a doorway, remember: You can make it a few inches smaller by removing the feet. This applies to any piece of furniture you need to make sleeker or lighter: Take off any knobs, drawers, shelves, racks and legs.

4 REMOVE YOUR DOOR STOP MOLDING

Sometimes an extra ½ in. is all it takes to get through a doorway. If removing the door doesn't open up enough space, pry off the door stop molding. That will give you another ¾ in.

5 RAMP IT UP (AND DOWN)

Use lumber, scaffold planks and blocks to create ramps to maneuver bulky items.

To load a wheeled generator into an SUV, one field editor built ramps using supported lengths of 2x6 and attached a come-along tool to the parking brake handle in the front seat. He was able to move the ratcheting lever with one hand and steer the item up the ramps with the other.

6 BREAK HEAVY THINGS INTO SMALLER PIECES

Need to replace a cast-iron tub or get rid of old radiators? Use your trusty sledgehammer to smash them into pieces.

4

5

6

7 **CARRY MIRRORS AND GLASS WITH SUCTION CUPS**
Available in single and double versions, these FastCap Handle on Demand suction cups can be attached to any nonporous surface. They're not for unfinished wood surfaces. A single pad can support 100 lbs. and the double pad twice that. The double-pad handle costs about $25 online.

8 **ROLL IT AWAY**
One field editor moved a 10 x 10-ft. shed himself by putting down 2x4s and using 10-ft. sections of PVC pipe to roll the shed into position.

9 **GET STUBBORN BOULDERS TO BUDGE**
Here are two potential methods for dealing with a boulder. First, consider burying it. Dig a slightly deeper hole next to it and just roll the boulder in. Another option is to use heat. Clear the grass from around the boulder and build a fire all around it. After a few hours, put bags of ice on top of the boulder and crack the boulder into pieces.

10 **USE PLASTIC WRAP, NOT TAPE, TO SECURE ITEMS**
Secure appliance doors, cords, tubing and other items with plastic wrap or moving bands rather than bungee cords or tape, which can damage the finish or leave a residue.

11 BRIBE HELPERS WITH PIZZA

A wise field editor told us that instead of using his head, he uses his 16-year-old son. "He's 6' 7" and strong as an ox. Pizzas and cans of soda are a lot cheaper than hernia surgery."

12 LIFT PLANTS THE SMART WAY

PotLifter plant straps let you tote up to 200 lbs. without straining. The straps are available for about $40 at online retailers such as Amazon.

13 USE CHAINS, NOT YOUR BACK

Here's a technique that can help you load just about anything into a vehicle without breaking a sweat. Beef up a garage roof truss, screwing and gluing ¾-in. plywood to both sides, then hang a chain hoist (starting around $70 at *harborfreight.com*) from the truss. Now you can lift a load a few feet off the floor, back a vehicle under it and lower the load into the bed.

14 DRAG A HEAVY LOG ... BEFORE IT DRAGS YOU

Moving heavy objects can be dangerous. Proceed with this cautionary tale in mind: "I was dragging a log with a four-wheeler. The log had a small branch sticking out, which caught a small standing tree. The tree broke off, hit my head, knocked me silly and flipped me off the vehicle. Nothing was hurt but my pride."

11

12

13

15

15 BUY MOVING BLANKETS— DON'T RENT THEM

Moving blankets are invaluable for protecting items, as well as floors. Sure, renting them is cheap, but you can get a blanket for about $15 at home centers or *uhaul.com* and have it on hand. These blankets work great for sliding appliances and furniture over hard floors and for hauling lumber home on a car roof.

16 GET ADJUSTABLE MOVING STRAPS

Moving and lifting straps ("hump straps") make carrying heavy items easier on your back by relying on stronger muscle groups like your legs and shoulders. The straps also leave your hands free to maneuver awkward items like mattresses. However, they can be tricky to use on stairs because weight shifts completely to the downhill mover.

Look for moving straps that can be adjusted for different length objects as well as for different-sized movers. Be careful not to trip on any slack from the straps. Since these straps are rarely padded, they can leave your shoulders sore (but that's better than your back!). The Forearm Forklift, Teamstrap Shoulder Dolly and others are available for about $30 to $50 at home centers and online.

17 SLIPPERY PADS REALLY WORK

You can buy furniture slides in many shapes and sizes at home centers and online. Use hard plastic sliders for carpeting, and use soft, carpeted sliders for hard flooring.

18 MOVE IT ON ICE

A mover shared with us a time when he was setting granite stair treads, and moving them around was tough. He poured bagged ice on the ground, set the treads on top and moved them easily into place. When the ice melted, the treads didn't move.

19 ALWAYS REMEMBER TO HAVE A PLAN B

Another mover reminded us to always have options. After measuring carefully, he thought he could get a fiberglass one-piece tub/shower up steps to a bathroom. After an hour of scratching the hardwood steps, the walls and ceiling—and destroying crown molding—he realized it would not fit. Plan B: Cut a hole in the second-floor exterior wall (it was coming out anyway) and use the excavator's backhoe as a crane to lift the tub to the second floor. Plan B took 15 minutes. It should've been Plan A.

USE MOBILE STORAGE CONTAINERS

///

BE PREPARED WITH THESE STORAGE TIPS

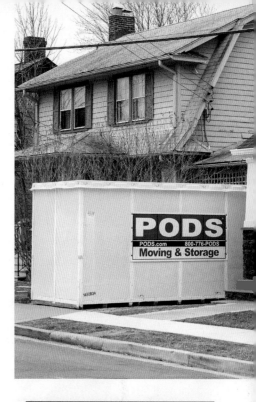

Ever wonder about those containers you see outside people's homes? If you need a place to put stuff temporarily, these storage containers are the perfect solution. Whether you're moving, decluttering or preparing to renovate, mobile storage containers offer the ultimate in convenience and flexibility. PODS, Pack Rat, Smartbox, U-Pack and U-Haul are a few companies that provide them. All you need is a level, paved surface for the container and maybe some professional or volunteer help to fill it.

GET THE BEST DEAL

With so many storage options to choose from, pricing is competitive. To compare bids, complete the form at each company's website. You'll need the ZIP codes where the container will be going (both empty and full), your anticipated dates of delivery, and the size and number of containers you want. Promo codes may be provided. If not, ask your real estate agent or contractor. Booking a container in the winter for a project you're doing in the summer can save you as much as 30%. You'll save even more money by using your own packing supplies—including blankets, boxes and bubble wrap—and by packing efficiently. All the companies offer videos on how to pack their containers.

RESERVE CONTAINERS EARLY

Most storage companies allow you to book containers without any deposit. Shop for a container as soon as you know you'll need one. "It doesn't matter how many containers you order," a salesman at PODS told us. "It's how many containers you receive." Plus, you can change the delivery dates without an additional charge.

HOW IT WORKS

Before taking a delivery, make sure you have all permits required by your city, apartment complex or homeowner's association. After it is delivered, you'll typically have three to 30 days to fill it before the company comes for it. Or you can leave it on-site. If you opt for off-site storage of your container, most companies will allow you to access it with 24 hours' notice. You can store your containers as long as needed or, if you're moving, have them delivered to your new home. If you store more than one container, keep a list of the container numbers and what each one holds.

IS MY STUFF SAFE?

In most cases, the container's contents are covered by renter's or homeowner's insurance. But once the container leaves your property, the coverage drops— typically to 10% of the policy's full value. You can also buy coverage from the storage companies.

MAKING A PLAN

REASONS TO USE MOBILE STORAGE CONTAINERS

- Preparing your house for sale or rent
- Decluttering your house or garage
- Renovations
- Sorting out an estate
- Storage of home office materials or equipment
- Emergency repairs

OTHER OPTIONS

If you're moving the contents of a small apartment, it might be cheaper to use FedEx, UPS or Amtrak instead of a temporary storage container. While you'll sacrifice some convenience, you could save hundreds of dollars. It depends on the weight of the shipment and the distance it will travel.

MAJOR SUPPLIERS

- 1-800-Pack-Rat: *1800packrat.com*
- PODS: *pods.com*
- Smartbox: *smartboxmovingandstorage.com*
- U-Pack Moving: *upack.com*
- U-Haul (U-Box): *uhaul.com*

CLEANING OR PEST CONTROL SERVICES

CLEAN THE THINGS YOU NEVER DO (BUT SHOULD)

//

ADD JUST AN ITEM OR TWO TO YOUR REGULAR ROUTINE, AND YOUR HOME WILL THANK YOU— NO CREW REQUIRED

You change your sheets often, but when was the last time you refreshed your mattress? You run your dishwasher regularly, but how long has it been since you gave the machine itself a wash? Chances are, you haven't thought to clean certain household items in a long while—and you may not think to clean them at all until they become bigger projects than they would have been if you'd given them a little TLC.

If you feel you already spend too much time cleaning, don't despair: There's no need to call a cleaning service. Many of these tasks are easy to tackle, especially if tacked on to existing chores.

We suggest routines for each, but these are simply standards to shoot for, not literal homework. To start, it is enough to notice these frequently overlooked items more often than you perhaps have before. The nicest part? As you build them into your cleaning routine, you won't have to pay much attention to them.

PRO TIP
Electronics are dust magnets— a very light dusting can help.

APPLIANCES

COFFEE MAKER

HOW TO CLEAN Over time, the oils from all your cups of joe build up inside your coffee maker. To remove them, along with any lime scale, first check the manual (or manufacturer's website) to see whether either advises against using any particular descaling agent. If not, mix one part white vinegar and nine parts water (or two parts lemon juice and eight parts water), fill the reservoir with the mixture and run a drip cycle. Pause it halfway to let the solution sit for about half an hour to break down any buildup. Then finish the brewing cycle and run two more full cycles with plain water to remove any lingering traces of vinegar or lemon.

HOW OFTEN When your machine starts to take an unusually long time to brew.

FAUCETS AND SHOWERHEADS

HOW TO CLEAN This is even easier than picking up the phone to call a pro: Fill a plastic bag about halfway with white vinegar. (Use quart-sized bags for faucets and gallon-sized bags for showerheads.) Wrap the bag around the fixture so any place where water exits is completely submerged in the vinegar. Use a rubber band to hold the bag in place, and leave it for an hour or so. Then remove the bag and rinse with water, using a toothbrush to scrub away any lingering residue.

HOW OFTEN Once a month.

HUMIDIFIER

HOW TO CLEAN Empty all water from the unit. Check the filters and replace any dirty ones. Then clean any mineral deposits with a small brush and whichever disinfectant the manual or company website recommends. (Remember to wear gloves and goggles if you're using a bleach solution.) Afterward, rinse the tank several times to wash away all cleaning chemicals.

HOW OFTEN Whenever you notice it looks dirty, and always before you put it away for the season. Let the humidifier dry completely before storing it.

DISHWASHER

HOW TO CLEAN Remove the filter, utensil holder and racks; wash them separately with soap and warm water to remove any greasy food residue, then replace the parts. Next, clear any debris from the dishwasher drain. (You'll be surprised by how many crumbs get stuck there.) Sprinkle baking soda across the bottom and set a bowl filled with vinegar on the top rack. Run a cycle on the hottest temperature setting.

HOW OFTEN Once a month.

WASHING MACHINE

HOW TO CLEAN For a top-loading machine, pour a pound of borax into the drum and add a gallon of vinegar. Then run the washer on the hottest and longest cycle available. For a front loader, pour ¾ cup of vinegar through the detergent compartment, wait 20 minutes, then run the self-cleaning cycle. Afterward, wipe the inside and leave the door open to let the machine air-dry.

HOW OFTEN Once or twice a year, or any time you notice mold or a foul odor.

REFRIGERATOR COILS

HOW TO CLEAN Pull the fridge away from the wall and run a handheld vacuum over the coils, exhaust fans and air vents.

HOW OFTEN Once a year.

PRO TIP
Anything cloth should
wind up in the laundry.

RANGE HOOD

HOW TO CLEAN Wipe the outside
and then the underside of the
hood with a soapy soft cloth. Next,
remove the filter and let it soak
in hot, soapy water for about
20 minutes. Let it dry completely
before putting it back. (The same
trick also works wonders on stove
burner grates.)

HOW OFTEN Once a month.
Vacuum the hood's exhaust
fans once a year.

ELECTRONICS

SCREENS

HOW TO CLEAN These surfaces
are delicate, so use a microfiber
cloth to prevent scratching—and
don't apply too much pressure. A
dry cloth is all you should need,
but to remove stubborn stains,
use a mild soap highly diluted
with water. Put the solution on
the cloth instead of directly on
the screen, then wipe. Wiping
in circles creates streaks, so be
sure to use straight strokes, either
vertical or horizontal. Don't use
glass or window cleaner for this
task—such cleaners often contain
acetone or ammonia, which can
discolor screens.

HOW OFTEN Once a week.

KEYBOARD

HOW TO CLEAN Turn the keyboard
upside down and gently shake it
to dislodge any dust and crumbs.
Flip it back over and sanitize with
a disinfecting wipe. It pays to run
one of these wipes over the mouse
(and your TV remote) as well.

HOW OFTEN Once a week.

EARBUDS

HOW TO CLEAN Wipe the plastic
part with a dry lint-free cloth and
scrub the mesh part with a dry
cotton swab. Never use alcohol
or disinfecting wipes on the mesh
part, but you can wipe it with a
slightly damp microfiber cloth if
it's really dirty. These tips also
work for the charging port in your
cellphone, although compressed
air is your best bet for cleaning
that out.

HOW OFTEN When you see gunk.

SURFACES

CABINET DOORS

HOW TO CLEAN Routine TLC helps
a home look as if a cleaning crew
just left. Wipe cabinet faces and
knobs with damp microfiber cloths.

HOW OFTEN Once a week. The
interiors, only once a year.

BACKSPLASH

HOW TO CLEAN Mix equal parts
baking soda and hydrogen
peroxide with a splash of
degreasing dish soap. This
combination breaks down the
greasy buildup common in kitchen
areas (but the solution loses its
effectiveness if it sits around too
long, so don't make too big a
batch). Apply the paste with a
microfiber cloth; rinse it off with
another damp microfiber cloth.

HOW OFTEN Once a month.

LAMPSHADES

HOW TO CLEAN Do a quick pass over each lampshade with a handheld vacuum—just not while the lightbulb is on. Use the same attachment you would on other upholstered surfaces. (Speaking of this, you'd be surprised by how much schmutz is hiding under your couch cushions, so vacuum there too.)

HOW OFTEN Once or twice a year.

CURTAINS

HOW TO CLEAN Toss them right into the washing machine, along with other seldom-washed fabric pieces such as oven mitts and reusable grocery bags. As for shower curtains, wash them every few months or so, and remember to replace the plastic interior liners when you do.

HOW OFTEN Once a year.

WINDOW SCREENS

HOW TO CLEAN Remove screens from windows; use an all-purpose cleaner mixed with warm water and apply it with a soft brush to loosen any debris. Then rinse with a hose. This is a job best done outdoors.

HOW OFTEN Once a year.

FIREPLACE WINDOW

HOW TO CLEAN Make sure the glass is cool, then use a commercial cleaner specially formulated for fireplace glass. It may be tempting to use a vacuum to remove the soot buildup, but don't—it could ruin the vacuum.

HOW OFTEN Once a year.

GARAGE DOOR TRACKS

HOW TO CLEAN Run a cloth along them to ensure that the door can roll up and down smoothly.

HOW OFTEN Once a year.

MATTRESS

HOW TO CLEAN Sprinkle the mattress with baking soda, let it sit about 20 minutes, then vacuum the entire surface. (Baking soda absorbs moisture and neutralizes odors.) At the same time, throw the duvet cover, mattress pad and bed skirt into the washing machine.

HOW OFTEN Once a month.

TRASH CANS AND RECYCLING BINS

HOW TO CLEAN Scrub them—inside and out—with an all-purpose cleaner.

HOW OFTEN Once a month.

CLEANING TOOLS

HOW TO CLEAN Finish any job by washing your cloths, sanitizing your sponges, wiping your vacuum and cleaning the vacuum filter.

HOW OFTEN Any time you clean.

PRO TIP
Sanitize your sponges. Dirty tools don't clean.

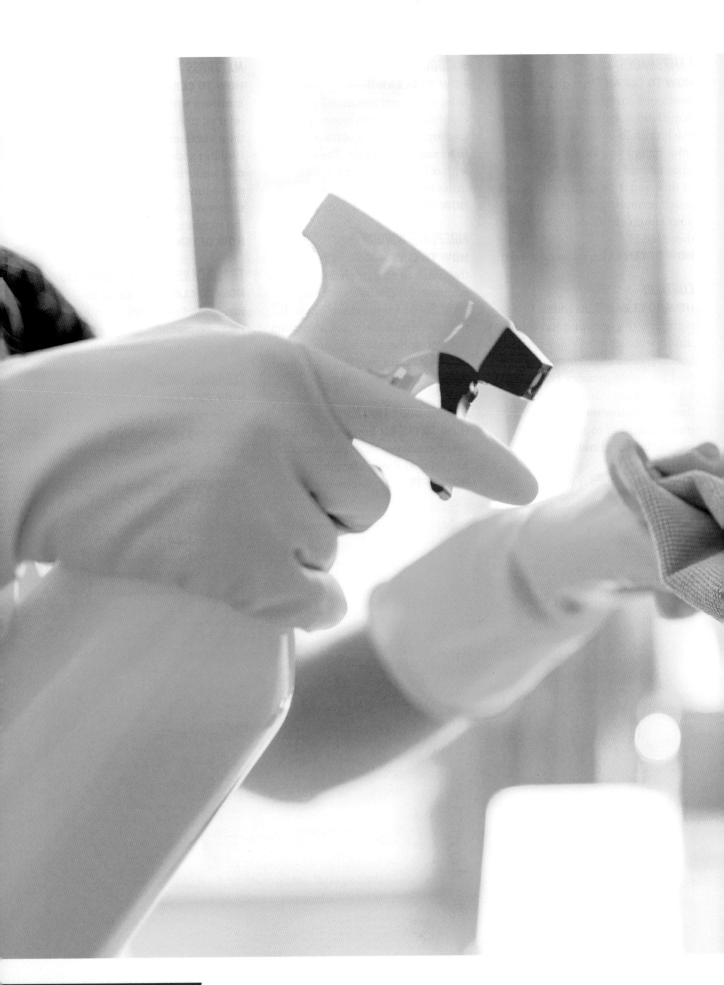

ZERO IN ON THE DETAILS

THESE HOME IMPROVEMENTS HAVE A HUGE PAYOFF

You probably don't think of cleaning as a home improvement, but a thorough cleaning really is a powerful way to improve your home. Things that look old, worn and in need of replacement sometimes just need a good scrubbing! Some of us at *Family Handyman* have learned that lesson recently.

DECLUTTER FIRST

Cleaning your house is far easier once you remove clutter, and that's something most of us need to do anyway. Don't just move everything to the garage. Go through items and decide what you want to donate, sell, throw away or store.

- **DONATE IT.** Donating your goods is a nice way to get rid of usable items without the hassles of selling them. This is perfect if you have a lot of stuff and a time constraint.

- **SELL IT.** If you have time and you'd like to make a little extra cash, sell unwanted things online. Keep in mind that you'll have to check messages and be available for people coming over to buy your stuff. It can be a big hassle.

- **PUT IT ON THE CURB.** Setting free stuff on the curb is probably the quickest and easiest way to get rid of it. People will take anything that's free! The drawback is that if you itemize deductions on your tax returns, you won't get a receipt to count it as a charitable donation. You can also list free items on *Craigslist.com*.

- **TRASH IT.** If you have a lot of junk, throwing it all in a dumpster or Bagster bag is an easy and gratifying experience. The cost for a small dumpster (about 10 cu. yds.) typically starts around $300.

- **STORE IT.** For the items you're keeping but not currently using, mobile storage containers are a great option. Have one dropped at your house, fill it up, and then the company will haul it off to a temporary storage facility. The cost varies depending on the container size, your time frame, and the location of your home and/or the storage site.

FOCUS ON THE BATHROOM

Cleaning the bathroom might take you more time than the rest of the house combined. But once it is done, your entire home will feel refreshed. A spotless bathroom can feel as good as a remodel, without all the time and expense of calling in pros.

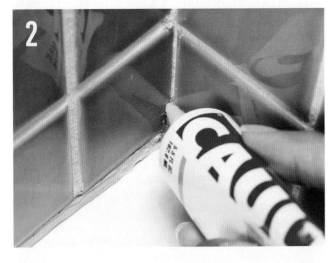

1 GLASS SHOWER DOORS

Built-up soap scum seems impossible to remove. Pick up polishing compound at a home center or an auto parts store, and use it with an auto buffer to polish off the offending scum. If you don't own a buffer, you can buy one for as little as $25 or borrow one from a gearhead friend. If possible, take the doors out to the garage to avoid messing up the bathroom.

2 CAULKING

Trying to clean caulk often isn't worth the effort. If it's covered with mold or mildew, just cut it out and recaulk.

3 EXHAUST FAN

Turn on the fan and blast out the dust with canned air. The fan will blow the dust outside. This works on the return air grilles of your central heating/cooling system too. Run the system so the return airflow will carry the dust to the filter. You'll find canned air at home centers, usually in the electrical supplies aisle.

4 RUST STAINS

To clean rust from toilets and other porcelain surfaces, add three parts water to one part rust remover (Acid Magic is one brand we like). Use a sprayer, brush or foam pad to apply the mixture to the rust stains, then watch them dissolve. Rinse with clear water. You can also use the remover at full strength for stubborn stains. Avoid getting the acid on metal parts because they can discolor. Acid Magic is available online and at hardware stores.

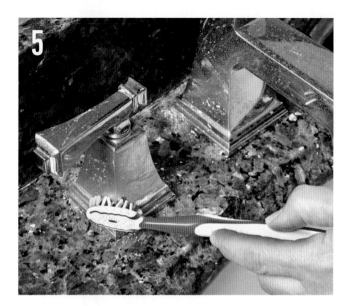

5

FAUCETS AND FIXTURES

Scrub faucets and fixtures with a calcium, lime and rust remover, such as CLR, and an old toothbrush. For an alternative method, see "Faucets and Showerheads" on p. 222.

6

TILE GROUT

Try a bleach pen to transform your grout from grungy to great. This method is tedious, but the payoff is crisp, clean grout lines. Use the pen to "draw" bleach across the grout lines. The pen allows you to target the grout without getting bleach all over the tile. Wait 10 minutes and then rinse.

7

TILE

Magic Eraser sponges (or other brands) make short work of cleaning tile. Just dampen the sponge and scrub off the offending mess. These sponges are especially useful for removing ground-in dirt from porous floor tile and cleaning those pesky nonslip strips in the bottom of your tub.

DIG INTO SPECIFIC JOBS

Some cleaning tasks are frequently overlooked. Pay attention to the following features to leave your home sparkling. For techniques and timelines, see "Clean the Things You Never Do (But Should)" on p. 220.

- Ceiling fan blades
- Light fixtures
- Baseboards/trim/ door frames
- Handrails
- Furniture feet
- Fingerprinted windows
- Furnace exterior
- Water heater exterior
- Exposed pipes and ductwork
- Washer and dryer
- Inside cabinets and drawers
- Walls and ceilings
- Curtains
- Under appliances
- Trash cans
- Doorknobs
- Dishwasher
- Throw pillows

WINDOWS

Your windows present the view as well as let in natural light. You can hire a window cleaning service, but if you'd like to do it yourself, go to *familyhandyman.com* and search for "how to clean windows."

CARPET

If the carpet needs a cleaning, machines are available to rent from many grocery or hardware stores. This route is more affordable than hiring a service. If there is hardwood underneath, consider removing the carpet.

CLEANING SERVICES

You could hire a pro to do a deep cleaning for about $500 for a 1,400-sq.-ft. home. But if you DIY the job, a weekend's worth of work could save you that money and allow you to invest it elsewhere in your home.

INVESTING IN REPLACEMENTS

Some things just aren't worth the effort to clean. You may save time and money and get better results by simply replacing the following items with new:

- Shower curtain liners
- Switch plates
- Mini blinds
- Showerheads

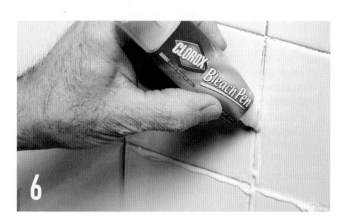

6

7

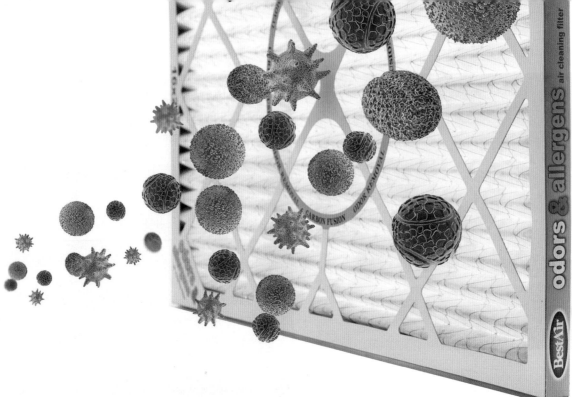

FIGHT ALLERGIES WITH FURNACE FILTERS

LEARN THE INS AND OUTS OF FILTER MAINTENANCE

The claims made by furnace filter manufacturers are true: A high-efficiency filter can provide some relief from allergies. By trapping smaller airborne particles, these filters make the air in your home cleaner and less irritating to allergy sufferers. But before you install a high-efficiency filter, there are a few things worth knowing:

- **HIGH-EFFICIENCY MEANS HIGHER COST.** If you're currently spending as little as $30 per year on cheapie filters, prepare for sticker shock. You can easily spend around $100 per year on high-efficiency filters.

- **THE NUMBERS ON THE LABELS MEAN SOMETHING.** Furnace filters are labeled with a numerical efficiency rating. A higher number indicates higher efficiency, which simply means the filter traps smaller particles. When it comes to furnace filters, "efficiency" does not mean energy savings.

- **THE RATINGS ARE TRICKY.** MERV is the most common rating system. But some filters carry MPR or FPR ratings (see "How Furnace Filters Are Rated"). For a MERV to FPR conversion chart, see p. 32. There are also several charts online to help

HOW FURNACE FILTERS ARE RATED

Many filter manufacturers follow the Minimum Efficiency Reporting Value (MERV) rating system established by the American Society of Heating, Refrigerating and Air-Conditioning Engineers (ASHRAE). The MERV number is an indication of the filter's effectiveness at trapping particles. A MERV 1 filter traps dust bunnies but allows most dust to pass right through, while a MERV 16 traps bacteria and particles as small as 0.3 to 1.0 micron and is used mostly in operating rooms. If you don't have allergies, a MERV 7 furnace filter will work just fine in your home. And if you do have family members with allergies, go up to a filter with a MERV 11 rating.

However, some filter manufacturers and retailers have developed proprietary rating systems such as Microparticle Performance Rating (MPR) or Filter Performance Rating (FPR). Before you buy a filter based on an MPR or FPR rating, look for a MERV to FPR/MPR chart online (*nordicpure.com/information/what-is-a-merv/* is one site) or contact your furnace service company for a filter recommendation based on your particular furnace.

PREVENT FURNACE DAMAGE WITH A FILTER MONITOR

A filter that's plugged with particles may not look dirty. And the manufacturers' life-span estimates are nearly worthless. So how can you tell when a filter is dirty enough to stress your heating/cooling system? You can't unless you install a filter monitor. They're available in two versions:

■ **MECHANICAL FILTER MONITORS** are inexpensive and take about five minutes to install even if you're a beginning DIYer. They're available online for about $20 (search for "furnace filter monitor"). The downside is that it relies on your memory. If you forget to check it, you won't know when the filter is clogged.

■ **ELECTRONIC FILTER MONITORS** let you know when the filter needs replacing. The unit shown (the FILTERSCAN WiFi, about $130 online), for example, connects to your home's Wi-Fi and sends an alert to your smartphone. Installation is as simple as driving a few screws. Just find a location on your return air duct and predrill holes **(Photo 1)**. Then mount the unit **(Photo 2)** and follow the calibration and Wi-Fi setup instructions.

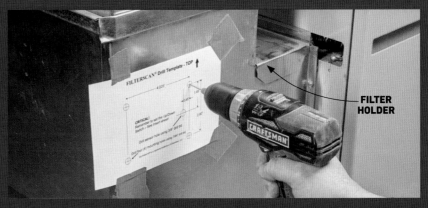

1 DRILL MOUNTING HOLES

Tape the template to the return air duct between the filter holder and the furnace. Stay at least 6 in. away from the filter holder. Then drill screw holes in the duct.

FILTER HOLDER

2 MOUNT AND CALIBRATE THE MONITOR

Screw the monitor to the duct and install the batteries. Turn off the furnace and press the calibrate button. Then install a new filter, turn on the furnace, raise the thermostat setting and wait until the blower kicks in. Press the calibrate button again. Then install the cover.

---

you convert the numbers. Just search for "MERV vs. MPR vs. FPR."

■ **HIGHER ISN'T ALWAYS BETTER.** If no one in your home suffers from allergies, there's no reason to go higher than MERV 7. For allergies, MERV 11 is your best choice because higher-rated filters cost more but don't provide much extra relief.

■ **DON'T TRUST THE LIFE-SPAN CLAIMS.** Filters carry claims such as "lasts up to 90 days." But the life span of a filter depends on how clean the air is in your home and how much your heating/cooling system runs. No manufacturer can possibly know that information.

■ **FILTERS ARE NOT ENOUGH.** Furnace filters help, but for allergy sufferers, reducing dust in your home is even more important. That mostly

consists of frequent vacuuming with high-quality vacuums and filters and/or eliminating carpeting and rugs as much as possible. For more guidance on dust control, see "Create a Dust-Free Home" on p. 232.

■ **"EFFICIENCY" CAN WRECK YOUR FURNACE.** High-efficiency filters have smaller pores, which can reduce airflow when the filters are new and even more as they clog. That can make the furnace overheat, causing it to shut down or burn out the expensive blower motor. The repair bills can easily run up to hundreds of dollars, not to mention the increased energy costs to run the stressed blower motor. (To protect your system, see "Prevent Furnace Damage with a Filter Monitor.")

CREATE A DUST-FREE HOME

DUST BUNNIES WON'T STAND A CHANCE AFTER YOU TAKE THESE 10 STEPS

Studies show that the average six-room home in the United States collects 40 lbs. of dust each year. Sounds impressively awful, right? But don't confuse all that dust with dirt and bad housekeeping. It's actually a combination of dead skin, animal fur, dander, decomposing insects, dust mites, food debris, lint, fabric fibers, drywall particles, tracked-in soil, soot and pollen. The dust also contains hazardous chemicals that migrate from home products and enter through open doors and windows or on the soles of your shoes. Household dust can trigger allergy and asthma symptoms. While it's impossible to get rid of dust completely, here are our top tips for keeping dust at a minimum so you and your family stay healthier.

1 CLEAN WITH MICROFIBER PRODUCTS

Microfiber products attract and hold dust with an electrostatic charge, unlike dry rags and feather dusters, which just spread dust around. Machine-washable microfiber products can save you money over disposable brands because you can use them over and over. Just make sure to let them air dry (so they'll stay soft), and don't use bleach or fabric softener, which degrades the fibers and reduces their ability to attract and hold dust.

Microfiber dusting tools for blinds, ceiling fans, floors and general cleaning are available online and at many stores. Buy your microfiber cloths in the automotive section. "Cleaning" and "detailing" towels are the same as "dusting" cloths, and they're often a lot cheaper.

2 BAG AND BOX IT

Stray fibers from clothes, bedding and pillows are a major source of dust. The solution is to store these things in bags and clear plastic containers. You can use space-saving vacuum-seal bags, garment bags or even large garbage bags to help cut down on dust from clothes and fabrics. Clear plastic containers will lock fibers in and lock dust out, and let you see what's inside. And because seasonal clothes shed fibers year-round, store your winter coats inside garment bags to help contain fibers and keep the coats themselves from becoming coated with dust.

3 UPGRADE YOUR FURNACE FILTER

Your home's forced-air heating or cooling system helps to control dust by filtering the air. A standard cheap fiberglass filter protects your furnace from large dust particles and provides maximum airflow, but it does little to reduce household dust. More expensive pleated filters usually provide a good balance between cost and filtration efficiency. These filters trap 80% to 95% of particles 5 microns and larger.

But if you have family members with allergies, consider spending more on high-efficiency filters that capture 99% of airborne particles as small as 0.3 microns (this includes bacteria and viruses, fumes and pollen). Be aware that you'll have to run your furnace fan full time to get the maximum benefit from a high-efficiency filter, and you'll have to change the filter frequently to prevent damage to your furnace from the reduced airflow.

If you go the high-efficiency route, install a filter monitor such as FILTERSCAN (about $130), which automatically alerts you when your furnace filter needs changing, or the GeneralAire G99 Filter Gage (about $25), which requires you to manually check it. For more information, see "Prevent Furnace Damage with a Filter Monitor" on p. 231.

PLEATED FILTERS TRAP MORE AIRBORNE PARTICLES THAN FIBERGLASS FILTERS

4 CLEAN THE AIR WHILE YOU CLEAN THE HOUSE

Your vacuum's agitator brush and exhaust whip up dust that eventually settles on the surfaces you've just cleaned. Filter out some of that dust before it settles by switching your thermostat to "fan on." This turns on the blower inside your furnace and filters the air even while the system isn't heating or cooling. Leave the blower on for about 15 minutes after you're done cleaning. But don't forget to switch it back to "auto." Most blowers aren't designed to run constantly.

DAMP TOWEL

5

6

5 DUST WITH YOUR DRYER

Blankets, pillows, slipcovers, drapes and other textiles not only trap household dust but create it as they shed and disintegrate. Curtains and drapes in particular get very dusty because they absorb moisture and dirt from the outside and act as a landing pad for dust from ceiling fans and air vents. The best idea is to buy machine-washable items and launder them twice a year (OK, at least once). For non-machine-washable textiles, throw them in the dryer on the air-fluff setting (no heat) for 20 minutes with a damp towel. The damp towel will attract pet hair, and the tumbling movement and airflow will remove the smaller particles for you.

6 DITCH YOUR CARPETING

In most homes, carpet is by far the biggest dust reservoir. It is a huge source of fibers and absorbs dust like a giant sponge. Even the padding underneath holds dust, which goes airborne with each footstep. Although ripping out your wall-to-wall carpet may sound radical, it's the best thing you can do if you suffer from serious allergies. Replace carpeting with hard flooring like laminate, wood or tile, and wet mop it regularly (with a microfiber cloth) instead of sweeping. Sweeping is more likely to stir up dust than to remove it.

7 MAKE THE MOST OF YOUR VACUUMING

The right vacuuming technique, combined with the right filters, bags and machine, has a significant impact on how much dust remains in both your carpeting and your house. Keep the following tips in mind:

- Vacuum entrance areas and high-traffic areas twice a week and the rest of the carpeting and large area rugs at least weekly.
- Make numerous slow passes over the same area in all directions (fast passes stir up more dust than they suck up).
- Take smaller rugs outside for a vigorous shaking every week, and take large area rugs outside several times a year and beat them with a broom or tennis racket.
- Use certified True High-Efficiency Particulate Air (HEPA) filters to remove invisible particles and allergens. Look for the word "True" on the label; otherwise you're wasting your money.
- If you have allergies, upgrade to a sealed-body bagged vacuum with an airtight sealed filtration system that works together with a True HEPA filter. This means all the exhaust will exit through the HEPA filter instead of leaking back into your house through the machine's housing. Sealed-body vacuums have rubber seals or gaskets around the lid and filter, and they will last 10 to 20 years. Brands include Riccar, Miele and Sanitaire. You can get a good bagged vacuum for $350 to $600.
- Buy high-quality vacuum bags. Inexpensive 2- or 3-ply paper bags leak more dust. Higher-quality cotton-lined paper bags are better, and top-quality synthetic cotton HEPA bags are the best. Bag capacity matters too. Higher-capacity bags capture more, smaller particles that would have otherwise clogged the filter.
- Clean all your bagless vacuum filters regularly and replace them every three months.
- Turn off the agitator brush on hard flooring so you're not blowing dust into the air.
- Maintain your vacuum: Empty the canister frequently (always outside), and change bags and belts when needed. Keep the agitator brush free of hair and other material. Check the vacuum for cracks and loose hinges, and get it serviced every so often to keep it running smoothly.

8 PURIFY THE AIR

Here are four things you can do to cleanse the dusty air in your home:

■ Place air purifiers in your most-used rooms to help suck up dust before it settles. Choose units with True HEPA filters (about $50 to $200 or more) rather than ionic cleaners that release ozone, a respiratory irritant. See purifier reviews at *cadr.org*.

■ Add a plant to every room. Plants naturally absorb common indoor pollutants such as benzene and formaldehyde. NASA studies have shown that many plants, including aloes, palms and ferns, can absorb as much as 80% of the formaldehyde in a room in 24 hours.

■ Keep the humidity in your house between 40% and 50% to help lower static electricity, which can cause dust to stick to surfaces and make them harder to clean. Both a humidifier (cleaned regularly) and leafy indoor plants will increase humidity levels. Just don't increase the level to more than 50%. This will promote the growth of mold, which is far more dangerous than dust. You can monitor humidity levels in your home with a cheap hydrometer from a gardening store.

■ Keep your windows closed on windy days. Dust enters through doors and windows in the form of pollen, mold spores and airborne pollutants.

9 REDUCE REMODELING DUST

Remodeling dust goes everywhere air flows, so the key to stopping this dust is stopping airflow. Create an airtight plastic dust barrier curtain, and completely seal the top and sides with tape. If you can't seal the bottom edge with tape, lay a board across it. Light plastic (1 mil or so) is fine for most jobs. If you need to pass through the dust barrier, use heavier 4- or 6-mil plastic and add an adhesive-backed zipper.

Also make sure to seal both supply and return air ducts with tape and plastic. That way you'll avoid plugging your furnace filter or coating every room in the house with a blanket of fine dust when the blower turns on. Note: Turn off the heating/cooling system while the ducts are covered. Operating the system with restricted airflow can damage it.

10 BAN SHOES INSIDE (BUT OFFER SLIPPERS)

More than half of household dust enters your home through windows, doors and vents, and on the soles of your shoes. Think about where you walk all day long (restrooms, city streets, construction sites, etc.) and all the bacteria and debris your shoes collect. Do you really want to track that inside? An EPA study of homes where a doormat was added at the entrance and shoes were banned indoors showed a 60% reduction of lead dust and other contaminants in the home, as well as a significant reduction of allergens and bacteria.

Your first line of defense should be a coarse-fiber heavy-duty doormat placed outside exterior doors. Inside, have everyone remove shoes at the door. Keep a bench, a shoe rack and a basket of cheap slippers available so no one has to walk around in their stocking feet on chilly floors.

8

EASY-RELEASE MASKING TAPE

STICK-ON ZIPPER

6-MIL PLASTIC

9

PRESSURE-WASH YOUR DRIVEWAY

//

USE THESE HANDY TIPS TO MAKE OLD CONCRETE LOOK NEW

With all the tools, nozzles, psi ratings and equipment, pressure-washing can be intimidating. But it was easier than we thought it would be. With advice from an expert and a little experimenting, we were able to make a driveway look like new in an afternoon. So whether you want to extend its life or add a little curb appeal, here are some tips to get your driveway clean in no time.

1 TIME IT RIGHT

Pressure washers use a lot of water. If your water is supplied by a well, it's best to tackle this job when other water use is light. You don't want to deplete your well on laundry day or when you have a house full of guests. And if you're in a drought, you may want to postpone for a few months.

CAUTION: WEAR SAFETY GEAR

Pressure washers are loud, the water and other debris can splash back in your face, and you'll be stepping around slick, soapy water. Always wear safety glasses, hearing protection and closed-toe shoes with good traction. A powerful pressure washer can actually cut skin. Use it with caution, and keep it away from children.

2 TARP YOUR PLANTS

Concrete detergent can harm plants; before you begin pressure-washing, cover them with tarps. We used canvas dropcloths, but they can be expensive. For a cheap, lightweight option, use a roll of painter's plastic. Remove the tarps as soon as possible to avoid overheating the plants.

3 CHOOSE THE RIGHT NOZZLE

Nozzles are calibrated in degrees—the lower the number, the narrower and more powerful the stream. We experimented with various nozzles and settled on three: For dousing concrete with detergent, a 65-degree worked well. For actual cleaning, a 25-degree was fastest. For tough areas, we used a 15-degree. Pick up a 5-in-1 dial nozzle (about $40 at home centers) to make changes quick and easy.

4 GO BIGGER TO GO FASTER

The greater the pressure washer's psi rating, the faster the cleaning job. We tested three pressure washers: 1,600, 2,300 and 3,100 psi. There's no doubt that electric pressure washers from 1,300 to 2,300 psi can wash a concrete driveway, but it'll take longer. If you have a large driveway with lots of stains, you'll want more power to do the job faster. We chose the 3,100-psi gas pressure washer and cut the job time in half.

5 BLOW AWAY DEBRIS

Moving piles of debris with a pressure washer is a waste of time and water. Instead, use a leaf blower to clear away smaller debris such as leaves, rocks, sticks and mulch. You can use a broom, but a blower is faster and easier. Don't rush this step, and clear away as much as possible.

6 PURGE THE HOSE

Once you've connected the garden hose from the spigot to the pressure washer, don't be too eager to turn on the pressure washer. Instead, squeeze the trigger for roughly 30 seconds until a nice, steady stream comes out. This releases the air from the hose and preps the machine for a strong blast.

7 EXPERIMENT ON A LESS VISIBLE SPOT

If you hold the nozzle too close to the driveway, the pressure can etch the concrete surface. The distance depends on the power of your pressure washer and the nozzle you're using. Experiment on an inconspicuous spot and see how close you can get without damaging the concrete.

2

3

5-IN-1 DIAL NOZZLE

4

8 WASH OTHER SURFACES FIRST

Plan ahead; work from top to bottom. If your roof, siding and retaining walls need to be washed, do them first. Otherwise, dirty water will run off the surfaces and ruin your clean driveway.

9 USE A DETERGENT

Concrete detergent is incredibly effective. We tried pressure-washing without it, and the result didn't come close. It helps remove stubborn oil, paint and dirt stains. We used Zep Driveway & Concrete Pressure Wash detergent, but many great options are available. Newer pressure washers often include a soap tank to apply the detergent. Wave the wand back and forth roughly 8 in. off the surface to create a nice lather. Let it sit for 10 minutes; then wash. Don't pour bleach or other chemicals into your pressure washer soap tank.

10 SPOT-TREAT STAINS

Before you clean the entire surface, spot-treat the oil stains. We saturated these stains with diluted concrete detergent solution from a spray bottle. Let the soap sit for 10 minutes, then rinse with the pressure washer. Some stains are tough to remove—paint stains clean up quickly, but oil and rust stains take longer. If your stain isn't disappearing, treat it a few more times with a less diluted solution.

11 START AT THE TOP

Start at the high end of your driveway and work your way down. You don't want dirty water running over the places just cleaned. Also, be sure to park the pressure washer near the high spot so you're dragging the hose behind you, rather than constantly kicking it out of your way.

12 WORK IN SMALL SECTIONS

If you spray your entire driveway with soap all at once, it'll settle and dry before you can wash it off, which could leave white stains and streaks. Instead, soap and wash in 10 x 10-ft. sections. On the driveway we cleaned, we found the concrete joints to be a natural guide.

13 EXTEND YOUR REACH

Pressure washers are no fun to lug around. Do yourself a favor and buy a pressure washer extension hose. Hoses come in 25-ft. and 50-ft. lengths (about $40 to $75). We attached a 50-ft. hose to the 25-ft. hose that came with the machine. Be sure the coupler you choose is compatible with your equipment.

14 MOVE TOWARD THE EDGES

Whether you're applying the soap or washing, start at the center of the driveway and work your way toward the edge. If you're using a nozzle, sweep the water back and forth.

15 GET A SURFACE CLEANER

It takes a lot of time and effort to clean a driveway with a nozzle. Cut both in half by using a pressure washer surface cleaner. Surface cleaners are affordable, ranging from about $20 to $90. The one we used cost about $90 online and was worth every penny. As you use it, pull it from side to side rather than pushing it. Also, hold the wand upright to avoid putting pressure on your back.

16 RINSE OFF YOUR PLANTS

Even with a tarp, soap can still find its way onto your plants. The plants also can absorb the soapy runoff at the roots. When you're finished

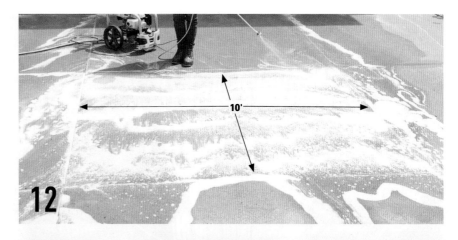

pressure washing, rinse the plants around your driveway with a garden hose.

17 WASH EDGES WITH A NOZZLE

The surface cleaner doesn't clean the edges along retaining walls, posts or other structures, so you have to clean those with a nozzle. Use a 25-degree nozzle for deep

cleaning and a 40-degree nozzle for rinsing away standing water.

18 PROTECT YOUR DRIVEWAY WITH A SEALANT

After you've cleaned the driveway, consider sealing it. A good sealer will protect your driveway, help it last longer and make future cleaning easier. Be sure it is dry before you begin.

PRO TIP
Sometimes you can locate pest passageways from indoors. On a sunny day, light peeking into a dark basement, garage or attic reveals gaps and cracks. A heavy concentration of cobwebs indoors can also indicate an entry point.

CRITTER-PROOF YOUR HOME

SHORE UP YOUR LINES OF DEFENSE AGAINST UNWANTED GUESTS

If mice, ants, spiders or other pests are getting into your home and claiming squatters' rights, it's time to evict them. Like any other guest, pests will visit only if you let them in. Once inside, they'll stay only if you make them comfortable. This article details three pest-fighting strategies. First we'll show you how to close the entryways through which the critters come in. Then we'll help you eliminate the moisture that sustains the pests as well as the clutter that provides their cozy habitat.

ANTS: Tree branches that touch the house become a "bug bridge" to your home. Ants will nest in clogged gutters.

BATS AND SQUIRRELS: Gaps along roof vents, dormers and adjoining rooflines become easy entrance points into your cozy attic.

COCKROACHES: Cardboard box clutter is the perfect habitat for a cockroach colony.

BEETLES: Loose sliding doors, windows and thresholds provide bugs an easy entrance.

MICE: Tiny holes in your home's exterior, such as gaps around utility lines and along foundations, offer rodents a thoroughfare into your home.

MOISTURE BUGS: Poorly directed downspouts, shallow slopes and thatchy lawns make basements moist for spiders, centipedes and other bugs to thrive.

FIRST LINE OF DEFENSE: ELIMINATE PEST ENTRANCES

Stop mice, squirrels, bats, beetles, ants and flies

Although your walls may appear solid, many walls are full of tiny pest passageways. Small insects can sneak through the tiniest cracks, so you may not be able to make your home absolutely bug-proof. But you can seal most gaps, especially the larger ones that let in mice and larger insects.

FIND THE PASSAGES THAT LET PESTS IN

Put on some old clothes—you'll have to get on the ground, slink behind bushes and even crawl under your deck to examine your home's exterior. Take a flashlight and a mirror along. If mice are your main concern, also bring a pencil. If you can slide the pencil into a crack, it's large enough for a young mouse to squeeze through. Take your time and examine every square foot of your home. Inspect these key areas:

WALL PENETRATIONS Search for gaps around anything that passes through your walls, such as gas, plumbing and A/C lines; phone and TV cables; and exhaust vents.

SIDING Gaps and holes in siding and around trim are usually obvious. Also look under the siding where it meets the foundation **(Photo 1)**. Rot, foundation shifting and sloppy building practices can leave openings there.

DOORS AND WINDOWS Look for torn screens and worn-out weatherstripping that might provide an entryway for bugs. If mice are a problem, make sure the rubber gasket under your garage door seals tightly to the floor (replace the gasket if it doesn't seal).

FOUNDATION Look for foundation settling cracks in masonry and make sure basement windows close and seal tightly **(Photo 2)**. If there's a crawl space under your house, all the floors above the space are potential entry zones. If the crawl space is accessible, put on safety glasses, crawl inside and inspect it with a flashlight.

FOLIAGE OR WOOD PILES Anything touching your house provides a freeway for bugs. Tree branches spell trouble even high above the ground. Ants use branches as bridges to your house. Trim them back.

DRYER VENTS AND EXHAUST FANS Be sure dampers open and close freely **(Photo 3)**. A damper that is stuck open leaves a welcoming entrance for pests.

SOFFITS AND ROOF Look for holes and gaps in soffits and fascia, especially those adjoining rooflines (they're favorite entries for squirrels, bats and wasps).

ROOF VENTS A missing or chewed-through screen on a roof vent lets squirrels or bats into your attic.

CHIMNEY CAPS Chimney caps prevent critters from making your fireplace's firebox a summer home.

GUTTERS Debris-filled gutters are a favorite nesting spot for corn ants.

1 SPOT OPENINGS WITH A MIRROR
Inspect the underside of your siding using a mirror. If you find a gap, mark the location with masking tape so you can seal it later.

2 SEAL EDGES WITH WEATHERSTRIPPING
Seal doors, windows and basement sashes with adhesive-backed weatherstripping. Clean the surface so the weatherstrip will adhere well.

3 MAKE SURE THE DAMPER ISN'T STUCK OPEN
Examine dryer vents to ensure the damper isn't stuck open or broken. Also check that the seal between the vent and the wall is tight.

4 CAULK GAPS SMALLER THAN ¼ INCH WIDE
Fill gaps between trim and siding with acrylic latex caulk. Keep a wet cloth handy to clean up any stray caulk. Smooth the bead with a wet finger.

5 INSERT COPPER MESH BEFORE ADDING FOAM
Stuff in a generous amount of copper mesh with a screwdriver, leaving about half an inch of space for expanding foam sealant. Seal gaps with foam.

EXPANDING FOAM

6 TRIM THE FOAM WITH A UTILITY KNIFE

Use a utility knife to trim the foam flush after allowing the foam to harden overnight. To trim off a thicker section of foam, use an old steak knife.

EXPANSION FOAM

7 FILL LARGE CAVITIES WITH FULL-EXPANSION FOAM

Pull nests from soffit gaps and then fill these openings with full-expansion foam. After the foam hardens, cut excess with a utility knife.

PLUG UP PASSAGES

Chances are you'll find several entry points in your walls, foundation or soffits. Fortunately, these gaps and cracks are easy to seal. For those smaller than ¼ in. wide, acrylic latex caulk (about $3 per tube) is a good filler because it's inexpensive, paintable and easy to apply **(Photo 4)**. But acrylic caulk won't last long in wider gaps. For gaps and cracks ¼ in. to ½ in. wide, use polyurethane caulk (less than $10 per tube). Polyurethane is gooey and more difficult to use than acrylic caulk, but you can smooth and paint it for a neat-looking job. Keep a rag and mineral spirits handy to clean up accidents.

Expanding foam (about $5 per can) is a fast, convenient filler for anything wider or for areas where appearance doesn't matter. It can fill gaps of any size but doesn't leave a smooth, neat-looking patch. Since rodents can gnaw right through foam, it's smart to stuff gaps with copper mesh before you add the foam **(Photo 5)**. Conventional steel wool can eventually rust away. If you have only a few gaps to fill, buy a box of Chore Boy copper scrubbing pads for about $4 from a hardware store or online. If you have holes galore, it may be cheaper to purchase a professional copper mesh product such as CopperBlocker, which is available online at *nixalite.com*. For most cracks, minimal expanding foam is the easiest to use (standard foam expands too much, flows out of the crack and makes a mess). A little overflow is no problem, since you can slice off the excess **(Photo 6)**. For large or hollow cavities, standard full-expansion foam is the best **(Photo 7)**.

MOUSETRAP TECHNIQUE

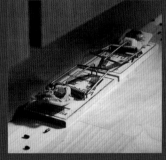

Snap-type mousetraps, when well placed, can be an effective way to rid your house of mice. Snap traps may seem cruel, but compared with a slow death from a glue trap or poisoned bait, they're a more humane way to exterminate mice. And because you toss the remains in the garbage, there are no dead mouse surprises to encounter later.

Common mistakes are poor placement of traps and using too few of them. Mice have poor vision and prefer to feel their way along walls. Place snap traps along walls in areas where you've seen the telltale brown pellets. For an average-size house, two dozen mousetraps would not be too many.

The best technique is to set two traps, parallel to the wall, with the triggers facing out. While mice can jump over one trap, they can't jump two. Favorite baits of professional exterminators are chocolate syrup and peanut butter.

Live traps are best used in pairs in the same manner as conventional mousetraps. Place them back-to-back with the open doors on each end.

SECOND LINE OF DEFENSE: DEPRIVE BUGS OF MOISTURE

Stop centipedes, millipedes, springtails, termites, spiders and silverfish

1 KEEP DAMP SOIL AND MULCH AWAY FROM WOOD

Rake moisture-wicking soil and mulch away from the window frames and low wood. Turn your mulch periodically to help keep dampness down, and keep bushes trimmed back as well.

2 REPLACE ROTTEN WOOD

If you suspect that an area is damp, use a screwdriver to probe the wood to determine if it's soft and moist. Eliminate the source of the moisture and replace rotten wood.

Insects and other small pests need to draw life-sustaining moisture from their surroundings, so they avoid dry places and are attracted to moist ones. If the soil around your house, foundation and walls is dry, it'll be less attractive to insects, spiders and centipedes.

There is no way to keep everything perfectly dry, of course, but you can help reduce moisture around your house. Here are common moisture sources and ways to reduce them:

DOWNSPOUTS AND GUTTERS Check that the downspouts are turned away from the house, and invest in a splash block or downspout extensions to disperse rainwater. Also, watch for major leaks in your gutter system that may be pouring water onto or near your foundation.

STANDING WATER If water is not absorbing into your lawn, your grass may have a buildup of thatch. The solution is to aerate your lawn to open up dense patches and better admit water.

POOR DRAINAGE Make sure that the soil is sloped away from the house at least 6 in. over 10 ft. This will reduce soil dampness near your foundation and keep your basement drier.

DAMP MULCH Mulch and soil trap moisture. Rake away from windowsills and other wood **(Photo 1)**.

HEAVY VEGETATION Plants growing against the house will keep siding damp. Trim back bushes and trees.

PLUMBING LEAKS Fix leaks such as a dripping hose bib. If your home is above a crawl space, look for leaks from any exposed plumbing under the house.

Moisture problems can come from inside the home too. A leaky sink trap, for example, can create a moist bug oasis under your kitchen cabinets. A poor seal around a bathtub can allow water into the surrounding floor and walls. Damp basements are a favorite home for spiders, centipedes, millipedes, silverfish and sowbugs.

SPIDER SOLUTION

You can virtually eliminate spiders in your basement by using a dehumidifier to maintain a 40% humidity level and by vigilantly sweeping down cobwebs whenever they appear. Keep the basement window-sills brushed clean too. In a matter of weeks, the spider population will die down significantly.

THIRD LINE OF DEFENSE: ELIMINATE CLUTTER
Stop mice and cockroaches

1 KEEP PET FOOD SECURE
Store pet food in a lidded metal trash can, since mice cannot climb the slick, vertical sides of the can. Sealed plastic containers are also a good option.

2 PLACE BOXES ON SHELVES FOR QUICK INSPECTION
Store items off the floor on wire rack shelving to prevent moisture from collecting underneath. Look for mouse droppings and other evidence of infestation with a flashlight and mirror.

SELF-ADHESIVE VINYL TILES

3 CLEAN AND ORGANIZE UNDER THE SINK
Tidy up under the kitchen sink. Store items in a caddy so you can easily clear out the cabinet for cleaning and inspection. Self-adhesive tiles provide an easy-to-clean surface.

Cluttered areas are a pest nirvana: They conceal initial infestations from homeowners and provide privacy and shelter for critters and pests to reproduce.

The best way to eliminate pest homes is to store items properly. Garages often harbor many clutter zones and are easily accessible to critters, so keep your area clean. Store birdseed and pet food in containers that mice and other rodents can't enter **(Photo 1)**. Avoid keeping old cardboard boxes in your garage, but if you must, break them down neatly, store them off the floor and inspect them regularly.

Neatness deters pests indoors too. Keep filled boxes and even plastic bins off the floor and on a wire rack or shelf. Be especially rigorous on concrete floors. Moisture forms between the concrete floor and the box bottom, forming an ideal environment for silverfish and other invaders. Plus, with boxes off the floor, you can quickly spot mouse droppings and other evidence of unwanted guests **(Photo 2)**.

A cabinet under the kitchen sink offers pests moisture, clutter and dark hiding places. Storing paper bags there is tempting, but it can create a cockroach condo. And once the cockroaches move in, they deposit their pheromone-laced fecal pellets,

attracting even more cockroaches to your kitchen. To make these infestations easy to spot, take everything out and stick self-adhesive vinyl tile squares to the cabinet floor. The tiles are cheap and easy to wipe clean. Then put all cleaning supplies in a tote so you can easily remove them to inspect and clean **(Photo 3)**.

If you find roaches, hire an exterminator. High-quality bait is expensive and effective only with proper placement. Spend just a bit more to hire a pro who will guarantee the job and know what to look for.

PREVENT A CALL TO EMERGENCY SERVICES

DANGEROUS CROSSCUT

BLADE IS TOO HIGH

AVOID COMMON TOOL INJURIES

STAY SAFE WHEN YOU USE DANGEROUS EQUIPMENT

Every year, emergency rooms report 120,000 visits for injuries caused by four tools: table saws, circular saws, nail guns and utility knives. Add to this the 200,000 ER visits for eye injuries—a large percentage of which occur during work around the house—and it's easy to see how we came up with this list of the most dangerous don'ts (bravely demonstrated by our crash test dummy, Nigel). When you start on your next project, keep these don'ts in mind so you don't become the next statistic.

1 DON'T CROSSCUT AGAINST THE TABLE SAW FENCE

If you cut a board to length using the fence as a guide, the board can get pinched between the blade and the fence and get thrown back into your body with lots of force. That nasty incident is called "kickback." Broken thumbs, cracked ribs, ruptured spleens and punctured eyes are only a few of the resultant injuries you can suffer. In addition to avoiding the dangerous technique shown, there are a few other ways to prevent kickback injuries:

- Don't cut anything that's longer than it is wide with the shorter side against the fence. If you want to crosscut with a table saw, use the miter gauge or a crosscutting sled.
- Avoid ripping wet, bowed or twisted lumber.
- Position your body to the right or left of the miter saw slots, not directly behind the blade.
- Don't let bystanders walk behind you when you're operating the saw.

2 DON'T REMOVE THE BLADE GUARD

Every table saw sold includes a blade guard, which has a splitter attached. The guard covers the blade, preventing you from accidentally touching it, and the splitter keeps wood from pinching on the blade and kicking back. Don't take them off! Sure, the guard may be a nuisance at times, but it's better to be inconvenienced than to lose one or more fingers. Even with a blade guard installed, you should keep your fingers away from the blade. Always use a push stick for rips less than 4 in. wide. If you're using your thumb to push the piece and the piece kicks back, you risk torn ligaments, tendons and broken bones. Push the cut piece past the blade, turn off the saw and wait for the blade to stop before retrieving the ripped piece. Don't reach near a spinning blade to remove a cutoff.

3 DON'T PUT YOUR HAND DIRECTLY BEHIND A CIRCULAR SAW

When you're using a circular saw, remember that if the blade binds, the saw can shoot backward a lot faster than you can move your hand out of the way. Anything in the blade's path, including fingers, hands, legs or feet, is in danger of getting cut. Avoid the risk by clamping your work and keeping both hands on the saw whenever possible. Also keep your body to the side of the saw rather than directly behind it.

4 DON'T PUT YOUR HANDS NEAR A NAIL GUN

Even if you're a nail gun expert, nails don't always go straight. Wood grain or knots can deflect the nail and cause it to shoot out the side of the board. If you're driving the nail at an angle to toenail a board, there's a good chance the nail could glance off and go shooting into space. If you must hold a board with your free hand, keep it well away from the nail gun muzzle. If you're reaching over a board to hold it down, move your hand out of the nail's path. Also avoid shooting into large knots that can deflect the nail. And, of course, always wear eye protection when you're using a nail gun.

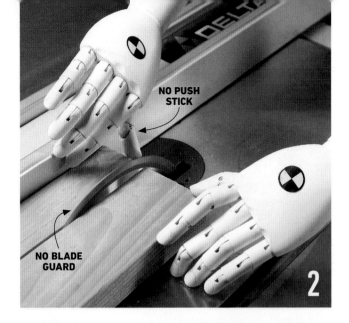

NO PUSH STICK

NO BLADE GUARD

2

DANGEROUS HAND POSITION

3

DANGEROUS HAND POSITION

4

FINGER ON TRIGGER

5

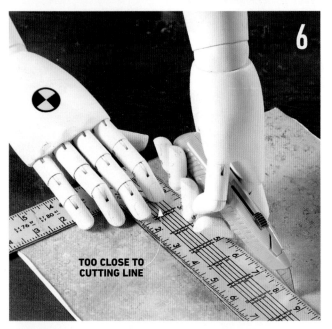

6

TOO CLOSE TO CUTTING LINE

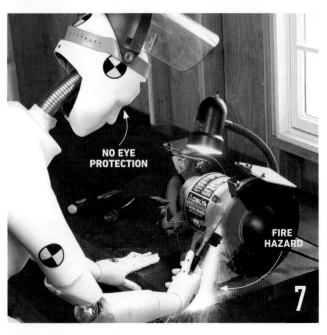

NO EYE PROTECTION

FIRE HAZARD

7

5 DON'T BE SLOPPY WITH NAIL GUNS

A tool powerful enough to shoot a 3-in.-long nail into wood can easily penetrate skin and bone. Just ask any carpenter—you're sure to hear a story about a nail that went through a finger or hand. Depending on the type, some nail guns can be set to "bump-trip." In this mode, the operator can simply hold down the trigger and bump the gun's nose against the surface to shoot a nail. This is great for speeding up jobs such as nailing down plywood sheathing, but it creates a risk if you hold the trigger while carrying the nail gun. Bump your leg, and you'll be heading to the hospital. In incidents where accidental contact caused an injury, more than 80% of the time the operator had a finger on the trigger.

There are two ways to avoid this. First, get out your owner's manual and see if you can set your nail gun to sequential mode. This requires you to push down the muzzle and then pull the trigger for each nail. Second, keep your hand off the trigger when you're carrying a nail gun, or better yet, unplug the hose. Then there's no chance of accidental firing.

6 DON'T GET CARELESS WITH A KNIFE

Utility knives account for a whopping 60,000 estimated emergency room visits a year. One slip is all it takes to put a deep cut in any body part that's in the way. While most cuts are superficial, permanent tendon and nerve damage is common. To avoid an injury, clamp materials whenever possible to avoid having to hand-hold them. If you do have to hold something while you're cutting, imagine a line at right angles to the cutting line and keep your hand behind it (on the dull side of the blade).

7 DON'T RISK YOUR EYES

It's hard to think of a good reason not to wear safety glasses, goggles or a face shield when you're working around the house. Wood chips, metal shards, bits of tile, household chemicals, paint, solvents and sticks are just a few of the many things that can injure eyes. It's important to choose the right eye protection for the task at hand. For general work around the house, wear ANSI-approved safety glasses or goggles. Look on the frame for the "Z87+" marking, which indicates that the glasses are rated for high impact. Buy several pairs of safety glasses and keep them in convenient locations so you'll always have them on hand. Wear a face shield for grinding operations—of the more than 200,000 emergency room visits a year for eye injuries, at least 10,000 of them involve grinders.

BE PREPARED FOR DISASTERS

//
HAVE PLANS AND TOOLS READY TO GO

When disaster strikes your home, you can text a friend, call a plumber or dial 911. But until help arrives, you're the one on the scene, the only one who can act fast. And what you do can make the difference between minor damage and major destruction. As usual, it all comes down to preparation and know-how. This article provides the know-how, and the prep work is quick and inexpensive. So read on—the payoff could be huge!

GET TO KNOW YOUR FIRE EXTINGUISHER
During a fire is not the time to learn

Household fire extinguishers are for small fires and have a short discharge time (10 seconds is typical), which means you can't learn as you go. Take a minute now to read the label. Check the

expiration date and the pressure gauge to be sure the extinguisher will work when you need it.

Luckily, basic fire extinguisher technique is not very complicated:

■ Stand a few feet from the fire, start blasting and move toward the fire. The instructions will tell you how far away to start.
■ Move the stream in a sweeping motion.
■ Aim at the base of the fire, not at the flames.

There are a couple other important things to know. First, extinguishers blast the area with chemicals and make a significant mess. For this reason, an extinguisher may not be the best tool for addressing every small fire. In the case of a stovetop grease fire, for example, it's usually best to smother the fire with a pot lid. Second, don't let your guard down too soon—any fire that seems to be out can reignite. Always keep an eye on the area where the fire was located for a few minutes afterward.

SEAL ROOF DAMAGE

With 30 bucks in materials, you're ready for almost anything

Minor roof damage can lead to major water damage inside your home. But if you keep a few simple materials on hand, you can seal most roof injuries in just a few minutes.

A section of flashing is the perfect patch for smaller holes, which are often caused by blown-down tree branches **(Photo 1)**. Don't forget to caulk around the hole. Special roof sealant is best, but any type of caulk is better than nothing.

For larger areas, a tarp is the best bandage. But before you spread a tarp, screw plywood over large holes in the roof. Left unsupported, a tarp will sag into a hole, fill with rainwater and possibly leak. If shingles have blown off but there are no holes in the roof, you can lay the tarp directly over the roof sheathing. Stretch the tarp so it lies smoothly over the roof and batten down the entire perimeter (except the ridge). Just a few inches of loose tarp will allow strong winds to drive in rain or rip the tarp to shreds. Use screws and any type of lumber you have on hand to secure the tarp. Whenever possible, extend the tarp over the roof ridge **(Photo 2)** so water won't flow down and under it. If there's no way to run the tarp over the ridge, slip sections of flashing under shingles and over the upper edge of the tarp. Then drive nails through both the flashing and the tarp.

CAUTION: ROOFS ARE DANGEROUS!

Emergency roof repairs often mean walking on a wet roof and wrestling with a tarp, which can catch the wind like a sail. We strongly recommend you wear a roof harness (a roofing safety kit is about $100 online).

A 9 x 12-ft. tarp (less than $15) is big enough to cover a large area but small enough for one person to manage. If you have a large roof, keep two or three of them on hand. A 14 x 10-ft. roll of aluminum flashing costs about $15.

1 PATCH A SMALL HOLE

Cover a small hole with metal flashing. Slide the flashing under the shingles above the hole, run a heavy bead of caulk around the hole and nail down the exposed corners of the flashing.

2 TARP LARGE AREAS

Even if the damage is near the lower end of the roof, extend the tarp over the ridge so water won't run under the tarp. Screw down boards to secure the tarp.

STOP SEWAGE BACKUP

During a flood, sewage can flow back into your house

Floodwater doesn't just fill streets and basements. It can also fill sewer or septic systems, causing sewage to backflow through drains and into homes. Sewage is a nasty, toxic soup—more damaging, dangerous and disgusting than ordinary floodwater. The lower the drain, the greater the risk—so homes with basements and homes in low-lying areas are the most vulnerable. To find out if this is a likely danger in your home, talk to your neighbors. If they've ever had sewage backflow during a flood, your house is probably at risk too. Don't wait to plan and prepare; at times home centers run out of backflow-stopping gear just before a flood is expected.

In some situations, blocking off individual drains is a good approach. In a basement with only a floor drain and a laundry tub, for example, you can stick a test plug in the tub drain and install a backwater valve (about $10 online) in the floor drain **(Photo 1)**. But other types of drains are more difficult: The best way to block a toilet drain, for example, is to remove the toilet and plug the pipe. The most reliable way to block a bath or kitchen sink is to remove the trap and cap the drain stub-out pipe. That's a lot of work.

So instead of fussing with individual drains, consider blocking the main drain line at the cleanout **(Photo 2)**. Most homes have a cleanout near the point where the main line exits the house. Unscrew the cleanout plug, insert a test plug and inflate it with a bicycle pump. This single solution protects your whole house but has three drawbacks: First, you have to do it immediately when flooding begins and the flow is weak. Strong backflow will make it impossible. Second, any water that seeps into your home (through basement walls, for example) can't flow out through floor drains. And third, since your entire drain system is blocked, you can't use toilets, sinks or tubs. To prevent accidental use, it's a good idea to shut off the water supply.

The ultimate solution is a whole-house backwater valve (not shown) installed in the main line. Prices start at about $50 online. Once installed, this valve will protect all your drains without any effort or inconvenience. Installation isn't tricky but usually requires breaking up the floor, which is a big, messy job.

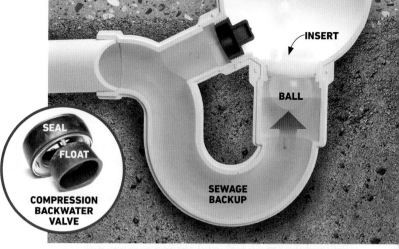

1 PROTECT FLOOR DRAINS WITH A BACKWATER VALVE

A backwater valve lets water flow into the drain but not out. To install the type shown above, drop the ball into the drain and screw in the threaded insert. When water rises, the ball seals against the insert. If you have a cast-iron floor drain, the threads inside are probably corroded, so choose a version with a rubber float and compression seal instead **(inset above)**.

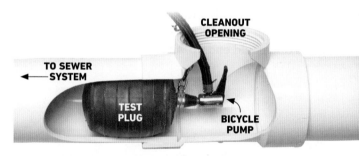

2 BLOCK THE MAIN LINE WITH A TEST PLUG

The fastest, easiest way to stop sewage backflow to all drains is to place an inflatable test plug in the main sewer line. Inflate the plug with a bicycle pump.

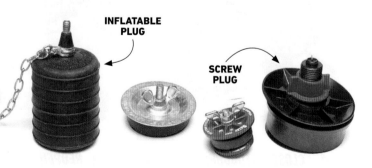

Test plugs are used when plumbing systems in new homes are pressure-tested. But the plugs can also be used to block drains and stop sewage backflow. Screw-type plugs cost less than $10. Inflatable plugs are more versatile and cost more ($20 to $40). Home centers carry some test plugs; shop online for the best selection.

TEST THE SHUTOFF
Don't wait for a disaster to see if it works

Your main shutoff valve is one of the most important disaster-stoppers in your home. When a pipe leaks or bursts, this valve lets you shut off water flow to your entire home. But your main valve may fail just when you need it. So take a few minutes now to make sure you can close it.

Ball valves rarely fail, and testing is easy. But if you have a gate valve, you might need a little patience and know-how. Turn the handle clockwise to close it. If you can't turn the handle, loosen the packing nut just a little **(Photo 1)**. A shot of lubricant or penetrating oil may also help. Then try again. Don't worry about cranking too hard. There's a small chance that you'll damage the valve, but a valve that won't close is useless anyway and needs to be replaced. For help with that project, search for "main valve" at *familyhandyman.com*.

Reopening a stubborn gate valve is more risky than closing it; you're more likely to break internal parts and could end up without running water. If the valve is stuck closed, tap it with a hammer **(Photo 2)**. When the valve opens a little, stop for a few minutes. That allows water pressure on both sides of the valve to equalize, instead of pressing against one side and locking the valve in place.

EMERGENCY SHUTOFF TIPS

■ If a toilet or faucet is leaking, try the shutoff valves below them first. If those valves won't close, head for the main valve.

■ If you're able to close your main valve most of the way but it's still allowing a trickle of water through, simply open the lowest faucet in your house. Water will trickle out of that faucet, but it won't flow to the higher pipes in the house.

■ If your home has a water meter, you have two valves—one on each side of the meter. If one won't close, try the other. Closing either will stop the flow.

■ If you have a hot water leak, you can stop the flow by turning off the valve at the water heater.

1 **CLOSE A STUBBORN GATE VALVE**
If the handle won't turn, loosen the packing nut. But be sure to hold the handle in position while you turn the nut. If the handle turns as you unscrew the nut, you risk breaking the valve.

STEM

PACKING NUT

2 **REOPEN A GATE VALVE**
If the valve is hard to open, tap the underside of the valve with a hammer as you turn it.

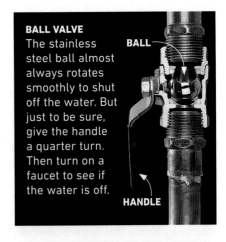

BALL VALVE
The stainless steel ball almost always rotates smoothly to shut off the water. But just to be sure, give the handle a quarter turn. Then turn on a faucet to see if the water is off.

BALL

HANDLE

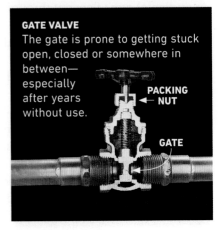

GATE VALVE
The gate is prone to getting stuck open, closed or somewhere in between—especially after years without use.

PACKING NUT

GATE

ACT WISELY IN EMERGENCIES

WHEN THINGS GO WRONG AT HOME, YOUR REACTION MATTERS

According to disaster experts, 9 out of 10 people either panic or freeze during an emergency; only one is able to jump into effective action. We have no doubt that *Family Handyman* readers are part of the 10% who deliver. To make sure you're ready for anything, here are steps you should take first to tackle a number of emergencies head-on.

KITCHEN FIRE

More than any other emergency, fire makes people panic and do dumb things. But armed with a few basic rules, you'll reduce the panic and respond effectively.

REACT FAST: For a toaster fire, unplug the cord and use an ABC (dry chemical) fire extinguisher, or pour baking soda into the toaster (and then get a new one). For a stovetop fire, turn off the burner and smother the flames by dousing them with baking soda or putting a lid on the pan.

OR DO NOTHING: If it's an oven fire, the most dangerous thing you can do is open the door. Just leave the oven door closed and turn off the heat to the oven. The fire will eventually smother itself.

BAD MOVE: Don't use water to put out a grease fire. It can splash burning grease and cause burns.

WORSE MOVE: Never carry a burning pan outside. A full-scale house fire can start if flaming grease spills and ignites something else.

TOP 5 CAUSES OF HOME FIRES

- Cooking fires
- Heating equipment
- Smoking
- Electrical (wiring, lamps, outlets, etc.)
- Children playing with lighters and matches

the lowest faucet in the house, which will let the water harmlessly drain out of the faucet instead of through the leaking pipe.

DON'T DELAY CLEANUP: The longer things stay wet, the more likely you'll have permanent damage. Delay can even lead to mold problems inside walls, which can cost thousands to eradicate. So before you run off to buy plumbing parts, clean up the mess. Pronto.

WILD ANIMAL INVASION

A squirrel or raccoon in the house may not seem like an emergency, but those critters can do a lot of damage quickly. If all else fails, you may have to call in a wildlife removal service or your town's animal control officer.

WHAT TO DO FIRST: Isolate the varmint by closing the doors to all other rooms in the house. Then open a window. Leave the room and shut the door. The animal will eventually find its way out the window.

WHAT NOT TO DO: Don't try to chase the invader out. It'll just panic and hide. If it crawls into a hidden spot and soils your house, has babies or dies, that's a whole set of different problems.

THE WORST THING TO DO: Don't let your dog or cat help with the animal's eviction. That could result in an expensive trip to the vet or a gory mess.

FLOODED BASEMENT

Your first impulse will be to wade in and rescue your stuff. But that water might be dangerous, so put on your boots and take these precautions.

DON'T GET FRIED: Any water in contact with electricity could be deadly. Even a shallow puddle could be electrified by a cord on the floor. Stay out of the water until you've turned off the power to your basement. If you can't reach the circuit breaker box, call an electrician or your utility to cut the power to your home.

DON'T GET SICK: If the flooding is due to flash floods or your belongings are leaching toxins, the floodwaters may contain toxic chemicals and will almost certainly breed dangerous bacteria. Protect cuts and open sores from floodwaters and wear plastic gloves when handling your possessions.

BURST PIPE

A gushing plumbing leak can dump several gallons per minute into your home. You have to act fast to stop the stream—and that is just the beginning.

STOP THE FLOW: Shutting off the main water valve is an obvious move. But there may still be a few gallons of water held in pipes above the leak. Turn on

BAT IN THE HOUSE

Bats cause a visceral reaction (like screaming and head covering) in most people. But keep in mind that a bat doesn't want to tangle with you (or your hair) any more than you want to tangle with it.

PLAN A: Open a window and then get out of the way. There's a good chance the bat will leave on its own.

PLAN B: If the bat lands before it can exit, look for it in places it can hang, such as behind drapes or upholstered furniture. When you find the bat, throw a thick towel over it and carry it outside (just to warn you, the bat will complain loudly, but don't drop it!). Shake out the towel so the bat can fly away.

WORST MOVE: Don't approach a bat with bare hands. Bats can carry rabies. Wear thick gloves to avoid bites.

DEAD FURNACE

As the temperature drops inside your house, your first worry may be the budget-busting cost of an after-hours service call. But there are several simple things you can troubleshoot before you pick up the phone and break out your checkbook.

IS THE FILTER FILTHY? A clogged filter can cause the furnace to shut down.

IS THE FURNACE GETTING POWER? A switch (just like a standard light switch) is located near the furnace. Make sure it's on. Check the circuit breaker or fuse box too. A natural gas furnace won't work without power either—the thermostat, fan motor and gas valve all need electricity to operate.

IS THE EXHAUST PIPE CLEAR? Sometimes heavy snow can cover up the exhaust vent to the outside.

IS THE GAS VALVE ON? The handle should be parallel to the gas pipe.

DOES THE THERMOSTAT NEED TO BE RESET? Turn it down, and then turn it back up.

If the inside temperature continues to fall, take action to prevent burst pipes. Turn off the main water valve and drain the pipes by turning on the faucets to let out the remaining water. Use a plunger to drive water out of the toilets and drain traps.

TORNADO OR HIGH WINDS

Straight-line winds can cause just as much damage as tornadoes, but they're more unpredictable. When a storm with high winds approaches, don't wait for sirens to sound before you take action.

TAKE COVER: Move to a protected interior room on the lowest floor of the house, as far as possible from exterior walls and windows. Use pillows, cushions, blankets or mattresses to protect yourself from flying debris.

IGNORE THE MYTHS: Don't open windows to "equalize the pressure" no matter what your grandparents told you. This can cause even greater damage. And the southwest corner of the basement may not be the safest spot to hunker down, especially if that corner is near an outside wall or window.

POWER OUTAGE

Surprisingly enough, the worst trouble caused by power outages often occurs when the problem is resolved and the power comes back on.

PREPARE FOR SURGES: Turn off and unplug all electrical equipment, including your tools, appliances and electronics, and turn your heating thermostat down (or turn up your cooling thermostat) to prevent damage from surges when the power returns. (Major appliances can be turned off at the breaker box.) Leave one light on so you'll know when the power is restored.

WHAT NOT TO DO: Once the power is restored, don't turn everything back on at once—that can create internal power surges. First, restore the thermostat setting on the heating or cooling system and turn on your larger appliances. Give the electrical system a few minutes to stabilize before plugging in your remaining appliances and electronics.

WATCH FOR MORE TROUBLE: If your lights are noticeably dimmer or brighter after the power is restored, turn off all the power at the breaker or fuse box and call your electric utility.

ELECTRICAL STORM

Lightning strikes can burn out circuit boards in appliances, computers and telephones, doing thousands of dollars in damage in less than a second. If you hear thunder, power surges are possible, even if you don't see any lightning.

PROTECT YOUR GADGETS: Unplug computers and phone lines, and also make sure to unplug corded telephones and sensitive electronics to prevent costly damage from power surges.

DON'T WAIT FOR FLAMES: If your home gets hit, call the fire department immediately. Lightning strikes can cause small fires inside walls that smolder for hours before you notice anything.

PLAY IT SAFE: Lightning may strike nearby electrical and phone lines and then travel to your home. Avoid contact with any electrical appliances and telephones (landlines) during a storm.

> **CAUTION:**
> Lightning is the second-leading weather-related killer in the United States. More deadly than hurricanes or tornadoes, lightning strikes kill an average of 70 people and injure 300 others each year.

WACKY BUT TRUE: Lightning strikes can travel through metal plumbing pipes. Avoid sitting on the toilet, and don't shower or bathe during electrical storms.

AFTER A HURRICANE

High winds and storm surges cause a lot of property damage during a hurricane. But the truth is that more people die in the aftermath of a hurricane than during the storm itself. These deaths are primarily from carbon monoxide poisoning and electrocution.

ACT WISELY: Don't use charcoal grills, propane camping stoves or generators indoors. And don't clear debris from your home and yard without surveying the area carefully. Downed or damaged power lines can send electrical currents through tree branches and metal fences.

CAUTION:
Hurricanes, tornadoes and winter storms are the top three causes of catastrophic home insurance losses.

WHAT NOT TO DO: Avoid an "every man for himself" mentality. Once officials have signaled the all-clear, survey the damage to your home and reach out to your neighbors. It will be difficult to drive anywhere for supplies (if stores are even open), and you'll conserve resources by pooling them. Assess your neighbors' stocks of food, water and other resources. Eating meals collectively will reduce the amount of food that spoils (use fresh foods first) and will conserve cooking fuel.

CARBON MONOXIDE ALERT

Carbon monoxide is the leading cause of accidental poisoning deaths in the United States. Take it seriously and make sure you have working CO detectors in your home.

CHECK FOR SYMPTOMS: The early symptoms of carbon monoxide poisoning resemble those of the flu. If the alarm sounds and anyone

PRO TIP
Emergencies are dramatic, but far more people are injured in ordinary household accidents. To find out how to make your home safer, visit *nsc.org/ community-safety*.

is experiencing headaches, dizziness, fatigue or vomiting, get everyone out of the house and call 911.

NEVER IGNORE THE ALARM: Don't assume all is well if no one feels ill. Open your doors and windows to thoroughly ventilate the house. Turn off all potential sources of CO— your oil or gas furnace, gas water heater, gas range and oven, gas dryer, gas or kerosene space heater, and any vehicle or small engine. Then have a qualified technician inspect your fuel-burning appliances and chimneys to make sure that they're operating correctly and that there's nothing blocking the vents that let fumes out of the house.

GET SMART ABOUT SMOKE ALARMS

PROPERLY MAINTAINING YOUR ALARMS WILL KEEP YOU SAFER

Smoke alarms—as long as they're functioning—may be the cheapest, easiest and most effective means for protecting your family and your home from a fire. According to the National Fire Protection Association, three out of four in-home fire deaths occur in homes without a working smoke alarm. We've gathered some great information to help you avoid becoming a tragic statistic. You'll learn where to put your smoke alarms, how to maintain them and when to replace them. We will also show you a range of innovative options on the market.

1 CONNECT ALARMS WIRELESSLY

If a fire triggers a basement alarm, will you hear it from a bedroom? Interconnected alarms provide better protection because if one goes off, all go off, and early detection is key to safely escaping.

Smoke alarms in new homes are required to be hardwired and interconnected, but you can get the same protection in an old house with alarms that speak to one another wirelessly. At about $60, these cost more but are a much cheaper option than installing new wires throughout the house.

1

2

WRITE DOWN THE INSTALL DATE

Smoke alarms should be changed every 10 years. Most manufacturers list the date a smoke alarm was made on the back. That's helpful information if you remember to look for it. Give yourself a proper reminder by writing the date you installed the alarm in big, bold letters on the base plate so you'll notice it every time you change the batteries.

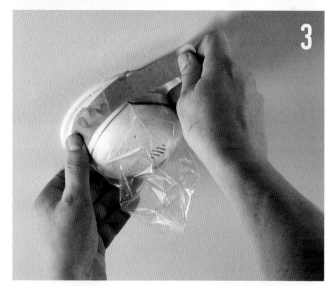

3

PROTECT SMOKE ALARMS FROM DUST

Excessive dust and paint overspray can wreak havoc with a smoke alarm's sensors. Before starting that messy remodeling project, temporarily cover or remove any alarm in harm's way. And if you are painting the ceiling, don't paint over the alarm—that will probably destroy it.

4

QUIET NUISANCE ALARMS

Kitchens are particularly susceptible to "nuisance" alarms. The horn on a typical alarm won't stop sounding until there's no more smoke to detect, which in a kitchen could take a while. Nuisance alarms are one of the main reasons people disable smoke alarms, and that's not a good idea, especially in the kitchen, where the majority of fires start. Now there are smoke alarms available with a "hush" button. Pushing it will kill the noise long enough for you to air out the room.

Some sensors are more sensitive than others, even if they're the same model. Before you go buy an alarm with a hush button, try swapping out the one in the kitchen with one from another part of the house.

- Check smoke alarms once a month
- Change batteries once a year
- Replace smoke alarms every 10 years

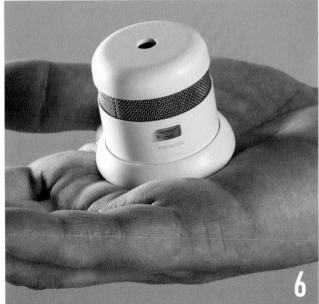

5 SAVE THE INSTRUCTIONS

Not all smoke alarms operate in the same way. Three chirps every minute may indicate "low batteries" for one unit and "end of life" for another. Save the instruction manual so you won't have to guess what your alarm is trying to tell you. Keep the manual in a place you'll remember. If you don't have a file or drawer for manuals, start one. If you have an unfinished basement, nail the manual right next to the alarm itself.

6 DOWNSIZE IF YOU PREFER

If you don't like the look of smoke alarms, then smaller is better. Smoke alarms don't have to be big to be effective. A few models on the market are a fraction of the size of standard alarms but perform just as well as their larger cousins.

7 INSTALL STROBE LIGHTS FOR THE HEARING IMPAIRED

People who can't hear an alarm need an alarm they can see. Some strobe alarms include smoke detection ($100 to $120). Others are strobe lights only ($50 to $70) and need to be connected with a compatible smoke alarm.

WHAT'S THE DIFFERENCE?

- **HARDWIRED** Hardwired smoke alarms operate off a home's electricity but still rely on batteries as a backup if the power goes out.

- **BATTERY-OPERATED** These units work on battery power alone. Some newer models have batteries that last 10 years.

- **INTERCONNECTED** Most hardwired alarms are interconnected, meaning if one goes off, they all do. Some battery-operated models can be wirelessly interconnected too (see "Connect Alarms Wirelessly" on p. 260).

8 HIDE A HOLE

Painting or retexturing a ceiling is no fun. If you have a hole from a hanging lamp or a small water stain, cover it up with a smoke alarm. Who cares if it's not interconnected with the other hardwired alarms? There's no such thing as too many smoke alarms.

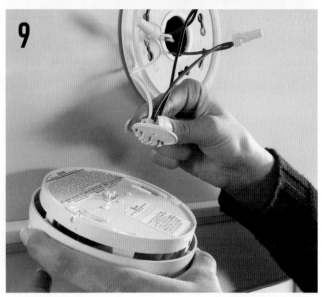

9 BUY A COMPATIBLE REPLACEMENT

Wiring a smoke alarm is pretty easy, but connecting it in a harness plug is even easier. When you need to replace your hardwired alarms, take an old one to the store. Save a bunch of time and buy new alarms that will accept the wiring harness on the old ones. That way all you have to do is plug in the new ones and maybe replace the base. Some new models come with wiring harness plug adapters, which makes matching easier. If your alarms are interconnected, never mix alarms made by different manufacturers.

10 KEEP THE SENSORS CLEAN

Dust can sometimes cause a smoke alarm to malfunction. Run a vacuum fitted with a soft brush over the alarm every time you change the batteries—at least once a year.

STAY WARM WHEN THE POWER'S OUT

THESE 10 TIPS WILL KEEP YOUR HOUSE FROM TURNING INTO A DEEP FREEZE

Heating systems need power. Even natural gas, propane and oil furnaces often use electricity for ignition, power dampers, fans or pumps. A power outage is always inconvenient—but in low temperatures it can be catastrophic. Frozen pipes can burst, causing thousands of dollars of damage in just a few minutes, and within a few hours, the damage costs can easily reach six figures. But there are ways to keep your home habitable and above freezing without power, even in the coldest weather.

CAUTION:
When using any fuel-powered heat source, it's imperative to have operating battery-powered carbon monoxide and smoke detectors.

FURNACE BACKUP TIPS

1 BUY A PERMANENT AUTOMATIC GENERATOR

This is the most efficient—and the most costly—option. You can easily spend $10,000 to $15,000, plus installation, but this will give you a seamless power transition. In the event of an outage, selected circuits, such as the one for your furnace, are on a subpanel and an automatic transfer switch, which is powered by the generator.

2 USE A PORTABLE GENERATOR

Portable generators aren't designed to take over any portion of your home's circuitry via a subpanel and transfer switch. Their outlets are for plugging in appliances.

But here's a safe method for powering just your furnace with a portable generator: Connect a heavy-duty double-pole, double-throw switch (such as Leviton No. 1262; about $35 online) to the furnace, along with a power inlet receptacle (such as Leviton No. 5278-CWP; about $45 online). If the utility power goes out, flip the double-pole switch to disconnect the permanent furnace circuit, and then run a cord from the portable generator to the inlet. The double-pole, double-throw switch prevents the portable generator from back-feeding the entire house or, worse, the utility's system. To be extra safe, turn off the main circuit breaker at the main service, disconnecting the house, to eliminate any chance of back-feeding the utility.

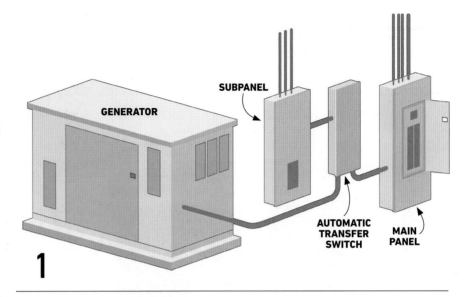

1

SUBPANEL · GENERATOR · AUTOMATIC TRANSFER SWITCH · MAIN PANEL

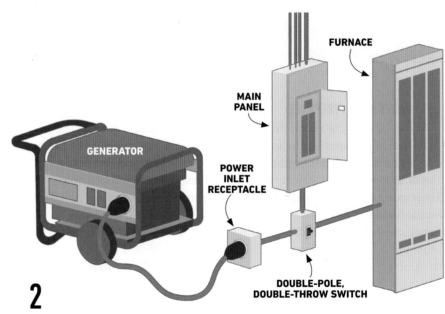

2

FURNACE · MAIN PANEL · GENERATOR · POWER INLET RECEPTACLE · DOUBLE-POLE, DOUBLE-THROW SWITCH

OTHER OPTIONS TO KEEP YOUR HOUSE WARM

If the generator methods are too expensive for your household, you can take other, less costly measures.

3 DON'T PANIC

If your home is well insulated, it's typically a matter of days, not hours, before pipes will freeze, even in subzero temps.

4 MOVE TO ONE ROOM

Each family member may want to keep cozy in their own bedroom, but it is far easier to keep one room in the house comfortable than to heat the whole house. A basement is a good choice because it's usually easier to maintain a constant temperature underground.

5 CLOSE YOUR BLINDS

Remember to keep the blinds closed except to let in direct sunlight.

6 LIGHT YOUR FIREPLACE

Fireplaces are notoriously inefficient heat sources, as a lot of heat goes up the chimney. But in an emergency, you can keep warm by a fire if you have enough wood to burn. A gas fireplace works, too, and is more efficient than a wood-burning fireplace.

7 BLOCK DRAFTS

Little drafts around doors and windows go unnoticed when the furnace is operating. But when the power's out, these drafts really bring on the chill. Block drafts with towels.

NOTE: Don't block drafts if you're running a fuel-powered heater. These small air intrusions help the heaters burn efficiently and provide ventilation.

8 PREHEAT YOUR HOME

If you have advance warning, set the thermostat higher than usual and heat typically unused spaces to boost thermal mass.

9 KEEP DOORS CLOSED

Opening a door to the cold lets out a lot of heat. Limit trips in and out of the house, opening doors only when necessary.

10 USE AN INDOOR-SAFE PROPANE OR KEROSENE HEATER

Propane or kerosene heaters are safe for indoor use only if they're labeled "indoor-safe" and only if the user follows the manufacturer's instructions. These portable heaters come in different sizes to suit different areas needing to be heated. The heaters, ranging in price from $80 to $500, are available at home centers and online. Manufacturers recommend opening a window an inch or so when using these heaters, particularly in a super-insulated home. If you're using a fuel-powered heater in a very small room, open a door to an adjoining room.

CAUTION:
Propane and kerosene heaters produce carbon monoxide just as gas stoves, ovens and fireplaces do. When running any fuel-powered heat appliance during a power outage, it's imperative to have operating battery-powered carbon monoxide and smoke detectors. Read and adhere to all the heater manufacturer's warnings.

RESERVE WATER BEFORE AN OUTAGE

PROPERLY COLLECT, STORE AND PURIFY YOUR EMERGENCY SUPPLY

When disaster strikes and no water is coming out of the tap, don't get left high and dry. Instead, follow our advice on storing water so you'll have an sufficient reserve to rely on. You'll also need to be prepared to purify water that may be unsafe and to conserve the water you've stored.

1 STORE WATER IN A FOOD-SAFE CONTAINER

Water doesn't have an expiration date, but it can become unsafe to drink if it's not stored properly. For long-term storage of large quantities of water, food-grade plastic is the gold standard. But in a last-minute stock-up for short-term storage, the gold standard changes to anything that's clean. In this case,

use a method of purification if there's any suspicion your water may be unsafe to drink.

2 CONSIDER SPECIALIZED WATER STORAGE CONTAINERS

Made for potable water or food, containers such as the WaterBrick (about $40 for two) have a tight seal and stack like blocks for easy storage.

3 STORE PLASTIC WATER CONTAINERS CORRECTLY

The chemicals used in concrete—not to mention the oil spills on a garage floor—can leach nasty chemicals into your water supply, giving it a bad taste or making it unsafe to drink. Store your plastic containers on cardboard or on a wooden pallet.

4

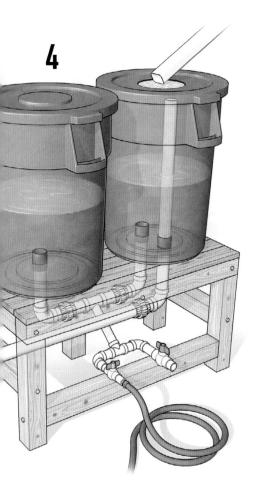

6 REMEMBER THE 40 GALLONS OF WATER IN YOUR WATER HEATER

To extract this water, turn off your water at the house's main shutoff and turn off the gas/power to your water heater. Open a couple of faucets above the water heater, if possible, to break the vacuum effect. Hook up a hose and drain the water from the tank. If there are solids in the water, filter them out before using it.

7 STOCK UP ON HAND SANITIZER

By using hand sanitizer instead of soap and water, you can stretch your water supply.

8 BUY A WATER BLADDER TO PUT IN YOUR TUB

The WaterBOB (about $35) holds 100 gallons of water for drinking. Just set it in your tub, wrap the spout around the faucet and fill it up before an anticipated outage.

9 CONSIDER INVESTING IN A CISTERN

It is very costly, but for serious water storage, you'll be able to reserve anywhere from 200 gallons to thousands of gallons of potable water.

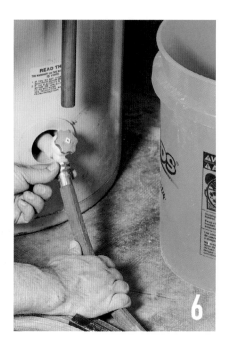

10 BUY FOOD-GRADE STAINLESS STEEL DRUMS

These drums are excellent for water storage because they don't let in UV light. On the downside, a 55-gallon stainless steel drum will set you back about $900.

11 AVOID STORING WATER IN AN UNSEALABLE CONTAINER

If a container doesn't have a tight seal, all sorts of contaminants can enter.

4 INSTALL A RAINWATER COLLECTION SYSTEM

You'll still need to purify the water, but it's a good way to take advantage of a natural resource.

5 STORE 1 GALLON PER DAY PER PERSON

The length of time you want to plan for is up to you. The Federal Emergency Management Agency (FEMA) recommends a two-week supply for each person. When you consider all water use—flushing, showers, handwashing, dishes, laundry, teeth brushing and outdoor watering—that's a LOT less water than we typically use daily. The U.S. Geological Survey estimates that we use an average of 80 to 100 gallons of water per day per person.

18

12 FRESHEN FLAT WATER
If stored water tastes flat, oxygenate it by pouring it back and forth between two clean containers.

13 MINIMIZE THE AMOUNT OF WATER YOU NEED
Decrease your activity and keep cool to minimize the amount of water you need to stay hydrated.

14 FILL UP YOUR POOL
You could even fill a wading pool. This water will need filtration and purification before you drink it.

15 DO LAUNDRY AHEAD OF TIME
If you know you'll likely be without water, be sure you have enough clean clothes to get you through.

16 FILL BATHTUBS AND SINKS
You shouldn't drink this water without purification, but you'll be able to use it as is for washing and flushing the toilet.

17 IF YOU HAVE POWER, USE THE WATER FROM YOUR DEHUMIDIFIER
Yes, it's distilled water, but you shouldn't drink it, as it's not purified or filtered. Use this water for washing, toilet flushing or watering plants.

18 FLUSH THE TOILET WITH A BUCKET OF WATER
Pour the water into the tank instead of the bowl. This method uses less water than pouring it directly into the bowl. Unpurified water, such as water stored in the tub without a container, is perfect for toilet flushing.

19 PURCHASE CAMP SHOWERS
For those who require a bit more luxury than a sponge bath, these are available for about $10 to $100. It's a good option if you have a plentiful water supply.

269

20 STOCK UP ON CLOROX WIPES AND HAND WIPES
Use these for general cleaning instead of using soap and water.

21 ROTATE YOUR SUPPLY OF PLASTIC BOTTLES
If you're storing plastic bottles of water for an emergency, use/rotate your supply once a year.

22 FILTER OUT SOLIDS
Filter solids through a coffee filter before purifying water.

23 STOCK UP ON DISPOSABLE PLATES AND UTENSILS
Conserve your supply of water by minimizing the number of dishes you have to wash.

24 FREEZE JUGS OF WATER
If the power is out, they will help keep your frozen food safe a bit longer. If it's potable water, you can drink it when the ice melts.

25 AVOID CONTACT WITH FLOODWATER
Floodwater can be extremely toxic. It likely contains all sorts of chemicals as well as raw sewage.

26 PROPERLY SANITIZE GLASS CONTAINERS
Glass containers are good if properly sanitized, but they're heavy to transport and they break easily.

27 DISPOSE OF TOILET PAPER IN A WASTEBASKET
Yes, you'll still be flushing your toilet, but the typical amount of water from other sources won't be going through the drain, so it's more likely that toilet paper could cause a backup.

HAVE A WAY TO PURIFY YOUR WATER

BOILING

Boiling kills parasites, bacteria and other pathogens in water. It does not, however, eliminate all forms of chemical pollution. Also, you'll still need to filter out any solids. A camp stove ($10 to $150) is a good item to have on hand for boiling because your power might be out as well. Any camp stove will do, but a portable stove that burns wood is nice in case there's a shortage of other fuel to purchase. Don't use camp stoves indoors—they generate carbon monoxide.

WATER PURIFICATION DEVICES

Water purification devices ($15 to $450) are available at camping supply stores. They come in sizes suitable for one person or large groups. Some of these devices are capable of purification as well as filtration.

WATER PURIFICATION TABLETS

Water purification tablets are available at camping supply stores. They fit neatly in an emergency kit, are easy to use and usually have a shelf life of up to five years.

BLEACH

Bleach is a readily available household item that can be used to purify water. Use only regular, unscented chlorine bleach with either 6 or 8.25% sodium hypochlorite as the active ingredient. With a clean eyedropper and 6% hypochlorite bleach, add 8 drops per gallon. For 8.25%, use 6 drops per gallon. Stir the water and let it stand for half an hour. If the water doesn't have a slight chlorine odor, repeat the dosage and let it stand for 15 more minutes. In general, you'll need more bleach if the water is cold or murky. Bleach has a six-month shelf life; be sure to keep a fresh supply.

IODINE

Iodine is another household chemical that can disinfect water. It is, however, a harsher chemical than bleach. On the upside, you can also use it to treat wounds. Using 10% povidone-iodine, add 8 to 16 drops per quart of water, depending on the water's level of cloudiness.

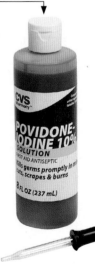